Relationship Anarchy

Relationship Anarchy
Occupy Intimacy!

Juan-Carlos Pérez-Cortés

Translated by
Amanda Foy

First edition in Spanish, April 2020
Author: Juan Carlos Pérez Cortés
Publisher: La Oveja Roja
Original Title: *Anarquía Relacional. La revolución desde los vínculos*

First edition in English, December 2022
Second edition in English, April 2023
Third edition in English (International Edition), July 2024
Title: *Relationship Anarchy. Occupy Intimacy!*
Translator: Amanda Foy
Cover design: Juan-Carlos Pérez-Cortés
This edition: Independently published

Copyright © 2020, Juan-Carlos Pérez-Cortés
All rights reserved.
ISBN: 978-84-09-62747-9

Dedicated

To those who have taught me and cared for me,
to those who are doing so now,
and to those who will in the future.
In the hopes of having known how to care for and teach some, too,
and of being able to continue to do so.

Table of contents

Foreword 13

Introduction to the International Edition 16

Preface 19

Introduction 23

Chapter 1. What is Relationship Anarchy? 28
1.1 The political becomes personal 28
   Starting from anarchism 28
   Moving closer towards a utopia 31

1.2 Where and when did all this come about? 31
   August 20, 2005: Anarkistfestival, Långholmen, Stockholm 31
   "A genderqueer relationship hacker" 34
   When everything is still new and something even newer comes along 35

1.3 Who's taken an interest in relationship anarchy so far? 36
   The academic world 36
   Queer collectives 41
   Non-monogamous collectives 44
   Asexual and aromantic individuals 45
   Colonized cultures 48
   Other communities 51

1.4 Perspectives, interpretations, and critical views 52
   Understanding based on privilege analysis 52
   The neoliberal, individualistic, apolitical gaze 55
   The gender perspective 58
   Critiques of relationship anarchy 62

1.5 What is relationship anarchy *not*? 68

Chapter 2. Cultural and historical perspective 73
2.1 Authority, family, private property, and anarchism 73
   The anarchist approach 74

Anarchism today 75
2.2 Feminism and anarcho-feminism 77
Early feminist authors 78
Alternatives to bourgeois feminism 82
Contemporary anarcho-feminism 86
2.3 Relationship anarchy and anarchism 88
The social contract and the marriage contract 88
Agreements, rights, and authority 92
Focus on the group 95
Personal or political activity? 96
2.4 Free love, polyamory, ethical non-monogamies, and affective networks 97
From the sexual revolution to free love 97
Outcomes of the sexual liberation movements 100
The rise of the ethical slut 102
2.5 Biological and anthropological perspective 106
Interpretations of natural forms of relationship 109
Moral and dogmatic models for regulating relationships 119

Chapter 3. I relate to others in a different way: labels, models, and practices 124
3.1 Labels and models 124
Descriptive and prescriptive labels 124
Models and self-management 129
3.2 The relationship escalator 133
Steps and their unrelenting ascent 133
Breakdowns and flaws in the mechanism 135
The price of dissent 137
3.3 Queer theory 139
Background 140
Feminisms and homosexual rights 141
Poststructuralism, sexuality, and identity subversion 142
Queer theory in five points 143

Five parallels with relationship anarchy..146

3.4 Axes of a multidimensional relational space 148
The axis of normative progress, or the escalator..............................149
The axis of normative labeling or the sense of security 151
The axis of the number of relationships or exclusivity 154
The axis of love and affection..156
The axis of physical intimacy...159
The axis of communication and transparency 161
The axis of identity 165
The axis of commitment...168
The axis of individualism, consideration, and responsibility...............169
The axis of hierarchy and authority..172
The political axis 174
The axis of the monogamy/non-monogamy binary 178

3.5 From amorous thought to non-normative practices 179
Romantic, monogamous, amorous – Disney – thinking......................181
Alternatives to hegemonic thinking..183

Chapter 4. The revolution that starts with bonds: ethical, collective keys 190

4.1 Privileges and resistance practices 190
Knowledges, truths, and submission...192
Power, relationships, and gender 194
Normative enforcement and emancipatory practices.........................199
Power imbalances 201
Anarchism, reason, and religion...204
From mysticism and dogma to witches and poetry 215

4.2 Identities and sensibilities..220
Political identities..222
Relationship Anarchy: from identity to sensibility...............................224
Contesting normative identities 225

4.3 Freedom, rights, entitlement, and agreements 234
Commitments versus transactions and contracts 236
Freedom doesn't exist (without equity at the starting point)..................240

4.4 Family of origin, chosen family, and raising children **242**
   Family normativity 243
   Raising kids outside a bubble 244

4.5 Models of life, cohabitation, and care **248**
   Intentional communities 248
   Cohabitation 252
   Legal recognition of bonds 254

Chapter 5. A way of sharing based on commitments and boundaries: relational keys 259

5.1 Touching down **259**
   Individual respect and cultural criticism 260
   Relationship cartography 261

5.2 Critical deconstruction of the ideology of the couple **263**
   Couple privilege 265
   Expectations 267
   Affective sexual scarcity 269
   Desire and desires 273
   Lack and precariousness as starting points 276
   Voluntary, intentional, responsible commitments 277
   Affective individualism 279
   Caretaking 280
   Recognition 283
   Delimitation in time 285
   Negotiation 287
   Communication 291
   Trust 293

5.3 Difficulties, obstacles, and collective ways of overcoming **295**
   Jealousy and compersion 295
   The need for symmetry and "feeling special" 299
   When the couple is no longer the measure of everything 301
   Obsessions, addictions, dependencies, and interdependence 303
   Blackmail 306
   Dangers of identarian feeling 307

The natural, the cultural, and the political 309
Continual management: relationship bureaucracy............................310
Who's with me? 311
Closets..314
And... what if I'm a woman? 316
And... what if I'm a cishet man?...319

5.4 Sustainable relationships 323
Dosage and sustainability 324
Well-being 326
Respect..327
Falling in love and limerence ("New Relationship Energy")..................328
Forms of cohabitation 330
Consent 331
Conclusions and proposals for starting to relate in a different way.......333

Chapter 6. Making what's nameless visible: relationship activism 336

6.1 What activism, and why? 340
Identity or cuddles 342
Hermeneutical dissent 344

6.2 Support networks and civil and economic rights 347
Liberation from or deregulation of relationships? 348

6.3 Collectives, spaces of socialization, and actions for visibility 350
Communities for non-normativity 350
OpenCons 351
A meeting on relationship anarchy 357

6.4 The future...357
Examples and reference points..358
Beyond bonds 359

Epilogue 362

Glossary... 363

About the author 385

Foreword

Years ago, when I first heard the phrase "Relationship Anarchy," it brought to my mind burning loveseats, people yelling, and other unsettling images of chaos. Like many others who know little about anarchy beyond stereotypes, I erroneously understood it to be a free-for-all of self-interest and mayhem. Over the years, however, talking to folks who identified as relationship anarchists has helped me better understand this idiosyncratic relationship style. What had initially seemed absolute bedlam turns out to be merely the rejection of automatic acceptance of relationship conventions and instead a negotiation of something that works better for those involved. In short – freedom. Too much freedom for some, without doubt, but, for others, relationship anarchy offers an unparalleled opportunity for authenticity. If you are one of those people who have hungered to escape from the social formulae that demand conformity to an unthinking norm and questioned fixed attitudes towards loving interactions that celebrate romance and belittle other forms of intimacy, then this book is for you.

Recently translated from Spanish to English, Juan-Carlos Pérez-Cortés' engaging and challenging book will appeal to readers interested in the philosophy of relationships. This is not to say that the book is challenging in the way that it is difficult to understand – that is not the case. While Pérez-Cortés uses the occasional big word like patriarchal or hegemonic, he does so when necessary to express big ideas rather than to intimidate readers or flex his intellectual muscles. Relationship Anarchy: Occupy Intimacy! is challenging because it examines and perhaps overturns some of the most deeply rooted – and often automatic – assumptions about what makes relationships "real" or "important."

Relationship Anarchy: Occupy Intimacy! is not your average self-help or how-to book. Instead, it is a philosophical thought experiment about the fundamental structure of relationships at the personal and collective levels. The first portion of the book offers a historical and intellectual overview of anarchic thought, grounding these ideas in the cradle of European feminism and politics from which anarchy originated. From the pioneering Swedes Andie Nordgren and Jon Jordas, who coined the term relationship anarchy, through works exploring the nature of intimacy from Anthony Giddens, Zygmunt Bauman, Jacob Strandell, and Ida Midnattsol (among others) to the speculative fiction of Octavia Butler, Ursula Le Guin, and Samuel Delany, Pérez-Cortés provides a thorough overview of the evolution of relationship anarchist thought. Along the way, Pérez-Cortés explores queer and non-monogamous collectives, asexuality, and indigenous reactions to colonized views of intimacy. At root, Pérez-Cortés' analysis focuses on the myriad ways that power is created, encoded, and enforced through defining and regulating intimate relationships.

The second portion of the book offers a more personal application, outlining how Pérez-Cortés applies these ideas to his own life and the practices of crafting relationships without authority. Pérez-Cortés asks some challenging questions that require readers to reconsider social norms and investigate what relationships might look like "if social mandates were replaced by mechanisms of self-management in small networks of bonds." For Pérez-Cortés, the personal is very much political, and his work points to a revolution that begins at the most basic level of interpersonal relationships. Pérez-Cortés points out that all of us are able to participate in the founding of this new social order by relating to each other in an additive way, focusing on self-management and collective well-being rather than imposed structures that dichotomize interactions into "important" (i.e., exclusive, sexual, ownership-based) and "just" friends.

Freedom outside of social mandates can be exhilarating but frightening as well. What happens when expectations fall away at both the personal and collective levels? What, then, is the basis of a society in which everything is done by choice? Who is free to make these choices, given that the menu of choices is written within the existing structures of oppression and systemic power relations that we might not be so free to ignore? Pérez-Cortés offers no easy answers to these questions but rather provides the full range of information that will assist readers in coming to their own conclusions. What could be better for anarchic enthusiasts than to think for themselves?

Elisabeth Sheff
Ph.D. in sociology, educational consultant, public speaker,
expert on polyamorous families and sexual minorities.
Author of "The Polyamorists Next Door," "When Someone
You Love is Polyamorous" and "Stories from the Polycule."

Introduction to the International Edition

It has been more than four years since the original publication of *"Anarquía Relacional. La revolución desde los vínculos"* in Spanish, in the spring of 2020, at the wake of the outbreak of the COVID-19 pandemic. It is likely that the consequences of the confinements and restrictions that we lived as a dystopia of the everyday also reached the relational sphere, that they highlighted aspects of the hegemonic structure of relationships, such as isolation in family bubbles, the veiled existence of care networks that this structure downplays and makes subordinate (but which saved us) or the evidence of couple relationships based more on resignation than on enthusiasm. I do not know if it is possible to establish a connection, but it is clear that the surprising reception of the book, the fact that one edition after another has sold out (in 2024, the sixth edition hit the bookstores in Spain and Latin America) and that several translations into other languages and publishing projects in other countries have been released or are underway, indicate that there was and still is a social need to know and understand alternative structures when it comes to relating to each other.

The two English editions that have appeared since December 2022 have also proved successful in terms of dissemination and public impact. The most enthusiastic reception has been in those communities already interested in radical alternatives to the hegemonic monogamous system and also in groups more focused on lifestyle-politics activism of anti-patriarchal, anarchist and anti-capitalist inspiration. In these areas, particularly, reading sessions, analysis, courses, seminars, and workshops of varied scopes, extensions, and approaches have been organized. Likewise, the proposals presented in the book have been collected in press articles, radio and TV programs, interviews, podcasts, and other digital and printed formats. All this activity continues and is even increasing as time goes by.

As I have been able to ascertain, the book's audience covers very different profiles in terms of interests and other traits such as age, gender, sexual orientation and preferences, geographical and sociocultural origin, etc. I believe that one reason for this is that the work brings together both visions: the political and the relational. The work historically structures the elements leading to the emergence of this framework, starting with the philosophical and political theoretical foundations, the freethought tradition, social developments, feminist, queer, sex-positive activisms, etc., while addressing the more personal and everyday aspects.

Reviewing the history of an area as crucial as social thought and the collective experience of relating to each other freely and without coercion provides an insight and perspective that is both reassuring and stimulating for those who are hopefully exploring the possibilities that may exist beyond the hegemonic framework.

Since the first editions of the book and from all the territories of Spanish-speaking countries, the feedback from readers has been constant, valuable, and incredibly moving for me. It shows that there was a need in many people who felt they did not fit into the only model available to them. Reading this volume has inspired and helped them not to "feel like weirdos" and to have pride and confidence in their own decisions and choices regarding relationships.

In these almost three years, the trends that led the book to be the way it is have been consolidated and generalized in what can be read in forums and other written works and, in many cases, in how many people intend to live. Relational anarchy is still a little-known framework in general, but increasingly recognizable and understood by collectives with revolutionary social concerns and individuals interested in building fairer, healthier, and more egalitarian relationships.

The daily experience of these people and these collectives reinforces the importance and the interest of spreading this and other alternatives that confront the normative monogamous relational model formed by functionally isolated bubbles, more and more to the general public. Robust networks of love, affection, help, support, and solidarity cannot be formed if there are no people around us who are aware of these options and try to be part of these networks to the extent of their emotional and material possibilities.

This International edition builds on the first English translation maintaining most of the original content, updating some topics, and adapting only the necessary contextual elements so that English-speaking readers can interpret the examples, references, comparisons, and anecdotes with greater familiarity. With the English and international editions, the potential audience for the work is significantly expanded. I am very excited about this step, which I hope will lead to a new adventure as fascinating as the book's original publication.

Juan-Carlos Pérez-Cortés
June 2024

Preface

"If there is a book that you want to read, but it hasn't been written yet, you must be the one to write it."

— Toni Morrison.

Like most personal and intellectual endeavors, whether the everyday and inconsequential or the most extraordinary one, individual or collective, immediate or long-term, this book has a lot to do with seeking identification. It's a balance between the need to tell and the need to understand.

It's been said that books should be written to reveal things to those who read them, not as a way to boast about what one knows. The paradox, though, is that writing is one of the best ways to learn. This work doesn't aim to instruct but to show, reveal, present — or put even more precisely, nothing short of revealing myself, putting myself on display. Getting undressed without the point being that image of nudity; getting behind the easel and painting portraits with my bare hands, fully exposed, skin splotched in paint; composing without avoiding the telltale mirrors in the background, instead opting for a wide lens. The search for identification can be a form of projection from the intimate to the structural, offering its own line of inquiry and gathering together a patchwork of perspectives, not so that they can compete with each other but so that they can be pieced together to create a suit that fits perfectly.

This book is not a ready-made garment, much less a uniform. This exhaustive path of exploration leads through back rooms and fitting rooms, as I carefully sketch and try out, with the utmost restraint, an outfit that I find particularly comfortable, motivating, and evocative; I hope these sketches and mock-ups can serve as something akin to inspiration. But inspiration for what, and for whom? Well... I trust that the answer will be given rather anarchically – that is to say, following a self-made order – in the pages ahead. And if, in the end, reading doesn't lead to any answers, I at least hope that it has raised a lot of questions. I haven't approached any part of this work as if it were a cookbook or a guide on self-help or personal growth. The approach is reflective and speculative, and it strives to be informative, as well – though without claiming some impossible objectivity or pursuing the veneer of impartiality.

In short, I'm sure that the general scheme and the specific aspects of my proposal will be surprising to some who are already acquainted with the approach and the practices of relationship anarchy to some degree. This is especially true with regard to the political and social anchor I use as the foundation for my interpretation, which strives for radicalism more than moderation or neutrality. As this topic grows and becomes more publicly recognized, the tendency to approach relationship anarchy from an apolitical – uncommitted – perspective is also increasing, as the search for a collective perspective and the importance of power relations and resisting gradients of oppression created by gender, race, class, and origin are slowly left behind. I intend to take the opposite road to confront that view, a view that I believe leads to splintering and individualism.

However, being on the side of relationship anarchy does not mean understanding this proposal in prescriptive terms. A regulated model of anarchy would be a laughable oxymoron. Throughout, the framing is descriptive and representative of my own experiences and thoughts as well as those of others; it is largely hypothetical and ultimately utopian. Nor does a firm ideological commitment entail renouncing subjectivity and social, relational, and affective particularity but simply establishing limitations. Both personally and politically, it is articulated according to the conviction that any analysis of relationships that doesn't account for the structures of oppression that permeate deep into the fabric of our societies — particularly the patriarchal model of thought and social organization that has become naturalized and hegemonic — is the product of an almost unbelievable lack of awareness (almost insulting at this point in history) or the product of involvement with and a vested interest in that oppressive and unjust system. The structure of the book isn't hard to follow; still, I find it helpful to map out the contents and the conceptual itineraries outlined in it to give an idea of where we're headed.

The first chapter defines relationship anarchy and expands on its anarchist, utopian, and transformational foundations, as well as its understanding in academic research and by different groups and its interpretations from both familiar and critical perspectives. The chapter defines the proposal's scope and compiles where and how this proposal, initially called "radical relationships," came about, first emerging in anarchist environments in Northern Europe. It also looks at how these ideas have reached the groups that those of us throughout the continent have organized to reflect on non-normative ways of relating and how it has spread throughout the world.

Chapters two and three situate relationship anarchy in relation to philosophical, social, legal, biological, anthropological, moral, religious, and political thought, starting from the first modern anarchism, bourgeois feminism, anarcho-feminism, the sexual revolution, and the free love movement of the 1960s and '70s, to the latest movements like queer activism and the most recent waves of feminism.

The fourth chapter focuses on the collective dimension of relationships and the factors that justify the search for other ways of relating, as well as why anarchism has always claimed reason as an alternative to the opium of alienating religious doctrines, which steer people towards gods or themselves, preventing practices of resistance from being articulated socially. Finally, in that regard, it presents the initiatives emerging from the principles of relationship anarchy, something of a transition from normativity in relationships to collective self-management: from identity to sensibility, from forming family bubbles to other models of life, coexistence, and care-taking.

The fifth chapter describes what I can do in my own everyday life if I choose to apply the ideas and convictions that stem from the principles of relationship anarchy. It delves into how the hegemonic conception of relationships works, its outcomes, and how I can overcome them if I set out to maintain relationships that are healthy, sustainable, and collectively developed with no authority. It attempts, now in a personal, practical, committed way, to ground all these ideas and reflections in real life. It goes over each of the daily implications of privileges, expectations, scarcity and lack, individualism, the need for recognition and boundaries, negotiation, commitments and limits, communication and trust… as well as difficulties and a few ideas to overcome them.

The sixth and last chapter presents the forms of relational activism that have been proposed, their characteristics, and which are being carried out effectively in different parts of the world. It also lays out this movement's path and what is0.63in0.38in to be expected in the near future.

Finally, the glossary includes several terms that appear in the text, offering definitions from this book's specific perspective and, therefore, providing information that goes beyond a mere inquiry into the meaning of the words. I think it might be of interest to read the glossary itself before, during, or after the main body of the book.

If you enjoy reading this a fraction as much as I've enjoyed writing it, that pleasure will make the work that went into it twice as precious. Thank you.

Introduction

"We'll meet tomorrow, then you'll tell me what
the Prince of Salina feels about the Revolution."
"I can tell you that at once and in a few words; he says there's
been no revolution and that all will go on as it did before."

— Giuseppe Tomasi di Lampedusa, *The Leopard*.

Is this an age of revolutions that aren't actually revolutions? Many aspects of daily life are moving forward at incredible speeds. Still, it seems like it gets harder every day to change certain aspects of the world, as if Lampedusa's words on changing everything so that nothing changes had become a prophecy – or maybe things have been like this forever. The second decade of the 21st century has seen significant socio-political events: the Arab Spring, the anti-austerity movements that followed the publication by Stéphane Hessel of *Indignez-vous* (Time for Outrage!) in several European countries, Occupy Wall Street in the United States, and so on. All these awakened high hopes and dreams, and they became valuable symbolic reference points, even though their practical outcomes (at least in the short- and medium-term), have not lived up to expectations.

Once again, changes in the collective imagination didn't transform reality; instead, reality adapted. It's with the same mixture of hope and concern that we're witnessing even more recent processes, such as the rise of feminist mobilizations around the world with the advent of what has been dubbed "fourth-wave feminism." But, to paraphrase James Branch Cabell,[1] optimism can lead us to think

---

1 North American writer whose early twentieth-century work is considered an aesthetic and, at the same time, anti-romantic reference.

that this is the best of all possible worlds, while pessimism leads us to fear just that. Regardless of which attitude we take, there is no doubt that we can see farther on the shoulders of new theoretical universes.

One of the chants repeated at the demonstrations for popular empowerment movements in 2011 was the phrase coined decades ago by Joan Fuster: "Politics: you either do it or get it done to you" ("La política, o la haces o te la hacen").[2] Adding this idea to the ever-relevant feminist slogan of the '70s, "the personal is political,"[3] we come up with the combined synthesis that the configuration of personal relations is political; you either do it or get it done to you. Indeed, the sphere of relationships is not exclusively determined and conducted on a personal level. It is not a collection of lived anecdotes and autonomous decisions, the result of some naïve dream of free will; it is the experiential result of a system of thought built on the predominant cultural patterns. For all these reasons, I'm proposing a route with a critical view of these models in order to reflect and define possible alternatives for individual and collective emancipation.

Relationship anarchy is a relatively recent proposal that has been evolving for just over a decade. It explores those paths in two ways. First, in terms of personal critique, suggesting that this could be undertaken with the question of whether I'm really living the life that I would have made for myself if I'd started from a blank slate. This is a question of whether the significant decisions I make in the relational and affective sphere originated in my needs, my desires, and my material conditions or if I've been led up a sort of escalator that's taken me from one story to another, leaving little room for analysis and dissent.[4]

---

[2] Gonçal Mayos's prologue to *Filosofía para indignados: textos situacionistas*, RBA, Barcelona, 2013.
[3] E. Parrondo Coppel, "Lo personal es político," *Trama y fondo*, 2009.
[4] A. Gahram, *Stepping Off the Relationship Escalator: Uncommon Love and Life*, Off the escalator enterprises LLC, Boulder, 2017.

It is possible to escape this escalator that is normativity by jumping off or even perhaps trying to turn back. But by doing so, I'm exposing myself to the danger of a painful fall, or to the reproaches and judgments of those who are ascending with me — and who may be annoyed by my U-turn. That will undoubtedly involve risk, as well as pushing and nudging. Using this image as an example, relationship anarchy sets out an initial hypothesis that looks into what would happen if we could confront these mechanized routes in a decisive way.

Secondly, as for the criticism expressed from the collective gaze, I formulate the question of what our societies could be like if the uniformity that governs personal relationships were drastically diminished, and if social mandates were replaced by mechanisms of self-management in small networks of bonds, not admitting pre-determined guidelines or implicit structural prerogatives. Here, the hypothesis is that the expansion of decision-making spaces for individuals and groups — in something as organic for the community as the networks of relationships between those of us that make it up — can fundamentally modify its structure.

Some of the most significant axes of social privilege are based on the normative formats of control that we've learned and consider to be "natural." This starts with sexual and reproductive control (structurally, over women) which ranges from the concept of fidelity in the traditional monogamous (and historically asymmetric) couple to reach all spheres and forms of social regulation, to radical individualism that's extrapolated to the nuclear family. The latter makes extreme selfishness morally praiseworthy and almost mandatory when it manifests as defense of the family group. It is *l'egoismo famigliare* (familial selfishness) that Natalia Ginzburg identified in the 1942 novel *La strada che va in città* (The Road to the City) as the seed of fascism in Italy, within the framework of a lucid reference to the relationship between the personal and the political.[5]

---

[5] A. M. Jeannet y G. Sanguinetti Katz, Natalia Ginzburg: A Voice of the Twentieth Century, University of Toronto Press, Toronto, 2000.

Thus, the objective of this book is to develop these two angles – the personal and the collective – and to offer arguments that support the validation of the proposed hypotheses. This effort has a vocation for optimism and knowledge that seeks a breath of fresh air in the realm of the intimate and particular. It also strives toward the possibility of overcoming a system that is continually endowed with defense mechanisms, each one more adaptive than the last, and overcoming it from the bottom up, out of the very fabric of relationships. Triumphing over dynamics that allow the system to assimilate and neutralize ideas, alternative proposals, collective perspectives, and less authoritarian options for administration and government.

It is an endeavor that will probably develop over time and with this generation's capacity for evolution and individual and social readjustment. Still, it may help to know and compare references beyond the traditional and dominant. This way, it is possible that the next wave of change is already being led by people who don't feel captive to a predefined, exclusive model of relating to others and to just one way of fulfilling their emotional, familial, social, and communal desires and aspirations.

Bennett coined the phrase *"lifestyle politics"*[6] to describe the practice of tailoring personal decisions and behaviors to political principles and intentions, especially when these dynamics radically challenge the *status quo* and therefore entail a small (but potentially massive) struggle towards a new social order.

Perhaps, if the revolution confronts the system's support structures not only through the assault on power but also through what's shared — that which connects us as affective beings and shapes the fabric of bonds, care, emotions, and feelings by defending dignity and combating privileges and abuses in the personal sphere — perhaps then the resources that protect the hegemonic scheme in its authoritarian and oppressive character will begin to fail. And perhaps that will help us, in our most emotional dimension, to prepare

---

6 W. L. Bennett, "The UnCivic Culture: communication, identity, and the rise of lifestyle politics," Political Science and Politics, 1998.

to finally act as people who support each other, who relate to each other in an additive way rather than by dividing based on nuances broken down to infinity, who have not only learned concepts that speak of popular empowerment, solidarity, mutual aid, and the fight against injustice, but who also live these out and experience them every day.

Demonstration, Wall Street, 2011. Source: Wikimedia.

The aim is to prepare ourselves to take on a social change collectively from the bottom up, from the intimate to the shared, from the public outrage of occupying Wall Street to our personal relationships: let's occupy intimacy![7]

---

[7] On the Occupy Movement, see: B. Berkowitz, "From a single hashtag, a protest circled the world," Brisbane Times, 19/10/2011.

Chapter 1. What is Relationship Anarchy?

> "Do you consider yourself a radical?"
> "We all consider ourselves moderate and reasonable."
> "Well, define yourself ideologically."
> "I think that all authority has to be justified. That any hierarchy is illegitimate until proven otherwise. Sometimes, it may be justified, but most of the time, it is not. And that... that is anarchism."
>
> – *Noam Chomsky*
> (interview in the Spanish newspaper *El País*, April 2018).

With nearly 200 years of history behind them, the terms "anarchy" and "anarchism" are present in much of humanity's language and common symbolic universe. From active militancy in its various forms or interpretations, from theoretical analysis, out of sympathy, curiosity, fear, and mistrust – or maybe even from a disdainful distance – almost everyone in our day and age has heard of anarchism and anarchy more than once.

1.1 The political becomes personal

Casual references to this ideology or this set of political movements are not only superficial but rarely come close to reflecting the term's actual meaning; they can even suggest its exact opposite. For many, anarchy evokes social disorder rather than the most essential, sustainable order imaginable: the kind that is self-driven and self-managed. In the third chapter, I'll discuss political anarchism, its history, and its place in the dominant cultural layout.

Starting from anarchism

Relationship anarchy is a proposal based on a vision of social relations rooted in anarchism. It emerges with the aim of going a little further, overcoming the classic approach of a movement that has above all addressed political and economic organization and collective forms of management in social coexistence. It is formulated with the goal of expanding the principles of anarchism to the realm of personal relationships.

Actually, the universe of affective relationships – the way they're established, regulated, and the social consequences they can have – is an area that has been written about and reflected on in the earliest anarchist articulations, and interest in it hasn't waned over time. However, with only a few exceptions, it hasn't been a primary driving element of an imagined social revolution, but just another feature of a supposed future model of coexistence, an expected outcome of the revolution that will overthrow the State based on principles of freedom and collective self-management.

So, relationship anarchy is inspired by concepts that anarchism has examined and discussed for years, as we'll see, ideas about family relationships, solidarity, support, mutual aid, fellowship, commitment, and companionship; institutions like marriage; and the gender roles and power dynamics that underpin all these ways of relating with others. This is the result of applying a new perspective to a current of thought that has examined, validated, and revisited time and again how all these relationships could be set up in the much longed-for anarchist society. To some extent, that line of thought has brought together a common representation of these reflections.

Specifically, relationship anarchy (initially called "radical relationships" by those who proposed it) offers a critique of the normativity of the personal realm, of intimate life, and of close-knit, affective, everyday ties. Starting from the traditional explicit opposition to the State, the Church, authority, and the hierarchical yoke of the political, religious, and economic elites, it shifts to another paradigm. This paradigm focuses on tackling the axes of power represented by patriarchy and the current social system, which is based on the reproductive, heterocentric, nuclear family and the normative monogamous system.

This move, therefore, challenges the apparent facts that the social structure revolves exclusively around the traditional family and that relational practices are necessarily limited to serial monogamy. Any conduct or behavior, including monogamy, fits into relationship anarchy as long as it is the product of self-management; this means that it is the result of shared reflection and decision-making, not involving authority or coercion of any kind.

However, this attempt to outline and contextualize the proposal immediately produces questions: sure, but what do these proposals look like in practice? Is there an actual movement pushing towards these goals? The answer to the second question is that there probably isn't – at least not in the sense of a group united around common definitions and projects. Relationship anarchy is emerging as a new reference point, a paradigm (or an "anti-paradigm," given its antinormative sense) that may be of interest for many at a time when they're searching for different relationship models. Nevertheless, given its experiential nature, it doesn't aim to give rise to an organized movement, except in terms of study and dissemination.

I'll spend the rest of the book, or at least most of it, discussing the first question of how these ideas are expressed in everyday life. For now, I'll try to offer an initial answer in the form of a circumstantial, shorthand synthesis: the thought and practices identified with relationship anarchy are characterized by rejecting hegemonic normativity, prescriptive categories, authority, prerogatives, privileges, and implicit rights that this normativity, when accepted without criticism, introduces into relationships, as well as the expectations, hopes, and idealizations that arise among individuals based on all these factors. The very labels and stereotypes established by the dominant culture come into question; the standardized descriptions of relationships are closely examined. Is it love or friendship, valuable or insubstantial, or even intimate or not intimate? These categories are imposed; they are not the product of critical personal reflection that is free from regulated patterns and specific to each situation, emotion, and time. These imperative labels don't just explain reality; they impose order and hierarchy on it.

Moving closer towards a utopia

Relationship anarchy absolutely does not dispute the existence of bonds with varying levels of affinity, commitment, dedication, trust, agreement, emotion, passion, or affection. It is indisputable that these features can show up in each relationship at different times and in totally different ways. It does, however, warn that dividing up and labeling lots based on these or other dimensions only serves to reinforce stereotypical privileges, rights, and expectations, as well as the emotional consequences of these. The result is the creation of a false sense of security and a constant need to manage standardized dichotomies of relational location: "we are or we aren't," "friends or more than that," "we're heading somewhere or we're not," "it's over or it's not," "all or nothing," "they love me, they love me not..." This dichotomous thinking can continue to escalate to dangerous projections of possessiveness, coercion, and threat: "you're either mine or no one's."

1.2 Where and when did all this come about?

August 20, 2005: Anarkistfestival, Långholmen, Stockholm

One Saturday in August, during the short but bright Swedish summer, there is an event that, as Anki Bengtsson describes in the now-defunct Swedish newspaper *Yelah*,[8] turns the tranquil island of Långholmen into a little anarchist paradise. There are workshops and conversations in the grass, music, and "no sexists allowed." The workshops range from introductory talks to colloquia on ideas and issues as varied as free transportation systems, anarcho-feminism,

---

8   A. Bengston, "Relationsanarki som frigörelseprocess, reportage 050823," *Yelah*, 23 Aug 2005 (*Yelah* was an anarchist socialist newspaper published from 1994 to 2014).

direct media, the Spanish Revolution,[9] Emma Goldman, or how to establish an anarchist house.

More than 50 people gather in this idyllic setting at the Långholmsparken park amphitheater to listen to Andie Nordgren and Jon Jordås talk about normativity and relationships. Jon begins by saying that we have the cultural habit of approaching the relationships we label as romantic and those we call friendship from different perspectives. We paradoxically grant the former both higher status and greater vulnerability. We think it normal for the passage of time to threaten a romantic relationship to a much greater extent than other types of relationships.

Andie adds that we build a pedestal that we call love, and it can only hold one person or, in non-monogamous situations, perhaps a few. Getting up onto that pedestal requires sacrifice and a process of constant confirmation that the level of affection and commitment is what's expected of such a high status. However, the level of contact and dedication for what we've learned to call friendship is more flexible, and it can vary over time without leading to a breakdown in the relationship. There are undoubtedly specific friendships that involve significant levels of control and demand for attention, but this is not the expectation that is structurally assigned to them.

The two speakers go on to emphasize that their proposal for breaking down the wall between the types of pre-packaged relationships that we're given does not mean that emotions and feelings must be the same in all cases or that passion disappears. It simply means that the fixed attitudes we currently have towards love on one hand and friendship on the other can be blended together and practiced naturally at each moment, depending on the circum-

---

[9]The Spanish Revolution of 1936 was a unique social process that developed during the first months of the Civil War. It was based on anarcho-syndicalist ideological roots and was cantonalist in terms of territory, horizontalist in administrative affairs, anticlerical and rationalist in education, and collectivist and self-run in terms of economy. For example, see: Rafael Cid, "80 años de la revolución española. VIVIR la utopia," *Rojo y Negro Digital,* 2016.

stances. Andie and Jon say that they don't want their vision of relationship anarchy, as they call it, to be confused with the increasingly popular trend of polyamory (the practice of having several affective-sexual relationships at the same time). They believe that this could be a secondary outcome of their proposal, but it is under no circumstances the goal.

This is the first documented appearance – as far as I've been able to tell – of a term, relationship anarchy, that is claimed, discussed, and experienced more than a decade later by individuals and groups around the world. There are even books written about it!

Unaware of the praise and the adventures that lay ahead, Långholmsparken's little assembly continues. It addresses the phenomenon of parenting (an aspect that they recognize is complex) and jealousy, which is presented in the hegemonic vision as proof of love, not as what it is: a controlling, possessive behavior. Andie also underscores the need to shift to a feminist perspective that is not heterocentric, getting beyond the logic of the free love of the '70s, which ultimately only benefited men, keeping women in their role as caregivers while their male counterparts were free to explore. Andie asserts that creating each relationship should be approached as a project of liberation through the gender lens.

Amphitheater in the Långholmsparken park on the island of Långholmen, Stockholm. Source: Wikimedia.

"A genderqueer relationship hacker"

Andie Nordgren, who describes themself as "a genderqueer relationship hacker,"[10] is considered to be the person at the start of relationship anarchy. This is due to their online outreach through posts on *"Interacting Arts"* and various personal web pages,[11] as well as the compilation *"Fråga Dr Andie,"*[12], whose full title could be translated as *Ask Dr. Andie: Relationship Anarchy in practice, questions and answers from a radical perspective.* Andie acknowledges that Jon Jordås and Leo Nordwall also participated in developing the term and the idea.

On November 2, 2006, Andie announced on their blog that relationship anarchy finally had an entry on Wikipedia (the Swedish edition, with the page created by Eriq Petersson). It took until June 2013 for it to become available in English; a few months later, in January 2014, the Spanish and Catalan editions went live (I created these articles myself from the little information I could find at that time). On May 12, 2007, on the Interacting Arts forum, Andie reported that Leo Nordwall had designed a logo for relationship anarchy.

Logo for relationship anarchy designed by Leo Nordwall

Finally, the most cited document that has had the greatest subsequent impact is "The Manifesto of Relationship Anarchy." This text

---

10 Description that refers to a non-binary identity combined with an interest in research on relationships from activist and deconstructivist angles.
11 Interacting Arts defined itself as a group of interdisciplinary artists who were critical of the media; a network of activists; a conspiracy; a research center; a newspaper and a blog.
12 Andie Nordgren, Fråga Dr Andie Relationsanarki i praktiken frågor och svar från en radikal hjärtespalt, Leanpub books, Victoria, 2012.

was initially titled "8 points on relationship anarchy" (*Relationsanarki i 8 punkte*), but it was translated into English and adapted by Andie Nordgren with the title *The short instructional manifesto for relationship anarchy*.[13]

When everything is still new and something even newer comes along

The first time that I and others in Southern Europe looking into these topics heard the term was at a meeting held by the Poliamor Catalunya collective in Barcelona one Friday in November 2013. About a year before that in Valencia, we'd started talking about relational and gender questions in open discussions spearheaded by Cristian Yapur, Sonia Pina, and myself. This raised enough interest for a small, informal group to take shape. Like a stealthy advance party on a recon mission, Sonia and I went to that meeting, which was held casually over drinks around the Barceloneta district in Barcelona.

We didn't personally know anyone, but it was easy to spot the group of 10 to 15 people gathering in Plaza Pau Vila. Shortly after, we were around a table chatting off of a terrace a stone's throw from Barcelona's shoreline. This heterogeneous, multicultural group was, as the years since have come to show, fascinating – a true gift. One of the people who had organized the gathering and led the discussion was David. After introductions and a few preliminary questions, he mentioned some international meetings called OpenCon that had been tackling questions related to non-monogamy and non-normativity for several years then. I'll say more on all this later on in the chapter on activism. At some point, one of the participants – Lina – asked if anyone had heard of something called "relationship anarchy."

No one at the table was familiar with the term. She explained what it meant without much detail. She told us that the movement

---

[13] http://log.andie.se

had originated in her home country of Sweden and was beginning to spread and gain recognition elsewhere.

1.3 Who's taken an interest in relationship anarchy so far?

The academic world

In 2010, Jacob Strandell carried out a pioneering study on relationship anarchy from an academic perspective at Lund University.[14] In it, he contextualizes the model within the framework of the most important contemporary theoretical analysis on forms of social relationship.

He first cites Anthony Giddens and his now-classic hypothesis of how more emancipatory normativities are displacing traditional ones. He also refers to Zygmunt Bauman and his theory of liquid love. This theory explains the trend towards a greater fluidity in ties by looking at how the world of relationships mirrors consumer behavior, all set against the backdrop of a wide range of products and services. His research argues that in serial monogamy, the prospect of finding something better is continually in the background, generating continual disagreement and anguish. The anxiety that the threat of replacement causes operates as a self-fulfilling prophecy, making relationships less satisfactory and more likely to be replaced. I'll talk more about this along with the idea of sustainable relationships.

The study also cites Ulrich Beck and Elisabeth Beck-Gernsheim's theory of individualization. The process of individualization is fundamentally based on the dissolution of stable social structures such as class, gender, tradition, and family. What was once pre-defined

---

[14] J. Strandell, Det fria subjektets diskurs: en analys av de diskurser som möjliggör relationsanarkins diskurs och praktik, Bachelor's degree project, sociology, Lund Universitet, 2010.

is now open to consideration and choice. Between what Giddens interprets as positive emancipatory liberation and Bauman's view of a dystopian source of anxiety and vertigo, there is, in the case of Beck and Beck-Gernsheim, the appreciation of a potentiality that can lead in one direction or another, depending on how it is developed.

Finally, Strandell references Sasha Roseneil, who uses queer theory to analyze this same phenomenon. Roseneil concludes that the processes of individualization, de-traditionalization, and growth in the capacity for personal reflection open up new opportunities and expectations in relationships. These processes lead to a deconstruction of sexual identities and normativity, and they bring essentialism into question. Roseneil calls these "queer tendencies" and sees them as the basis for destabilizing heteronormative relationships.

In 2012, Ida Midnattsol carried out a scholarly analysis of testimony from a group of people who identify with the relationship anarchy model. This was part of another research project at Umeå University's Centre for Gender Studies; 20 it drew on Ernesto Laclau and Chantal Mouffe's theory of discourse. Midnattsol's aim was to examine the ideological and identarian substratum underlying their understanding of the model and relate it to its specific practices. The project sets out by recognizing that it deals with fragmentary, individual positions and discourses on a topic that is defined in a highly unspecific way and recoded differently by each individual, yet which give rise to a recognizable group identity despite its diffuse nature.

Discourse analysis is based on a social constructionist approach built on the premise that knowledge cannot be considered an objective truth. This is because our vision of the world is built on how we define our categories, and this task of definition is carried out in a specific cultural and historical context. This method of analysis doesn't jump to the conclusion that some particular meaning is essential or intrinsic rather than determined as a function of social interaction. It supports the notion that these learned meanings are perceived as natural by individuals. This makes criticism difficult –

not to mention the idea that these norms are simply one of many options instead of being a pre-existing, insurmountable reality.

Midnattsol concludes that relationship anarchy – as perceived by those first individuals who identified with its practice in those early years in its home country of Sweden – shows a clear conceptual connection with anarchism. Relationship anarchy takes up the idea that norms shouldn't come from a pre-established, hierarchical imposition but should instead be proposed and developed from the ground up for each situation and specificity, not for general purposes.

Another conclusion drawn in that study is that a dichotomy arises in the discourse: relationship anarchy is either clearly characterized and has some identifiable guidelines for those who practice it to follow, meaning that we've replaced one norm with another; or we renounce that normative dimension by underscoring total freedom to determine how we relate to one another, leading us to find that relationship anarchy can be anything and therefore stripping the model of meaning. As we continue in this search and try to get beyond binarisms, an essential premise is trusting that there is a middle ground. What is clear in this author's study is that the individuals who adhere to relationship anarchy question traditional social normativity, visibilize the possibility of forming relationships in a different way, and consider their practices to be an alternative that challenges existing social, legal, and economic frameworks, including the latter's clear distinction between relationships that possess the right to recognition as a family unit and everything else.

Other academic studies that independently work from the anarchist perspective – without explicitly citing relationship anarchy, which is why their extraordinary coincidence is particularly significant – appear in the book "Anarchism and Sexuality"[15] compiled by Jamie Heckert and Richard Cleminson from contributions to the conference of the same name held in Leeds in 2006. In "Nobody

---

15   J. Heckert, R. Cleminson, *Anarchism and Sexuality*, Routledge, Bingdon/New York, 2011.

knows what an insurgent body can do,"[16] Stevphen Shukaitis notes that politics is no stranger to personal interactions and relationships; that, as Antonio Negri says, affection and care are an expansive, creative form of power; that the power of freedom, ontological openness, and omnilateral diffusion creates value from the bottom up and applies transformations at the rhythm of the commonplace, the everyday. He discusses creating communities of resistance where there are high densities of relationships and affections that offer us support and mutual understanding in all aspects of life. He calls this sustainable culture one "of aeffective resistance," which links the notion of effectiveness with that of affectivity over the long term – two concepts that are far removed from one another in the neoliberal capitalist imaginary.

In "Love and Revolution in Ursula Le Guin's 'Four Ways to Forgiveness,'"[17] Laurence Davis examines the connection between the titular themes of love and revolution. Revolutions don't only take place with the overthrow of or change in governments, nor does a new regime necessarily entail a revolutionary transformation of society. He points out that, unlike their political "cousins," the progressives and Marxists, most anarchists – as well as feminists, environmentalists, anti-imperialists, and socialists who have freethought and utopian leanings – see the liberation of their daily life, their way of life, as a defining element of their ideas; at the same time, it's a means by which those ideas can be achieved. That's why they have incorporated revolutionary change into their lives, generating an enormously creative counterculture of free art, free schools, free media, and... free relationships.

In "Structures of desire: Postanarchist kink in the speculative fiction of Octavia Butler and Samuel Delany,"[18] Lewis Call analyzes

---

16   Ibid.: S. Shukaitis, "Nobody knows what an insurgent body can do"
17   Ibid.: L. Davis, "Love and Revolution in Ursula Le Guin's 'Four Ways to Forgiveness"
18   Ibid.: L. Call, "Structures of desire. Postanarchist kink in the speculative fiction of Octavia Butler and Samuel Delany."

the problems of power and subjectivity in society and how post-anarchism, which he defines as a form of contemporary anarchist theory – an heir of postmodernism and poststructuralism, seeks to take anarchism beyond its traditional limits. This includes the deconstruction of conventional forms of sexual identity through Michel Foucault, Judith Butler, and Gayle Rubin, and it leads to queer and kink universes.

In "Amateurism and Anarchism in the creation of autonomous queer spaces,"[19] Gavin Brown studies new forms of radical politics that incorporate ethical goals, such as cooperative, non-hierarchical, sex-positive relationships, and how they are put into practice as free collective processes that are created and maintained through relationships built on reciprocity and recognition. These processes create spaces that haven't been handed down from institutions or people in positions of authority, hierarchy, or power. That is why they are truly autonomous and self-run.

Finally, the Non-Monogamies and Contemporary Intimacies Conference (NMCI), which is organized within the framework of the European project Citizenship, Care and Choice: The Micropolitics of Intimacy in Southern Europe (INTIMATE),[20] offers different descriptors in the call, which are directly related to relationship anarchy. The contributions accepted for the three conferences held so far include analyses that are very much in line with all these concepts.[21]

These include: "Non-sexual and/or non-romantic relationships and emerging identities, such as asexuality and a-romanticism," "Intersections between non-monogamies and feminist theories, LGBT studies, gender, and queer studies, post/de-colonialism and

---

[19] Ibid.: G. Brown, "Amateurism and Anarchism in the creation of autonomous queer spaces"
[20] https://ces.uc.pt/intimate
[21] Among many others: "What is a family? Sexual and dependency ties in law and utopia," by Daniela Danna; "Non-Conventional Relationship Choices for the Over-Sixties," by John Button; "Relationship Anarchy: Breaking the paradigm" by Amanda Rose, and "Polynormativity!? – Revisiting the relationship anarchist critique of polyamory," by Gesa Mayer

other anti-oppressive strands," "Sex work, pornographies (mainstream or otherwise) and other capitalist-sexual crossovers within the broader field of intimacies," "Connections between religion and non-monogamies considered hegemonic," "New normativities and new resistances: polynormativity and relationship anarchy, neo-liberalism and political contestation." Related projects were also presented at other academic events held by the INTIMATE project.[22]

Academic activity focused on relationship anarchy continues to grow. Interest in this new proposal suggests that it is likely here to stay and that its ubiquitous influence may become increasingly significant.

Queer collectives

The queer gaze questions essentialism and power relations in the dominant society and culture in the West. Regarding gender, it rejects the hegemonic idea that this identity category is binary, natural, innate, essential, and unchanging – that it's dictated by biology. Instead, it suggests that it is a product of cultural construction, social norms, and individual situations. With this broad, critical questioning of what's "normal" and what's normative, queer theory holds the potential to deconstruct hierarchies, differences, and axes of control and domination by social structures, as well as those that some individuals hold over others.

Relationship anarchy, on the other hand, proposes not dividing relationships into the binary of affective-sexual or friendship. It questions the idea that the traditional family – specifically, the reproductive, heteronormative couple – is the natural, innate form of relationship. It also discusses how some types of relationships are privileged over others, including their characteristics in terms of

---

[22] Such as "Thinking Relationship Anarchy (RA) from a Transfeminist Perspective" by Roma De Las Heras (an expanded, more developed version appears in R. De las Heras, "Thinking Relationship Anarchy from a Queer Feminist Approach," *Sociological Research Online*, 2018), "Queer Friendship, Support and Vulnerability" by Varpu Alassutari, or "Chosen Families: Seeking the Possibilities of the Concept in the Case of Communal Living" by Anna Heinonen.

sexual orientations, gender identities, practices of greater or lesser intimacy, or adapting to social expectations. As I've already mentioned, Andie Nordgren defines themself as "a genderqueer relationship hacker."

Both proposals, therefore, share multiple suppositions, including the premise that gender stereotypes have historically been a way of articulating an axis of privilege where men position themselves on top and assume power, as well as sexual and reproductive control, over women. For this framework to work, the heterosexual mold must be preserved and highlighted to the greatest extent possible by condemning, invisiblizing, and eradicating any expression that moves away from heteronormative principles and sexual binarism. Blueprints for relationships, which are also stereotyped, heteronormative, and amatonormative (founded in conventional views on romantic relationships), are another fundamental pillar of this historically determined model of social construction.

The word "queer" first started to be used in this sense in the United States during the 1990s, as part of what has been called the third wave of sexual radicalism (the first two waves were the initial movements that defended the rights of homosexuals at the beginning of the 20th century and the gay and lesbian liberation movement in the '60s and '70s). This was part of a growing effort to foreground the diversity of sexual forms of expression, inclinations, desires, and gazes by distancing them from normative patterns. In the 21st century, though, its meaning has evolved towards more fundamental approaches that challenge gender categories, as previously noted. These approaches also encourage deconstructing the cultural and formative frameworks that shape our attitudes and relational guidelines by bridging dualities like male/female, heterosexual/homosexual, and, in what would be a proposal that would inevitably converge with relationship anarchy: intimate relationship/friendship.

Essentialism, which the queer gaze brings into question, suggests that there are certain characteristics that define the category assigned to each human being. It can be challenging to grasp just how significant these stereotyped, rigid, absolute canons are when it comes to keeping societies channeled within limits that don't threaten the normative order and the system. As we reach those first stages of life where we recognize what seems to be personal autonomy, we start building an idealized version of our identity and our future according to these canons. All of a sudden, we start hearing categorical statements like, "now you're a man," "you'll be a woman soon," or "it's about time you have a boyfriend (or girlfriend)." We go through rituals of affirmation in terms of gender, entering the relationship market, being praised for responsibility, and a near-urgency to start shaping a future by achieving the typical academic background and professional career, a normative family, a socio-economic level that suits the expectations put on us by our environment, and ultimately, a path to success and social integration.

Through expectations, chimerical projections of ideal futures (the American dream), and the monolithic, iron-clad conceptions of identity that we've inherited, we keep the mechanisms of power working, safe from dissent and dangerous metamorphoses. Each axis of identity determines its own affinities and antagonisms. The intersection of all these dimensions of disparity gives rise to an equilibrium built through the dissolution and detours of struggles and rebellions. This equilibrium steers us towards confrontations that are innocuous for the system, as they are incapable of challenging the true axes of privilege, subordination, and oppression. In *Polyamory and Queer Anarchism: Infinite Possibilities for Resistance*,[23] Susan Song (United States) says the following despite not yet knowing about (or at least, not mentioning) relationship anarchy, which had already begun to spread throughout Europe:

---

23 S. Song, "Polyamory and Queer Anarchism: Infinite Possibilities for Resistance," in C.B. Daring, J. Rogue, Deric Shannon, and Abbey Volcano. *Queering Anarchism: Essays on Gender, Power, and Desire*, AK Press, Oakland, 2012

"As anarchists interested and working in areas of sexual politics and in fighting all oppressions, we can create a new "queer-anarchist" form of relating that combines anarchist concepts of mutual aid, solidarity, and voluntary association with a queer analysis of normativity and power. (...) We can use queer theory to conceptualize new relationship forms and social relations that resist patriarchy and other oppressions by creating a distinctly "queer-anarchist" form of social relation. By allowing for multiple and fluid forms of identifying and relating sexually that go beyond a gay/straight binary, a queer anarchist practice allows for challenging the state and capitalism, as well as challenging sexual oppressions and norms that are often embedded in the state and other hierarchical social relations."

Non-monogamous collectives

The concept of relationship anarchy is still seeing quite modest social diffusion. Still, it has for a while now enjoyed some popularity in blog posts, articles, and meetings of collectives that are interested in non-normative relationships, especially non-monogamous relationship models. As we will see in the chapter on relational activism, few collectives specifically geared towards relationship anarchy actually meet regularly. Rather, those who identify totally or partially with the label form part of a larger group. In that context, various levels of relational normativity are questioned and often grouped under the umbrella terms of "polyamory," "ethical non-monogamies," or "non-normative relationships."

Currently, there is a growing trend around the term "polyamory" on social networks and in media around the world, though it is not always defined in a polished or rigorous manner. The informative handling and prominence given to it, which often veers towards sensationalism, has given rise to particular stigmatization due to hypersexualization, objectification, and marginalization of the practices and approaches broadly grouped under this term.[24]

---

[24] This effect is less pronounced in European media than on other continents, likely thanks to a more responsible journalistic criterion in this case and to the special care and dedication of those representing activist groups.

As a result, some of the people who are starting to call themselves relationship anarchists do so perhaps to escape this stigma. It's a new label that's less tainted (for now) and sounds good – both radical and rebellious. Their views and relational practices may actually fit into the model of relationship anarchy, but I think it's important for this identification to be conscious and informed, not the result of simply rushing forward.

And that is precisely one of the reasons for writing this book. It's not meant to define or stake out a "Universal Reference Book on Relationship Anarchy," propose some "Relationship Anarchy Seal of Approval," or create card-carrying members of relationship anarchy. It is the defense of a specific, defined interpretation backed with arguments and sincere enthusiasm that — without trying to quell discussion — offers a personal approach that strives to be as clear as possible while avoiding the thoughtless, sterile "anything goes" attitude that threatens to hollow out the content of a proposal that I find so interesting and valuable.

In many non-monogamous forms of relationship, strains of the hegemonic model always re-emerge, creating a privileged situation without any discussion or critique. Agreements with the existing "loves" determine the limits and obligations of whoever has agreed to them, as well as anyone else who may become involved. We could call this a kind of dictatorship of prior agreements. This culture of consensus sometimes justifies hierarchies, privileges, prerogatives, vetoes, power dynamics... all under the motto, "if it's consensual, it's ethical." I'll talk more about this in the chapter on relationship models and practices.

Asexual and aromantic individuals

Another group that has shown special interest in relationship anarchy's approaches is sexual and aromantic people. They can find in this model the possibility of creating relationships in a more flexible way, not in terms of stability but in terms of what is expected of them. More specifically, some individuals don't feel sexual attraction but do experience romantic passion or affinity of a personal, intellectual, or playful nature, to name a few possibilities. Others (rightly) want to break the mold for romantic love, either because they fail to fit into that scheme based on personal, ideological, or pragmatic decisions.

However, relating to these dissident identities doesn't mean that these people don't also experience a deep need to connect with others in a non-trivial way. This doesn't fit neatly into the hegemonic relationship model. In an environment where the behaviors expected in a more or less intimate relationship are not pre-defined, though, the pressure is undoubtedly much lower, and the possibilities are infinite.

For those who belong to the asexual community, relationship anarchy is important because it is the only approach that offers a way to combat allosexism, meaning that it removes sex as an indicator for and measure of a relationship's value. In common social settings – even open-minded, liberal, non-monogamous ones – the answer to the question "So are you having sex (yet) or not?" can mean the difference between a less-important relationship ("just friends") and a significant one.

In fact, one of the most cited texts in the field of relationship anarchy in recent years is the entry "Relationship Anarchy Basics"[25] on the blog The Thinking Asexual (now, The Thinking Aro, short for *aromantic*). There, as in other analyses, the author starts with the competing models at the time: monogamy and polyamory. It's assumed that relationship anarchy has to be compared with the latter or (mistakenly) that it's a form of polyamory.

The key factors highlighted are, of course, those related to sex and romance. As such, the text starts by stating that a polyamorous person can be just as amatonormative as a monogamous person (as

---

25 Relationship Anarchy Basics, on thethinkingasexual.wordpress.com.

I see it, this is obvious: both types of relationships are amatonormative by construction). In both cases, there are distinguishable expectations and behaviors, and there are specific times and places for a relationship that's assigned the label "romance + sex." Intimacy, care, commitment, and certain levels of attention are therefore limited according to these relational traits. The author goes on to say that those who identify with relationship anarchy, however, start from a place of indeterminacy and go about developing each relationship without expectations or behaviors that have been specified in advance.

For an asexual person who has spent years explaining that they don't have a disease, that they're not missing anything, that not everyone perceives sexual attraction as a need to be happy,[26] it's hard to face each new relationship with the demand to accept sexual practice in order to gain access to the level of intimacy, connection, and mutual understanding that they want. The same goes for those who don't want to share the codes, obligations, and myths of romantic love. It's the feeling that they're barred from forming relationships according to their own wishes and conditions, at least in part. In other words (going back to what I've listed several times as features of the "partner brand"), if an asexual person is seeking to build a project of coexistence, tenderness and deep emotional intimacy, physical and sensual closeness, one where they share vulnerabilities, child-raising, and long-term commitment, they have to step outside of the normative categories offered. In the realm of friendship, they would find something quite different from what they desire; by participating in a normative couple, they would be leading the other person to abstinence or infidelity.

---

26 See the accessible, interesting, and well-documented article "Cuando la atracción sexual no existe" on huffingtonpost.es.

Colonized cultures

The processes of colonization, both physical — territorial — and cultural, entail the phenomenon of colonizing forces progressively imposing their morality and way of life on the colonized people. The cultural assumptions of the conqueror become hegemonic, and previous customs and practices are considered atavistic, backward, and immoral. In the case of indigenous peoples, especially in North America, academic Kim TallBear[27] and other authors[28] have investigated these processes of colonization in terms of social relations. They describe traditional ways of life where relationships, coexistence, and care show very clear and interesting collective components. These structures have been destroyed due to the moral prejudices of colonizing forces and their cultural impositions.

The author of the blog The Critical Polyamorist, as well as other works, analyzes these cultural changes, which were primarily backed by the imperative of the couple-centric nuclear family. This *settler sexuality*, based on Scott Lauria Morgensen's work on *settler homonationalism,* is defined as "a white national heteronormativity that regulates Indigenous sexuality and gender by supplanting them with the sexual modernity of settler subjects" – which is also increasingly true of homonormativity.

TallBear, who was born and raised in an indigenous community, reveals the extent to which she perceived the influence of settler morality every time that white people, or even the majority of indigenous individuals who had been subjected to the same narratives, judged the families that followed the customs of their people as unsuccessful, failed, broken, or dysfunctional. They pigeonholed adolescents that had early pregnancies or single mothers, though these people would have been perfectly integrated and happy in the native

---

[27] K. TallBear, "Making Love and Relations Beyond Settler Sex and Family" in Adele E. Clarke and Donna Haraway, *Making Kin Not Population*, op. Cit.
[28] S. L. Morgensen, "Settler Homonationalism: Theorizing Settler Colonialism within Queer Modernities," *GLQ: A Journal of Lesbian and Gay Studies*, 2010 and A. Willey *Undoing Monogamy: The Politics of Science and the Possibilities of Biology.* Duke University Press, Durham/London, 2016.

culture, free from stigmatizing labels and supported by a fully functional and loving network of care. The point is that culturally imposed, heterosexual forms of amatonormativity have been adopted by homosexual forms that took on the former without actually being any less imposing or ethnocentric.

New norms like consensual non-monogamies and polyamory threaten to create a similar situation. This is because the settler sexuality is challenged only in part, extending the couple-centric model to a model of multiple couples.[29] This normative structure still does not recognize indigenous forms of family, the importance of collective solidarity, networks of care and affection, or a sustainable relationship with others and the natural environment as successful models of life and relationship structures. In TallBear's words:[30]

> "... nonmonogamous people also often privilege sexual relating in their definitions of what constitutes ethical nonmonogamy, or plural loves. Might we have great loves that don't involve sex? Loves whom we do not compartmentalize into friend versus lover, with the word "just" preceding "friends?" Most of the great loves of my life are humans who I do or did not relate to sexually. They include my closest family members, and also a man who I have had sexual desire for, but that is not the relationship it is possible for us to have. I love him without regret. We have never been physically intimate. Is this somehow a "just" friends relationship? I do not love him less than the people I have been "in love" with. Might we also not have great and important loves that do not even involve other humans, but rather vocations, art, and other practices?"

Western culture still has strong supremacist convictions on other cultural traditions. This idea of superiority is anchored in material facts, such as military, scientific, and technological dominance, yet it automatically extends to religious and moral aspects, such as

---

29 "Couple-centricity, polyamory and colonialism," on criticalpolyamorist.com.
30 "Looking for love in too many languages...," on criticalpolyamorist.com.

monotheism versus polytheism, the relationship with nature (dominance versus fusion), or the relationships between people (structural monogamy versus different forms of polygyny and polyandry). There are strong and established cultural certainties as to which is the true God (even atheistic people show some level of respect so as not to hurt the "religious sentiment" of those who believe in these great gods) and which are the childish idols of backward tribes, figures we have no qualms joking about and caricaturing.

The same is true of nature, which we're altering at levels leading to worldwide catastrophe, and of relationships and love. The free, rapturous, inspiring, Western romantic love that has been the subject of countless works of art is the only "true" form. Any other way of relating to others is an atrocity imposed by primitive cultures. See that? Imposed! Everything I don't do is imposed by tyrannical cultural mandates. As for everything that I do, of course, that isn't the case – even if a billion other people are doing the same thing.

Much like how not recognizing one elevated, sublime, sacred, supreme God is a sign of primitivism, not recognizing one elevated, sublime, sacred, supreme Love is a sign of immorality, inferiority, heretical and savage ignorance. Of course, I (author or reader) don't identify with this description of narrow ethnocentrism. I'm progressive, I'm open-minded about all cultures and worldviews, everybody has their own perspective... utmost respect for it! But some part of that ethnocentrism has burrowed down into the deep recesses of my mind and my emotions and is there to stay. Maybe, if I think about it carefully, it isn't actually that small or residual. We carry everything that has built our personality and our morals within us. Being aware that it's there and that it is racism, xenophobia, and aporophobia isn't a solution, but perhaps it is a first step.

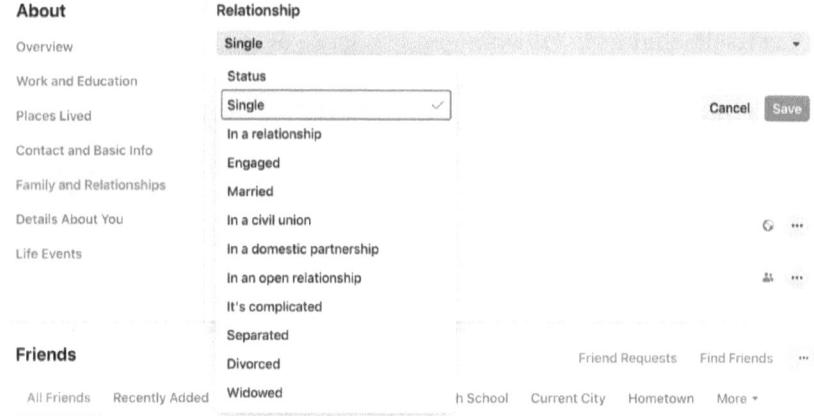

Relationship statuses on Facebook. The option for relationship anarchy might be: Has unique, valuable ties (and not all of them include sex or romance).

Other communities

In the following chapters, I will analyze other options that we could qualify as pseudo-normative, such as open relationships, swingers, or even sexual infidelity. However, there are many more dimensions of sexual and gender expression, orientation, and identity. Facebook, for instance, offers up to 71 identity options and various pronouns, depending on the language. A list of 108 identities appears on the Genderfluid Support[31] blog. This proliferation started in the 1960s and became more formalized in the '80s especially through Judith Butler's work; the aim is to sort out plural, diverse feelings.

The logical evolution of this increasingly necessary recognition of the diversity of people's perceptions, experiences, expressions, and attractions may expand to ways of relating and subjectivize those ties, moving away from uniformity and amatonormative binarism. In this case, perhaps it's not a question of expanding the list of relationship statuses on social networks beyond "engaged," "married,"

---

31 "Gender Master List," on genderfluidsupport.tumblr.com

"open relationship," or even "it's complicated," but rather that the box itself, that list, will stop making sense over time.

1.4 Perspectives, interpretations, and critical views

Understanding based on privilege analysis

The way a society is organized and its set of normative values always involve the legitimation of privileges and the censorship of behaviors that are atypical or critical of those values. The prevailing structure in our environment grants the couple (the normative couple, whether dating, married, in a domestic partnership... or even non-ritualized but socially read as such) a series of rights: couple privilege.

I'm not just talking about legal or economic prerogatives, which are clear enough. I also mean how automatically legible a relationship is in terms of emotional and life importance without the need for further clarification. Such is the case in terms of care expectations ("What's your relationship to them?" we're asked at the hospital or other institutions when we ask about or want to visit or care for someone there), respect (how does the average heterosexual, cisgender man act differently towards someone who he perceives as a woman depending on whether or not he thinks she has a partner – especially if she is heterosexual and even more so if the partner, another cis hetero man, is present?), social value (again, especially for women: can we identify any difference in the value given to words like girl, miss, ma'am?), long-term commitment, robustness, and much more.

Over a century ago, Emma Goldman was already thinking about how the institution of marriage, which was obviously much more coercive and inescapable at that time, was a tool of oppression used by the State and the patriarchy against women to subjugate them even in the most intimate spheres of personal life. Goldman suggested rebelling against this structure of men's control and ownership over women's bodies through the idea of free love; this marked a true symbolic revolution against the entire hegemonic scheme of authoritarian ideologies.[32]

Today, there may be a clearer awareness that someone possessing another is not acceptable and that no one should ever exercise control over someone else's behavior, much less within the framework of a social structure that automatically positions some individuals over others. Still, recognizing the existence of structures of control does not assure that I'm immune from the possibility of unconsciously adopting this thought, a notion that has surrounded us and shaped us our entire lives, time and time again.

I've been taught to believe that I'm entitled to give permission to those I have relationships with that are of a certain degree of intensity; to tell them (without any further consideration, per the privilege I've acquired) that something they do bothers me (even when I am not there); to hold them responsible for my happiness; to know the details of their private lives; to blame them for my insecurities, jealousy, lacks; to tolerate their emotions and actions (as long as they don't affect me too much); to insist that they understand my needs without me having to express them (because they're determined by the norm: they should know how to take care of a man/how to treat a woman); to get angry when something doesn't meet my expectations...

Even though something so commonplace and intimate may seem far-removed from the social axes of power and oppression, there's probably not another more singularly political act than trying to identify involuntary authoritarian actions, the nearly invisible components of the hegemonic instructions we've received. Any relationship model that aims to be ethical must have at its very core an analysis of power relations and proposals aimed at changing them.

---

32 E. Goldman, Emma Goldman's anarchism and other essays, Mother Earth, New York/London, 1911.

Another example of power relations are those that show up in romantic, sexual interactions, per the heteronormative model. Expressing yourself, talking to someone, behaving, socializing, flirting, or fucking in a way that is fully aligned with and defined by the gender roles you identify with can be an important, healthy statement if your identity is not hegemonic. However, it is generally an exercise of power if you're cisgender, especially a cis man (assigned male at birth and identifying with that category). Transforming – or at least softening – the behaviors, traits, and habits associated with the binary male-female interaction while trying to build relationships that are less shaped by gender is, therefore, another tool that's of great political interest.

The same can be said of other dimensions of privilege that heavily determine the ways we relate to each other: socio-economic status, culture, ability, race, origin, age, functional diversity, the very axis of privilege defined by differences in erotic, social, and sexual capital... These are important aims in terms of deconstruction and criticism that a relationship anarchist approach must prioritize.

It's precisely those who are most vulnerable, individuals with less power and privilege, who could benefit the most from the shift from a society of atomized, nuclear, individualistic relationships to a system based on broad networks, where relationships are not subject to cultural mandates on being labelled and defined by anything other than the needs, desires, and capacities of their members, where reciprocity is not determined on an individual basis but between each person and the group. Whoever can buy care with money or social and relational capital, whoever can get around freely, communicate effectively, anyone with access to a family of origin that has financial ability, and so on – they don't need much else.

For all these reasons, collective awareness, activism, and building networks based on affection, solidarity, support, and common identification against oppressions are fundamental aspects and deeply rooted in social anarchist culture. These, along with everything else, make up the axes of the revolutionary gears and the articulation of a paradigm shift that will not result in the assault on any institution (such as the couple or romantic love) or even a war over positions. Instead, this constitutes a utopian horizon that's looking towards the future, a horizon it is moving towards through example, visibility, and normalization over what will surely be generations.

The neoliberal, individualistic, apolitical gaze

This would be the exact opposite point of view: tailoring the blueprint for relationship anarchy to hegemonic logic (under the model that was called statist and bourgeois and is now labeled as democratic, capitalist, and neoliberal in Western societies; this would take other socio-economic forms in different places, but they always result in structural inequality, power, and privilege). It's common – almost universal – for any interesting or successful approach to be swallowed up by the dominant dialectic and for a moderate, sugar-coated version to be woven into the common parlance of the day. That way, it poses less of a threat to the *status quo* or may even be beneficial for it in its constant process of preparing to reach new markets.

In this field, the apolitical interpretation — which is always just as political as any other form — generally focuses on defending personal freedom, individualism,[33] and upholding the entire capitalist, consumerist, objectifying, heteropatriarchal imaginary. In most cases, this approach is likely not consciously chosen but a spontaneous process of accommodating the dominant cultural structure. In other words, in the absence of clear critical reference points that are collectively prepared and shared through deliberative processes where personal visions and experiences are reflected in a broad, diverse way, unestablished signifiers are filled with the prevailing

---

33 I'm not talking about individualistic anarchism, which I'll refer to later on and which represents a philosophical tradition of anarchism that emphasizes personal autonomy and opposition to state or social control over individuals.

meanings. We could, then, say that the understanding I'm analyzing here entails a naturalized reading and, as such, the default route, which is what I'm interested in highlighting and questioning.

Materially, the concept of "freedom" is not usually used in its virtuous meaning of conscious, responsible autonomy, emancipation, and empowerment prevailing, but in the sense of "freedom of the most powerful" and, specifically, exemption from commitment and responsibility over those who have less power. This clashes with the prevailing meaning in anarchist contexts, where the notion of freedom is examined – or should be examined – in a framework that's closely tied to the collective aspect and power dynamics.

An excerpt from a blog post on "Queer Anarchism"[34] offers a personal experience and a reflection that illustrates these ideas quite well:

> "I need to tell you something" the guy I just took to my tiny hotel room tells me as we lie down on the bed "I am a relationship anarchist". This is of little importance to me. We just hooked up in a bar (an anarchist bar so this is also no surprise to me). I am on vacation and moving out in 3 days. Why should I care about how he conducts his relationships? But he seems to think this requires further clarification. "That means I have sex with multiple people and I do not label those contacts as relationships. I see people when I want to see them." Again, this is of little importance to me.
>
> But his words linger. Is that what relationship anarchy is? Polyamory combined with non-commitment? I really hope not. That kind of individual freedom, the freedom to not form lasting relationships, the freedom to always follow your own desires, the commitmentless fucking around, sounds more like relationship capitalism to me. Yet this guy wasn't the first 'relationship anarchist' I've met who defined relationship anarchism as 'I do whatever I want'.

---

[34] "Relationship anarchy could be about so much more than the freedom to fuck," on queeranarchism.tumblr.com

I guess why relationship anarchy rarely appeals to me is because its practitioners often seem too obsessed with nonmonogamy. Anarchism, to me, is very much about commitment. About building communities. Communities that reject the 'rules' of capitalism, of ownership, of jobs, of productive and unproductive members, of competition. Communities that instead choose care, cooperation, equality, acknowledgement that our differences make our strengths, and each to contribute according to their ability and to receive according to their need. And in that community, we make the rules that suit us, and end them when they no longer suit our community.

Relationship anarchism then, to me, means community. A community of two or of many. A community that rejects the 'rules' of relationships, of enforced heterosexuality, enforced monogamy, of partners being entitled to sex, of marriage, of childcare being a two-person job and of the idea that we need a romantic or sexual relationship to be complete. A community that instead choses care, cooperation, equality, acknowledgement that we are more than our relationship and that we all have different needs. And in that community, we make the rules that suit us, and end them when they no longer suit our community.

By that definition, an anarchist relationship is first and foremost one of cooperation and setting our own rules. By that definition, it is not self-serving but always mutually beneficial. By that definition, it can be a monogamous relationship if that's what makes the people involved feel happiest. By that definition, it can be about friendship, about romance, about sex, about a selection of those things, but by definition it will be about care. And intuitively, I'd say an anarchist relationship is a mutual support system against the brutal, oppressive capitalist world around us. The world is an extremely fucked up oppressive place that seeks to divide us but we have chosen to support each other, to create a safe space within the rooms that we share when we share them, to help each other through tough days and tough years, to remind each other that we're in this together.

> This automatically-polyamorous commitment-free 'I do whatever I want' version of relationship anarchism feels nothing like that."

As we've seen before, the cultural context and the literalness of many of the proposals by Andie Nordgren and others who initially developed the approach of relationship anarchy clearly locate their starting point in the realm of anarchism (anarchism applied to relationships). However, most of the literature, reviews, references, and articles published since curiously define and approach it from an apolitical perspective. It seems that the word "anarchy," which has been present in the label itself from the very start, has become inexplicably transparent, invisible. Undoubtedly, how the prevailing concept of anarchy is understood in the current symbolic universe of the majority — an interpretation that is deeply flawed and evokes disorder, chaos, and confusion, rather than order and solidarity without recourse to imposition and authority — has contributed to this general invisibility, which even suggests a certain collective psychological defense mechanism.

The gender perspective

One particularly relevant axis of privilege in terms of the normativity of relationships is obviously that of gender. First and foremost, this is because this axis intersects virtually every dimension of society and life. This is especially true in the realm of relationships, and significantly so; it is the first link in a long chain that patriarchy uses in its structural control and subordination of women.

In Western society over the last two centuries, the hetero-monogamous romantic myth has been the main cultural weapon deployed to sustain a model that is morally acceptable to broad social majorities[35] and which allows women to occupy a well-differentiated place dedicated to reproduction, family, and care-taking. This myth places

---

[35] Before, at least since Hellenic culture, in many parts of the world during various historical periods (with interesting exceptions), similar objectives were imposed via the argument of women's inferior intellectual capacity and moral character.

women in what is supposedly a symbolically superior position (the object that men desire to conquer), yet this position is objectified and materially subordinated to the standards of being attractive and worthy of the love of the most powerful men. They're put into competition with other women, into permanent insecurity and fear of their physical beauty declining, of the failure associated with being an "old maid," forced sweetness and meek submission to the rules – all under the threat of marginalization and expulsion from the race for that romantic ideal at the slightest disobedience.

The nature of relationships, according to this omnipresent cultural construction, is materialized as a scheme of acquisition, possession, guarantees, security, shielding, and protection of the strength of the bond. This life event has a starting point – falling in love – and becomes a position to defend, a bulwark: the marital relationship (monogamous or not). It's no coincidence that there are echoes of wartime in this vocabulary: this construct has been designed by men and specially adapted to the capacities and aptitudes attributed to masculinity.

Aspects associated with hegemonic femininity, such as care-taking and communication, are part of the daily routine of relationships, but they're kept discreetly in the background. They're processes that are carried out organically, continually. It's affection, warmth, attention, love – but not "The Relationship." The conventional relationship is an object that almost has a life of its own, a project, a link, an alliance – not a daily process of offering mutual aid, experiences, attention, affinities, trust. I don't mean to say that a romantic relationship doesn't include all this (at least for some time, and in some lucky cases, without an expiration date), but that the relationship *is not* this. The stereotypical relationship is epically built on the traits of the masculine cliché, object and property, not the traits imposed on female socialization, which are more human and have to do with processes and solidarity.

Relationship anarchy — with its aim of not dealing with the norm's prescriptive aspect defining each relationship, like some object or box with a tag on it — leads to considering relationships as a process of development, an evolution, a transformation. Instead of "we are" or "we want (or consider ourselves) to be," "we do" or "we want to do." A path where insecurities and lacks are points along the way, much like emotions, passions, and mutual understandings, rather than markers of a condition or a (civil) status. Without those means of control available as levers of a coercive mechanism – the threat of failure; the fear of loneliness, exclusion, or going unlabeled – patriarchy loses a fundamental weapon, one that resides in each happy (or settled) and integrated monogamous, heterosexual couple, each in their own semi-detached house, townhouse, or neighborhood apartment.

In her most influential work, *Sexual Politics*,[36] Kate Millet, the leading voice of second-wave feminism in North America, writes:

> "Patriarchy's chief institution is the family. It is both a mirror of and a connection with the larger society; a patriarchal unit within a patriarchal whole. Mediating between the individual and the social structure, the family effects control and conformity where political and other authorities are insufficient. As the fundamental instrument and the foundation unit of patriarchal society the family and its roles are prototypical. Serving as an agent of the larger society, the family not only encourages its own members to adjust and conform, but acts as a unit in the government of the patriarchal state which rules its citizens through its family heads. Even in patriarchal societies where they are granted legal citizenship, women tend to be ruled through the family alone and have little or no formal relation to the state."

The logic of success, competitiveness, and individualism built for two is a race where the strongest wins, a tailor-made contest to reinforce the patriarchal capitalist structure (modeled on States with

---

36 K. Millet, *Sexual Politics*, Granada Publishing, London, 1969.

diverse economic regimes, which are also patriarchal). When relationships of a certified quality – love, the couple, the traditional family – are seen as resources (meaning they are scarce and exclusive) that must be obtained and conserved, the result can only be the most privileged members getting the upper hand and control, thereby reinforcing the axes of oppression, especially that of gender.

Going back to the origins of anarchist thought is interesting and quite surprising, as we can trace the already long history of these ideas; statements made by women more than a century ago can still be provocative and utopian. I'm leaving an orderly catalog and a multitude of examples for the section dedicated to anarcho-feminism; these include the ideas of Mary Wollstonecraft, Voltarine De Cleyre, Emma Goldman, and other authors who defended women's emancipation through solidarity and mutual aid; access to education and contraception; critique of the nuclear family, marriage, motherhood, economic dependence, marginalization and contempt of women without a husband; and objectification and hyper-sexualization.

In recent years, one of the victories won by feminist movements has been that the culture of consent has, little by little, found a stronger foothold in society. This culture insists that individual limits must be scrupulously respected and personal freedom defended in the form of bodily and emotional autonomy – agency and the power to make decisions for one's own body. These limits must be expressed clearly, but above all, that expression must be understood as a firm decision that is specific to that moment and situation, while also being revocable at any time. This culture perfectly reflects the character of the freedom that relationship anarchy upholds and encourages. This is not the freedom to do anything that is pleasurable or beneficial without thinking about others, abuse privileges in an individualistic way, or make decisions without considering anyone else. It's the freedom to decide about one's own time, space, and body, while also upholding consideration for and mutual aid between everyone in a network of affection and ties, in accordance with the principles of supportive, collective anarchism.

On the other hand, we must remember that, in this society, neither anarchism as a whole nor relationship anarchy – or practically any other relational model or behavior – is currently free from an inevitable sexist bias. The history of anarchism is told, written, and thought primarily in terms of men. Relationship anarchy is created with an anti-patriarchal sentiment and queer influences; however, the practices it inspires are still subject to the same privilege and power gradients that are at play in society at large. No one idea or proposal is going to end patriarchal privileges. The best we can aspire to in the medium-term is recognizing the importance of gender as a determining factor in all our practices and expressions.

As the author of this book, I admit that it is written from a masculine point of view. I'll explain this away with a smile, saying that this just so happens to be the case, it's a coincidence – at least I recognize it and say it out loud. And it's true that recognizing gender's role in each relational interaction and attempting to address it – minimize it – is a first step. But recognizing and rejecting a phenomenon is not the same as pretending it won't come up. This takes place every day, and its victims "just so happen" to always be the same people – and they're not cis-het men.

Critiques of relationship anarchy

Of course, this concept hasn't only garnered support. Objections, questions, difficulties, failures, and disappointments are often raised, both from ideological points of view as well as life experience. Not everyone shares the idea of politicizing the personal; moreover, the relational practices associated with an anarchist approach require important life changes that entail making efforts in communication, involvement, commitment, and generosity.

First, political motivation as a desire to contribute to transforming society is not a big factor for many who express interest in a non-normative relationship style. In fact, as Laura Portwood-Stacer says in her book *Lifestyle Politics and Radical Activism*[37]:

> "A puristic anti-normativity position risks reproducing the liberal model of free choice that treats individual acts as pure expressions of personal agency, even though systemic power relations are always at work in structuring those acts. To invoke this discourse is both to dismiss the real obstacles that work against the adoption of oppositional identifications and practices and to excuse people when their choices happen to replicate traditional oppressive relationships. The likely effect of a movement purporting to reject norms altogether is the invisible conservation of dominant norms from within and beyond that movement."

However, it is not exactly anti-normative purism that leads to reluctance among non-politicized groups that often don't have a conscious view of gender. It's the lack of recognition around the existence of structures of oppression, such as patriarchy, homophobia, growing inequality in capitalist societies, and so on, that generates the greatest opposition to an understanding of the new proposals for relationship models that is both based on free-thought and supportive. Anyone who isn't aware of how far these axes of oppression can reach – cutting through societies and compounding their effects by positioning some in places of privilege and others under multiple gradients of domination – can believe that they have the right to act freely from their position, which is usually one of power, and that rules only get in the way.

For those who are privileged in hegemonic dimensions, it's hard to recognize (to perceive, even more than acknowledge) their position or the very existence of these axes of power. This is due to not only a lack of motivation to do so (assuming even a minimum degree of intellectual honesty) but also because of the naturalization that cultural hegemony imposes on those privileges: the feeling of "I'm worth it." Thus, a very common attitude in practice responds to the

---

[37] L. Portwood-Stacer, *Lifestyle Politics and Radical Activism*, Bloomsbury, London, 2013.

assumption that all people have the same possibilities to be happy, communicate, socialize, attract, to free ourselves from our fears, lacks, and insecurities. From that reading, the temptation that often snares us is that of the free market of relationships: everyone has their own cross to bear. In such cases, an interpretation of relationship anarchy in the terms that I'm developing in this book is obviously nothing more than an annoying Jiminy Cricket, some unnecessary complication that elicits something along the lines of, "you're always politicizing everything!"

The second critique (the first was the question about the need for a political vision of the personal) seems much more significant and transcendent to me. It is about the difficulty and considerable degree of commitment and dedication that the move to an anarchist relationship model entails for someone born and raised in a society where structural serial monogamy (although this may only be apparent monogamy, given the frequency with which infidelity occurs) and patriarchal heterocentrism (which is also imperfect, given the more or less clandestine disruptive practices of heteronormativity) are not only dominant, but virtually the only widely available reference points. Grappling with the ubiquitous idea of the couple as a basic social construct isn't easy. Overcoming – truly overcoming – the strong, deeply-rooted emotions that inhabit the complex feeling of jealousy often requires work, discipline, and repeated failure. The same is needed to put the principle of having no authority and the agency and well-being of others on par with one's own needs for safety and comfort, or with the needs of one's crushes and loves. All these difficulties are real; they appear over and over on a daily basis in non-normative relationships and practices. I'll delve into this topic in Chapter 5.

The culture I've grown up in is like a multidimensional starting point that sets the limits and boundaries of where I can go, even when I'm trying my hardest to push past the various ethical, aesthetic, intellectual, and emotional aspects. Pushing against these is a painful process that takes me out of the comfort of my position, the comfortable support I receive from my surroundings, the protection of the mainstream that lets me take a break, instead of having to paddle constantly just to stay on course.

Material and economic sustainability aren't out of this cultural octopus's reach. In the short-term, it's hard for many to renounce the support of the nuclear family to set out on an adventure in search of other forms of coexistence and mutual care, usually without any references at hand. On such an adventure, everything can blow up at any time because we haven't experienced cultural assimilation of the new conditions, nor do we have experience in how to take the steps needed, nor do we even know where to take them or where they may lead us.

But once the decision has been made, perhaps the most complicated part isn't keeping up with the daily behaviors and practices on the path that I've set for myself (to try to be happy, to honor my ethical principles, and to take care of those around me), but keeping the expectations associated with my cultural construct from constantly appearing in my thought process. Expectations can be the most toxic, destructive, and complex ingredients in the entire cocktail of obstacles and impediments to a shift in the relationship model.

Another objection that may be made to relationship anarchy's approach has to do with the risk involved in seeing this proposal as going a step further in comparison to other non-normative relationship models – seeing this as the final frontier for those who have challenged some hegemonic relationship guidelines but have (ironically) not arrived at the highest realm of emotional bonds, the divine essence of free, supportive love.

The danger of delegitimizing other counter-hegemonic models, which may still have more normative components or involve less ambitious or radical alternatives, is quite real, and it often rears its head with negative consequences. Each individual decides to what extent they can or want to challenge social normality according to their interests, possibilities, and circumstances. Presenting relationship anarchy as the "good" version of open relationships, swinging, free love, polyamory, or consensual non-monogamies has the secondary effect of censorship or disapproval of those or other models that actually involve interesting disruptive processes that are very important. Any challenge to the universal criteria imposed by the norm is a valuable crack in the hegemonic structure that I believe must always be taken positively.

For a more specific example, this occurs at multiple levels when polyamorous individuals disparage open partnerships or swingers for getting beyond the norm of sexual exclusivity but not affective exclusivity. Another instance is when the dubious ethical validity of agreements about the veto power that some relationships have over others is cited in defense of non-hierarchical polyamory. Or when the lens of relationship anarchy is used to criticize the amatonormativity of polyamory (even when non-hierarchical), the focus on the number of relationships instead of their nature, the tyranny of agreements that perpetuate monogamous thinking, and the distinction between the ties of friendship and those based on authority and the transfer of personal sovereignty (just what I'm doing in these pages).

In this regard, I believe that the most reasonable formula is one that leads to a discourse that defends the particularities and contributions of my own proposal, yet simultaneously highlights the value of all the models challenging normativity insofar as these are useful life experiences (which are always extremely necessary) and can be adapted to the needs of different people starting at different points, levels of involvement, possibilities of transitioning to new models, and capacities (or desires) to adapt.

As for the fundamental critiques on essential aspects of the proposal of relationship anarchy, it's worth noting the one that suggests that it is possible to reject amatonormativity without needing to erase the borders between what are conventionally perceived as different types of relationships. After all, these labels can provide security and balance for some. In fact, I believe that this point is correct in part (while adding that those feelings of security and balance are only superficial in nature), and I do take it into consideration in the framing developed here.

What I'm proposing in this regard, as reflected throughout the various epigraphs and chapters, is that using descriptive labels is compatible with the anarchist vision of relationships. However, I also suggest that using categories for relationships in a prescriptive way – defined spaces that delimit what can and should be done (and what shouldn't), or as what can and should be expected (and what shouldn't) – is not. Even if these boundaries take the form of freely-made agreements. This is because these prescriptive and restrictive categories are the framework and the substrate for dynamics of subjugation and authoritarianism. From the amatonormative model, they inherit the concept of borders that mark the dividing line between one affective situation and another. Being on the right side of things depends on meeting certain expectations (structural expectations in monogamy; personal and consensual expectations in ethical non-monogamy). In that case, commitment, support, care, and respect for limits (elements I always believe to be essential) are not the product of basic solidarity with philosophical roots and principles; they are instead features associated exclusively with being within the bounds of that relationship.

Finally, I think it is quite important to make it clear that relationship anarchy is not a solution, neither as a relationship model for personal matters, nor as the seed of an actual revolution. It is akin to how a demonstration or protest doesn't automatically address the injustice it denounces. It is one of the tools we have at our disposal to change things, though. It's a reference point, and reference points make it possible for something to exist; something that doesn't have a name doesn't exist in some ways, after all.

For what, for whom, and to what extent can it be useful? It has been for me and for many others I know, as well, whether in a more conscious, direct way or more subtly and indirectly – yet real, all the same. It has helped our way of living be more in line with our way of thinking, feeling, and being happy. It has warded off individualistic tendencies; emotional armor; dissonance between what we thought, what we felt, and what we did. It has turned a downcast, "Sorry, I'm not quite normal," into, "I interact in a different way, and I like it," with bright, hopeful eyes. It's not magic, but it works well enough. It works for some of us.

1.5 What is relationship anarchy *not*?

Sometimes, it's interesting to enrich a perspective by describing views that complement it, specifying what it could be but isn't. This could be due to semantic similarity, a common confusion, or some broader or narrower idea. The objective is to clarify; this does, however, run the risk of creating a definition solely by opposition: underlining a series of alterities in a way that leads us to delineate an identity that once again ends up acting as a cage. To start with, relationship anarchy is opposed to relationship hierarchies. It is as far removed from the monogamous structure (which is hegemonic in the capitalist West and in many other places) as it is from religious or traditional polygamies associated with equally normative structures (both polyandry and polygyny) that can be found in different cultures (also in the West, as with Mormon communities). It is not a question of establishing comparisons or awful cultural supremacisms but rather defending the secular, non-normative nature of the anarchist framework. In any case, it is more closely related to some cultural customs of so-called indigenous peoples that have been considered primitive precisely because of the doctrines of those more widespread, dominant cultures.

In ideological terms, relationship anarchy is by no means a praise of individualism and freedom as a rejection of commitment and solidarity. It isn't related to the liberal tradition. Just as how the solution to low wages is not another side hustle, the answer to the problem of the normative couple as a bubble that isolates and prevents relationships from forming a network of support, care, and mutual understanding is not the "freedom" to multiply the bubbles. Relationship anarchy does not explicitly define affective-sexual practices. It is therefore not a kind of ethical or consensual non-monogamy, a category that would encompass swinging (which consists of a couple's joint sexual activities with other people or partners), open relationships (sex outside the couple is tolerated but never has an affective component), and polyamory, both hierarchical and non-hierarchical (acceptance of the possibility of multiple affective-sexual partners with some relationships being subordinate to others or all being on equal footing), to name a few.

The possibility of maintaining non-monogamous relationships constitutes a secondary effect of the anti-normative approaches of relationship anarchy. Sexual and affective exclusivity as the rule is not admissible in relationship anarchy. This is because that involves coercion or a veto right, not because there is an inherent inclination towards a specific number of relationships ("mono," "non-mono," or "poly"). Obviously, this propensity for an abundance of relationships does appear directly as the main focus in all the so-called non-monogamies.[38] In other words, both monogamous and non-monogamous relationships fit into the paradigm of relationship anarchy.

---

38 As Gesa Mayer wrote in the abstract of her contribution to the 2017 edition of the *Non-Monogamies and Contemporary Intimacies Conference* (NMCI): "In recent years, the concept of polyamory has not only gained growing popularity but has as well given rise to scrutiny. Critical questioning by proponents of relationship anarchy has reproached polyamory – to name only a few points – for being inherently hierarchical, for being based in regulation frenzy instead of spontaneity and trust, for fashioning itself as a tame apolitical lifestyle of the privileged, and for affirming key tenets of romantic love. From this angle, polyamory appears to foster normativity rather than challenge it. (...) A special focus will be placed on the question of to what extent poly echoes or deconstructs the ideal of romantic love and its craze for couples and the separation of sexuality and friendship. As I would like to argue, polyamory and related styles of non-monogamy cannot be adequately addressed by a one-size-fits-all criticism as they host a diversity of desires, constellations, and discourses. Even though definitely not immune to normativity, these poly multiplicities resourcefully subvert some of the stale categories and boundaries relationships and intimacies are usually shaped by."

Structural monogamy does not, however, because it implies a normative limitation on personal autonomy. This is because it establishes some cultural mandates that pre-define the commitments, meaning that these cannot be voluntary, responsible, or self-determined. For instance, if my own commitment to affective-sexual fidelity is the product of my personal decision after shared discussion, it is compatible with relationship anarchy; the requirement of exclusivity or any specific behavior from others, beyond what affects my personal and bodily limits, is not. I'll discuss commitment and boundaries in depth later on.

In phenomenological terms, relationship anarchy is not a mystical, enlightening proposal that seeks to liberate the human being and reveal the truth; to point out the snares that love, passion, and the flesh have set for us; or to show us the way to a higher level of awareness in relationships. Nor is it an extreme positivist formula that judges and despises the subjective, immaterial universes of individuals and their emotional outcomes. Relationship anarchy is not a model that challenges the value of relationships and the importance of love and commitment (as self-constituted in a personal or shared way, and not inherited or structural), nor does it underestimate the depth of feelings, passions, and emotions, the intimacy, trust, and union for mutual care, support, and love – quite the opposite. It does not promote emotional individualism; it confronts it from the widest possible angle. As such, it's also not a cynical option to save oneself from disappointment.

Relationship anarchy is not a reckless notion proposing new relationship models, arbitrarily substituting some normativities for others. It doesn't annul love, desire or desires, their orientations, identities, or anything of the sort to establish a repressive norm. It is not an improvised ethical reformulation. It is the product of thought forged and shared by generations of authors, activists, and organizations of an anarchist stripe through experiences, efforts, sacrifices, failures, and successes over the last two centuries. Here, it is applied to a theory of social construction where utopia is focused around relationships as the seed of a new form of collective organization, not just the result of it.

Relationship anarchy is not a moralistic discipline that condemns infatuation or passionate exaltation the same way that inquisitorial puritanisms have historically condemned free sexual behavior, alcohol, hallucinogenic psychotropics, etc. (and continue to do so). The more or less altered emotional states associated with the euphoria of love, the processes of idealization, projection, hope, anxiety, and dreams are surely not highly recommended for daily survival or making important decisions (like how drunkenness or psychedelic experiences aren't recommended for driving a car, for instance). They may, however, constitute a legitimate exploration of our limits, abandon or surrender to an investigative exercise, or simply the enjoyment of an inalienable personal freedom.

Beyond models and relationship schemes, managing when, how, and within what limits these behaviors or experiences are carried out is what defines whether there is some risk of significant negative consequences (physical or emotional) or if we have simply enjoyed yet another exhilarating possibility with the intensity that life offers and deserves.

Finally, relationship anarchy is not an extravagant fantasy that denies the fragility of those who have suffered or are suffering, either due to the structural violence of the construction of identities in this society or to personal violence or deprivation. It does not intend to leave them out of some superior, innovative model or, worse yet, harass and torment them on a daily basis for not being able to hang ten on this "fresh, groundbreaking, frothing wave of modernity." Jealousy, the need to feel special and unique, the feeling of abandonment in the face of loneliness, the difficulty of enjoying a chosen, healthy retreat, overcoming feelings of helplessness, sadness, failures, rejections... these are not signs of bad behavior or awkwardness. They're not defects or indications of the lack of maturity or willpower to get better. They aren't flaws to be ashamed of for failing to live up to the expectations defined by some innovative, cutting-edge doctrine.

No. They are behaviors that require support and solidarity, basic principles of anarchist thought. They also require significant amounts of introspection, communication, and assertiveness to prevent needs and hurts from being the justification for authoritarian guidelines. It's quite easy to confuse care with submission in our daily practices. It happens constantly. Turning sorrow into coercion is almost inevitable if there's no warning or an ever-present set of clear reference points. Relationship anarchy's exact aim is to contribute to building that landmark, the beacon that's always visible, reminding us of the importance of fellowship and the danger of tyranny. Coercive dynamics aren't sustainable, and they end up hurting more than helping, or even turning into dangerous oppressions in the long term.

Chapter 2. Cultural and historical perspective

> Oh, how beautiful, those by-gone days when we spoke of revolution.
>
> — Mario Benedetti, *Haikus*, no. 198, Inventario III.

In his 1884 text *The Origin of the Family, Private Property and the State*,[39] Friedrich Engels posits that modern societies' models of authority date back to the Neolithic transition from hunting and gathering in cooperative groups to cultivation and livestock, resulting in the emergence of the concept of property. This would have led to the shift from nomadic, matrilineal societies, where descent was exclusively linked to motherhood, to sedentary societies based on the State and the patrilineal nuclear family.

2.1 Authority, family, private property, and anarchism

Indeed, the ability to imagine the notion of long-term property ownership may have appeared with settled ways of life. Coexistence with livestock in enclosed areas, where male and female animals could be kept apart, was perhaps what led to the intuition or the confirmation and generalization of the thought that there is a link between sexual activity and reproduction – thus, the concept of paternity.[40] The combination of these two rational rudiments – property and paternity, along with the material and physical possibility for men to exercise sexual and reproductive control over women – would be the seed of the patriarchal nuclear family structure, which

---

39 F. Engels, The Origin of the Family, Private Property and the State, Penguin, 2010.
40 C. Ryan, C. Jethá, Sex at Dawn: The Prehistoric Origins of Modern Sexuality, Harper Collins, 2010.

is present in most of the societies currently prevailing around the world. This structure has historically had the role of ensuring the preservation of property and its ownership by men as the dominant group across generations. The State, law, dogmas, and doctrinal moral orders emerge as complementary features that guarantee the effective defense of this model. The State and militaristic, hieratic, and religious hierarchies in their various forms are, then, the keepers of the monopoly on authority through coercion by laws, punishments, supernatural threats, and sin.

The anarchist approach

The social anarchist approach challenges this organization, a structure that is based on the family as the subject of long-term property, on the authority of the State as the upholder of legal coercion based on force, and on the power of the Church and other religious hierarchies as sources of moral coercion based on superstition. It proposes alternatives that replace the institutions and the hierarchy by articulating mechanisms for self-management. Rules and decisions are agreed on collectively, and resources are created and distributed according to people's capacities and needs.

In the economic sphere, the self-managed anarchist organization would be based on association and cooperation, not on competition and the accumulation of assets. Functional maintenance for this associative, cooperative social model must be rooted in the rational will of the people, not just linked to another coercive dynamic arising from the group, other individuals, or the institutions representing them. The other essential functional feature is solidarity or mutual aid among equals that is always free, reciprocal, and based on a direct balance between resources and needs.

In 1918[41], Bertrand Russell defined anarchism as follows:

---

41 B. Russell, Proposed Roads to Freedom: Socialism, Anarchism and Syndicalism, Cornwall Press, Cornwall, 1918

"The modern Anarchism, in the sense in which we shall be concerned with it, is associated with belief in the communal ownership of land and capital, and is thus in an important respect akin to Socialism. This doctrine is properly called Anarchist Communism, but as it embraces practically all modern Anarchism, we may ignore individualist Anarchism altogether and concentrate attention upon the communistic form. Socialism and Anarchist Communism alike have arisen from the perception that private capital is a source of tyranny by certain individuals over others. Orthodox Socialism believes that the individual will become free if the State becomes the sole capitalist. Anarchism, on the contrary, fears that in that case the State might merely inherit the tyrannical propensities of the private capitalist. Accordingly, it seeks for a means of reconciling communal ownership with the utmost possible diminution in the powers of the State, and indeed ultimately with the complete abolition of the State. It has arisen mainly within the Socialist movement as its extreme left wing."

Anarchism today

One hundred years later – after a century of proposals, ideas, experiences, and struggle – is anarchism now dying out? Is this noble intellectual and political adventure of humanity and its peoples fading? Laura Portwood-Stacer's perspective[42] connects with the present and looks towards the future:

"The core philosophy of anarchism is that human well-being is best ensured by a decentralized, non-hierarchical, radically democratic society. Anarchists seek revolutionary change to existing society in the pursuit of a more just world. Although anarchy is often misperceived as being synonymous with chaos or violence, it denotes only an absence of hierarchy. Anarchists are not against organization or structure; rather, they object to organizations or structures that are based on unequal relations of power or are maintained coercively. Because of their critique of hierarchy, anarchists often work in solidarity with feminists, anti-racists, socialists, environmentalists, and any number of other radical and

---

42 L. Portwood-Stacer, *Lifestyle Politics and Radical Activism,* op. cit.

progressive movements that share this critique. Capitalism and the state are chief among anarchists 'targets of critique, since these structures are seen as centralizing authority in people and institutions that are unaccountable to the people who are subject to their power. Anarchists are also critical of other systems of oppression, such as patriarchy and colonialism. Thus, they are interested in mounting challenges to authoritarianism in many cultural spheres, not just in the capitalist market or in state governments. To put the anarchist project more positively, anarchists try to cultivate social forms that will foster egalitarian relationships of voluntary association and freedom of creative expression for all. While anarchism is clearly a utopian philosophy, it is also a philosophy for the here and now."

Journalist Rafael Cid offers still more views from the present:[43]

"Anarchism is still alive today, but without any designation of origin, without clichés or IDs; it shows up pollinating everything, as the leading vital alternative to the oxymoron of "capitalist democracy." At both the individual and collective levels, emancipatory activism has set up shop in real life, joining forces with networks for mutual aid, direct action, and self-management that "are growing every minute" to constitute a new social imaginary on a human scale. Even at the risk of falling into the vice of presentism, it could be said that this breath of life has ended up infecting other cultural traditions that are theoretically different and distant, such as the "Arab Spring." An Egyptian rioter in Tahrir Square explained his experience on a blog, saying, "We realized that the state organization was actually the ultimate form of disorganization because it was based on denying the human power to organize."

Or in the words of anarchist historian and theorist Miquel Amorós:[44]

"Rather, I understand anarchism as an aspiration to a full life, one that is fraternal and communitarian, without institutions

---

43 R. Cid, "80 años de la revolución española. VIVIR la utopía," *Rojo y Negro Digital*, 2016.
44 Jaime Gonzalo's interview with Miquel Amorós for *Ruta 66*, July 2016.

that escape collective control, where the connections between individuals are direct and egalitarian, not mediated by things. To the extent that social struggles are oriented towards these goals and use means that do not contradict them, anarchism has a future."

In any case, it is clear that now, in the 21st century, anarchism is not the predominant form of social regulation on a large scale anywhere around the world. This fact, plus the necessary premise of a sustained, universal, unanimous will to cooperate, help each other, and use the necessary resources free from self-interest or greed – which is hard to imagine in our current societies – lead the anarchist approach as a whole to be considered utopian in the short term by even the most revolutionary spirits. But if we shift our thinking from the organization of an entire society to the structure of our relationships, network of affections, and important people in our lives, do these same elements seem so utopian? A little less so, I think.

2.2 Feminism and anarcho-feminism

I've mentioned the historical conception of the Church-State conglomerate as the holder of exclusive command over souls, bodies, and territories, as well as over the hierarchical order of institutions and people. Even at its now-remote origins, we can find connections between these authoritarian values and the patriarchal worldview. In Antigone, a magnificent classic exploration of power relations written no less than 2,460 years ago, Sophocles issues these words through Creon:

> "There is no greater evil than anarchy, which destroys cities, ruins houses, breaks ranks, and leads to rout and retreat. In the final analysis, it is obedience which saves most men, and thus we must preserve the proper order of things. And there is no way we can allow a woman to triumph. Better to be defeated by any sort of man than seen as weaker than a woman."

Early feminist authors

Anarchist ideas developed in the 19th and early 20th centuries suggested that the patriarchal system was linked to the existence of the State, the Church, and social classes, and they prioritized ending these structures to eradicate patriarchy. In contrast, the first feminist views born out of anarchism suggest confronting patriarchy itself directly. In fact, this was the anarchist breeding ground where the personal and the political were first linked, where free love and women's sexual emancipation was addressed with an understanding of unjust secular subordination rooted in religious morality, the clerical establishment's power, the institution of marriage, and the economic and legal dependence enshrined in that institution.

Graffiti in a wall in Spain.

Some aspects, however, remained out of reach at that time. Anarchist critique's transformative audacity and thirst for justice and inclusion focused the spotlight on the family (described as a trap built out of love), how women's place in history had been devalued, contempt of female sexuality, denial of their pleasure, and many other issues. Nevertheless, they failed to undermine moral bastions such as the abhorrence of homosexuality, the sacralization of motherhood, or the condemnation of contraception, masturbation, and abortion.

Indeed, anarchist visions of what relationships would be like in a truly free society[45] ranged from recognizing egalitarian monogamous unions that could be dissolved simply by the will of one of the parties to the defense of potentially multiple unions where one person could have several simultaneous affective-sexual relationships. However, none of these forms of relationships between people of the same sex were recognized at all. Homosexuality was still an inviolable taboo.

As for motherhood, part of the anarchist epic focused on the figure of the brave, tireless, tenacious mother. This meant that any act of rebellion or autonomy that challenged the transcendent destiny of womanhood – mother and guarantor of the human race's perpetuity – was seen as an abominable perversion; such disgraces included abortion and contraception.

Another stereotype in the 19th-century anarchist narrative is that of the prostitute; she is portrayed as the victim of a system that leads her to her tragic fate. This discourse takes on a moralizing tone that is similar to previous ones: anarchist men are urged not to participate in such bourgeois practices and not to be complicit in using women's bodies. In publications, these women are never encouraged to organize to defend their rights or to participate in the revolution. They're rarely given a voice, and when they are, it's so that they can rid themselves of their guilt and mourn their misfortune. Besides this moral orthodoxy, militant women were seen as compatriots fighting alongside men. Anarchism generally recognized the political, economic, and sexual oppressions women were subjected to, even by fellow male anarchists, who often recognized themselves as being oppressors as well as oppressed. We know that some men signed texts as women to visibilize this perspective (perhaps when

---

45 L. Fernández Cordero, *Amor y anarquismo*, Siglo XXI, Buenos Aires, 2017.

there were no female authors who could or dared to do so for the publications); at other times, some women signed documents with male names for various reasons.

However, achieving relative co-leadership among women in anarchist movements required overcoming major obstacles. To start with, Pierre-Joseph Proudhon, who is considered the "founding father" of anarchism, was a markedly misogynistic figure, even for his day and age. He was a raging enemy of any form of female emancipation[46] (or any advances in expressions of love and sexuality). Other influential authors, such as Bakunin and Engels, demonstrated more open attitudes in their work. Still, in the end, women had to square off with the narrative of the passive, sacrificial victim of the system (invariably female) who is saved by the anarchist struggle led by men. The women in the movement added their own discourse by calling on male anarchists to stop behaving as oppressors or saviors and start being their equals, comrades in the revolution.

The historical current called bourgeois feminism took shape during the French Revolution with the 1791 *Declaration of the Rights of Woman and of the [Female] Citizen* by Marie Gouze (known as Olympe de Gouges), which was a response to the *Declaration of the Rights of Man and of the [Male] Citizen* from two years earlier. The reaction came swiftly. On November 3, 1793, she was guillotined by the Jacobins.

Around that same time in England, Mary Wollstonecraft was fighting for women's right to education with works such as her 1792 *A Vindication of the Rights of Woman*. Over the next century, many feminist demands and efforts centered around the right to vote. The suffragettes had to wait until the end of the 19th century and the beginning of the 20th for various democratic states to begin to include full female suffrage in their legislation.

---

46 Proudhon suggested that women should contribute to society from the private sphere and that the women's revolution would have to take place by contributing through domestic work.

As such, it wasn't only anarchist thought that addressed what we now call patriarchal oppression at that time in history. Bourgeois feminism, Marxism, socialism, and liberalism considered the question and made it part of their ideology. It was the liveliness of the social anarchist movement, though, with its radical consideration of all struggles as equally urgent and pressing, that led the greatest contribution to this first emancipatory phase to take place at anarchism's cutting edge.

In Spain, the first feminist organization created by women for women was founded in 1889: Sociedad Autónoma de Mujeres de Barcelona (Barcelona's Autonomous Society of Women). *Humanidad Libre (Free Humanity)* appeared in 1902, a biweekly anarcho-feminist publication by Valencia's women's society. Its first issue announced contributions from Teresa Claramunt, Soledad Gustavo, María Caro, Rosa Lidón, Louise Michel, and Emma Goldman, and other female authors (as well as male authors in the background). Its only precedent was *La voz de la Mujer (Woman's Voice):* this publication appeared in 1896 in Buenos Aires, and it was pioneering on a global scale.

Another noteworthy publication directed by a woman, Soledad Gustavo, was *La Revista Blanca (The White Magazine)*.[47] This author, whose real name was Teresa Mañé Miravent, was a lay teacher and anarchist who[48] wrote numerous pieces on women's emancipation in various spheres, including relationships. She wrote, for instance, "Men think it is a good thing for women to have greater freedom, but not so much for her to use it. After all, he will covet his neighbor's wife but lock up his own."[49]

---

47 A. Prado, *Matrimonio, familia y estado: escritoras anarco-feministas en La Revista Blanca (1898-1936)*, Fundación Anselmo Lorenzo, Madrid, 2011.
48 She was also the mother of Federica Montseny Mañé, the first woman to be named a minister in the Spanish government and one of the first in Western Europe.
49 Teresa Mañé, "Hablemos de la mujer," *La Revista Blanca*, 1923, cit. in G. Puente Pérez, "Al margen del feminismo: las vindicaciones de las anarquistas italianas y españolas por la liberación de las mujeres (1868-1939)," *Chronica Mundi*, 2017 .

Cover of the first issue of "Humanidad Libre" (Free Humanity)

However, the label "feminism" —which was accepted and used in some anarchist circles at the end of the 19th century— was gradually falling out of anarchist vocabulary, as it was considered a bourgeois current. This was because it in part defended women's right to participate in State institutions (participating in party politics, active and passive suffrage, etc.), thus contributing to perpetuating the system.

Alternatives to bourgeois feminism

The discourse that we would today call anarcho-feminist went beyond the general anarchist struggle. It revolved around the oppression linked to marriage; the question of whether it was better to abolish or reform that institution; the role that love played as a trap destined to cloud reason and lead to women's subjugation; and the

Church's role as an accomplice in the model that subjugated the female gender through proselytism and the fear of hell and purgatory.

Some issues that are still quite present in today's feminism appear in anarchist texts as early as the 19th century, such as these from *La voz de la mujer* (1896) compiled by Laura Fernández Cordero in *Amor y Anarquismo (Love and Anarchism)*:[50]

> "My steps slow and mechanical, I headed down some street to some place I can't recall, pensive, my head down, right up against the wall, with the sole aim of avoiding any encounters and vulgar comments, which I didn't manage to do, since it seems that those gentlemen of the bearded sex do not believe themselves to be so if they do not say some of those stupid phrases that constitute the well-worn repertoire (...) of the street art of... foolishness when they pass by a woman.
>
> (...) Such disdain is even reflected in language. To signify all beings of our species, we say: man, mankind, humanity. Womankind is also understood to have a lower title, and for that reason, she is not even named."

At that lively starting point in the 20th century, authors like He Zhen (a Chinese anarchist who carried out some of her work in Japan) began to show up on other continents, raising questions that still sound familiar to us today. Among them is the idea that the presence of powerful women in the political, economic, and social spheres could be an indicator of fairness in appearance only; such a veneer would actually create and normalize a new structure of oppression. It is a strikingly prescient idea, and a century later, it evokes contemporary figures like Margaret Thatcher, Marine Le Pen, Sarah Palin, and Esperanza Aguirre. Indeed, in 1907 He Zhen wrote:[51]

---

50 Laura Fernández Cordero, *Amor y anarquismo*, Siglo XXI, Buenos Aires, 2017.
51 He Zhen, "Women liberation," in Robert Graham, *Anarchism: a documentary history of libertarian ideas*, v. 1, Black Rose Books, Montreal, 2005.

> "The majority of women are already oppressed by both the government and by men. The electoral system simply increases their oppression by introducing a third ruling group: elite women."

In the United States, Helena Born, Marie Ganz, Mollie Steimer, Voltairine de Cleyre, and Emma Goldman are among the most recognized authors in the history of anarchism. Goldman appears in most monographs as one of the individuals who have contributed the most to this movement's spread and understanding. Her definition of anarchism suggests a more intersectional point of view that is in line with the fact that women were – and still are – subjected to the effects of more vectors of oppression than men:

> "Anarchism, then, really stands for the liberation of the human mind from the dominion of religion; the liberation of the human body from the dominion of property; liberation from the shackles and restraint of government."[52]

In her work Marriage and Love,[53] she defines marital union as a structure of control, deception, a transaction where the man buys the woman's name, intimacy, agency, and very existence for the rest of her life. In that text, Goldman offers statistics from over 100 years ago that we'd hardly bat an eye at today – overlooking the dates and figures – while flipping through a magazine or the Sunday paper:

> "(...) first, every twelfth marriage ends in divorce; second, that since 1870 divorces have increased from 28 to 73 for every hundred thousand population; third, that adultery, since 1867, as ground for divorce, has increased 270.8 per cent.; fourth, that desertion increased 369.8 per cent."

Emma Goldman backed the ideas and proposals she produced with tireless activism and an ability to spread her enthusiasm for life, freedom, and revolution against authority and oppression. There was a reason she was known as "the most dangerous woman in

---

[52] E. Goldman, "Anarchism: what it really stands for," in *Anarchism and Other Essays*, Dover Publications, New York, 1910.
[53] E. Goldman, "Marriage and Love," in *Anarchism and Other Essays*, op. cit.

America."⁵⁴ On the other side of the Atlantic, in Spain, the 1930s brought social advances and an intense transformative energy (as well as the subsequent fascist reaction). It was against that backdrop that the anarchist organization *Mujeres Libres* (*Free Women*) appeared to lead a twofold struggle: women's liberation and social revolution, with both of these objectives holding the same level of importance. The group had as many as 30,000 affiliates, who created networks of anarchist women and launched various initiatives, such as training centers, obstetric care, rural groups, exercises for denouncing sexist behavior and defending feminism, articles in the press, a magazine, and radio programs.

Mujeres Libres was a living example of many central aspects of anarchist theory. It focused on seeking collective liberation through empowerment, associative support, solidarity, horizontal organization, and direct action, confronting the then-dominant idea that women's liberation would "automatically" result from the social revolution's triumph. Throughout the 20th century, authors such as Margaret Mead, Simone de Beauvoir, Kate Millet, and Marcela Lagarde advanced the analysis of the structural domain associated with couples and amorous relationships. In her *Crítica del pensamiento amoroso*⁵⁵ (*Critique of Amorous Thought*), Mari Luz Esteban says that these analyses:

> "(...) contribute a strong, resounding critique of the love that makes women worthy of recognition only when they love selflessly and uncritically. Through the feminist lens, love is seen for the first time in human history as something that isn't irreparable, nor does it act like an avalanche, dragging you along and laying waste to your life. For the first time, love appears an experience where it is possible to get involved, decide, choose, select – all characteristics that have to do with freedom."

---

54 C. Bríd Nicholson, *Emma Goldman: still dangerous*, Black Rose Books, Montreal, 2010.
55 M.L. Esteban, *Crítica del pensamiento amoroso*, Bellaterra, Barcelona, 2011.

Contemporary anarcho-feminism

The term "anarchist-feminist" appeared explicitly in the latter part of the century, and it has since rubbed elbows with "anarcho-feminist" and "anarcha-feminist." According to Julia Tanenbaum,[56] one of the term's first appearances was in an editorial in the newspaper *It Ain't Me Babe*, dated August 1970. This publication exemplifies the "intuitive anarchism" of the American radical feminist movement; that era saw the beginning of a major trend in visibilizing all forms of subjugation and abuse, as well as opposing them.

An issue of the anarcho-feminist magazine *Siren* and two publications by *Come! Unity Press*. Source: anarchiststudies.org

Many initial theoretical formulations from the same time when anarcho-feminism was already gaining ground appear in the magazine *Siren* and in publications by *Come! Unity Press*. The manifesto published by Arlene Wilson in *Siren* under the title, *Who We Are: The Anarcho-Feminist Manifesto* intended to underscore what set anarcho-feminism apart by emphasizing the feminist struggle against domination by religion, the family, and the state. Until it went de-

---

[56] Julia Tanenbaum "To Destroy Domination in All Its Forms: Anarcha-Feminist Theory, Organization and Action 1970-1978," in *Perspectives On Anarchist Theory*, Institute For Anarchist Studies, AK Press, Edinburg, 2018.

funct in 1973, *Siren* shared works that addressed issues such as prefigurative politics,[57] lesbian feminism, gender identity and expression, gender binarism as a form of authoritarianism, and the inclusion of transgender people in the movement.

In short, the key aspect linking radical feminist theory with anarchism is the correspondence between patriarchal authoritarianism and the nuclear family. This structure treats women and children as property; it teaches them to obey authority in all areas of life and to follow hierarchical, patriarchal patterns of thought tied to dominance and submission. The proposed alternative to hierarchy is fraternity (now sisterhood)[58] among women, with relationships based on autonomy, equality, trust, and friendship, forging deeper bonds than male friendships based on patterns of competitive relationship. First introduced nearly 50 years ago, this discourse's strong resonance with the current thread of relationship anarchy cannot be overlooked.

Julia Tanenbaum says[59] that, for feminists who are familiar with anarchism, the connections between the theory and practice of radical feminism and anarchist discourse and activism are quite clear. Anarchist feminism was essentially a step in self-conscious theoretical development. Anarchist feminists believed that explicit anarchist analysis and knowledge of the history of anarchism, including how it confronted similar empirical and structural obstacles, would help women overcome coercion from the elites and help them create

---

57 According to Carl Boggs, who proposed the term, this is the desire to embody the forms of social relationship, decision-making, culture, and human experiences that represent the long-term goal in a movement's political practices. In C. Boggs, "Marxism, Prefigurative Communism, and the Problem of Workers' Control," *Radical America*, 1977.
58 According to Marcela Lagarde, *La politica de las mujeres*, Cátedra, Madrid, 1997, *sororidad* (sorority or sisterhood) "... is an experience that leads to the search for positive relationships between women and political and existential alliance, in order to contribute to the social elimination of all forms of oppression and to mutual aid with specific actions to achieve the general power of all and the vital empowerment of each woman." A complementary term is the Italian *affidamento* (reliance), which incorporates trust and affection within the group into this alliance as a way of managing discrepancies and conflicts.
59 Ibid.

structured working groups that were accountable to their members yet were not hierarchical. They built an independent women's movement and offered a feminist critique of anarchism, as well as an anarchist critique of feminism. For anarcho-feminists, the radical women's liberation movement meant a new opportunity for revolution, for taking on forms of domination and personal and political hierarchy. Unlike the anarchists of the 19th and early 20th centuries, radical feminists of the late 20th century were feminists first and anarchists second.

2.3 Relationship anarchy and anarchism

I've already mentioned that the concepts of anarchism and anarchy appear in the language of most people (the hegemonic semantic universe) with a profoundly skewed meaning.

Carlos Taibo provides an example of this distorted vision when[60] talking about Jorge Fernández Díaz, Spain's Minister of the Interior from 2011 to 2016:

> "(...) a few words from this stimulating intellectual figure, the Spanish Minister of the Interior, who a few months ago stated that a surprisingly well-organized anarchist group had been neutralized. This gentleman should read a basic guidebook on political theory: anarchists aren't against organization, they are against coercive forms of organization, which is 'a little different.'"

Along the same lines, we could say that an anarchist vision of relationships would not position itself against personal relations (whether these were founded in affection, love, commitment, emotions, or passion) but against coercive forms of relating.

The social contract and the marriage contract

Political anarchism identifies the State as the main element of authority and coercion. The social contract (an adhesion contract,

---

60 Various speeches and conferences, such as "Decrecimiento / anticapitalismo," on arrezafe.blogspot.com.

which is not negotiated by each contractor individually) gives the State the ability to enact laws and enforce them. In the models of society we live in, this capacity is exclusive: if a group decides to organize itself through other codes of conduct that contradict some part of the State's laws, the State has the right and the capacity to repress such behaviors, thanks to the authority granted to it by the social contract. This is a form of organization with centralized regulation; it's what I'm referring to specifically when I use the term normativity. When the rules of coexistence are collectively agreed on with each individual having the choice to accept or discuss them and to participate, I will use the phrase self-management.

In this regard, relationship anarchy shares most of the same foundations as political anarchism, but it shifts anarchism's attention from laws and the State to relationship guidelines and the hegemonic cultural construction of bonds. All of this means that the central question now is not about submission to a social contract and the right that emanates from it, but compliance with the moral and cultural norms embodied in the various forms of prescriptive relationships.

These forms of relationship are given exclusive names and well-defined boundaries that firmly delineate systems of action. If our relationship is defined as a couple, we have the obligations and rights (or expectations of rights) that belong to that label. These are obligations and rights that we have not personally stipulated. As such, our relationship is normative. If we relate to one another as friends, then we have the obligations and rights (or expectations) corresponding to that relational form. These are also obligations and rights that we have not explicitly agreed upon. As such, our relationship is once again normative. The same is true for all culturally stereotyped forms of relationship.

Relationship anarchy proposes replacing normativity with self-management in how we relate to each other. This doesn't arise from individualism (in this case, the prefix "self-" extends to a group, a relational network) but from the basic principles that have already been mentioned several times. Still, they bear repeating: mutual aid, responsible autonomy, horizontality, rejecting hidden power structures, the individual sovereignty to associate or split up, not representing some individuals through others, and non-interference in the self-management of others except to request that commitments be fulfilled.

It's important to note that a highly attentive, determined attitude is necessary to be aware of and prevent the parameters of self-management from cloaking behaviors and configurations of power and authority. The constructions of possession, control, and submission function subconsciously as cultural mandates, and they're defined along axes of gender, socio-economic status, relational and erotic capital, age, and so on. I will delve into this question of relationship practices and vectors of oppression in later chapters.

We'll move from the intimate to a more global point of view to analyze the implications of these premises on the forms of social organization; relationship anarchy involves a critical look at normative structures of relating to one another and the role of those structures in the configuration, maintenance, and evolution of the system. These are driving and stabilizing elements of the status quo. For example, bonds tend to be nuclear rather than networked or collective; they develop according to homogeneous, predictable models; responsibility for another's welfare is concentrated in one individual; the character, form, and arrangement of the entity that holds ownership of essential goods like housing, material support for raising children, and so on, are clearly established, etc.

Logically, this firm, disciplined model of relationships also functions as a normative-formative environment for the next generation, which can be expected to reproduce this model with few changes. The fact that care, affectivity, and above all, authority and power during childhood are fundamentally centralized in two well-identified people clearly favors adapting to a logic built around possession or submission rather than dynamics of cooperation, alliance, harmonization, management, and collective decisions from the very earliest stages of building our identities and personalities.

As for specific practices arising from the perspective of relationship anarchy, it isn't easy to put together a full characterization. Challenging normativity doesn't mean that the possible relationship models and those embodied in practical reality follow a simple pattern. For example, the number of people that you can interact intensively at a given time in life, regardless of the specific ways you relate to them, is not limited to one, but it can be one – or none, or several. As I've mentioned before, the number of relationships is not a specific attribute of the practice of relationship anarchy, though an extensive network does mean more support, stability, and affection.

The sort of projects you take on with other people isn't, either. We can share housing, basic resources, different levels of economy, dreams, intellectual or artistic creations, travel, sports, passion, adventure, sex, reproduction, raising kids, culture, fun, and so on. All of this can be either in the short term or may be longer-term commitments, or they may not even have a set end date. They may be more mystical or more pragmatic, romantic (the parts of romanticism that don't involve control or authority), platonic,[61] poetic or prosaic, regular or sporadic, involving constant or occasional communication.

The only characteristic features that cannot be absent in the very foundation of a non-normative organization that is responsibly self-managed (which would be, in an informal parallel, "the fundamental rights in relationships") are the articulation of the mechanics of the relationships through voluntary commitments made by each person

---

61. The meaning of "platonic love" varies across cultures. In most cultural contexts, it generally retains the original meaning from Plato's work as "love without romantic attraction or sexual attraction." In others, it's usually understood as "idealized, unrequited, unattainable love."

with boundaries circumscribed to their own body, space, and feelings. Commitments must be honored, and if they change, it must be through a process of reflection that entails responsibility and communication. Scrupulously adhering to others' boundaries must be firmly ingrained in the context of a culture of consent. This articulation of boundaries and commitments must give rise to relational networks where consideration, personal respect, and a minimum level of care, support, and solidarity are ensured.

Agreements, rights, and authority

Agreements, rights, and authority inform basic elements of anarchist thought. As a radically non-normative proposition, relationship anarchy suggests creating and developing relationships based on their specificity, not in terms of pre-existing sets of rules. Therefore, it is about expressing my wishes, listening to yours, and looking for a path we can take together comfortably, enthusiastically, and passionately.

But can these wishes, the agreements around them, and their implications be delimited? Can those wishes affect other people? Obviously, that depends on the analysis's moral framework. In the moral paradigm of majority religions (as well as many secular ideologies) whose softened, humanized versions continue to have a stronghold in our societies, these aspirations cannot challenge the exclusivity of the most intimate sphere restricted to the couple. This is especially true for women, given their subaltern position that is subject to stricter moral control.

In more open, non-monogamous models, there may be intimacy and even affectivity with others, according to their different limitations. These restrictions respond to learned social constructions or convictions, lacks, insecurities, ambitions for control, possessive holdovers, or even specific needs for care. Each situation is undoubtedly different; it may be the product of honest reflection with communication and respect between parties – or the result of more dogmatic, irrational positions.

But since we're talking about anarchism, is there an anarchist moral framework? The answer to that would require many long volumes to dig deeper, but we'll approach it with a general overview. Anarchism is based on values like individual sovereignty: no one has the right to coerce another person, and defending oneself against coercion is recognized as fair; on consensus-based agreements that are free from underlying power structures; on the right to associate freely or not and the right to split and form new associations; on singularity: everything carries its own law; on horizontality: each individual is their own representative, so no one has command over another; on mutual aid under the moral imperative of solidarity; on responsible autonomy: non-interference in personal or collective management, beyond the requirement to comply with what has been agreed on; and on conflict resolution through mechanisms that are in accordance with anarchist organization: they're voluntary, free from coercion, and held under conditions of equality.

I mentioned the social contract earlier. One of the basic theses of Bakunin's anarchist thought posited that this concept – which was proposed by Hobbes, Locke, and Rousseau – was a dialectical straw man used to obscure the inherent illegitimacy of the process of imposing authority instead of achieving popular sovereignty by working from the basis of rational principles. By tailoring the commitments and pacts in the sphere of relationships to this framework of values, we find the main points to be the rejection of coercion (the wishes of some imposed on those of others) and authority (the rights of some imposed over those of others). Given their weight and breadth, these references directly exclude any idea of possession and control.

So let's go back to the initial questions about wishes, agreements, and their implications: are they delimited? Can they affect others? According to the anarchist ethical approach, the limits are authority and coercion between each of the people involved. Any voluntary commitment that arises from one's own will fits in this model. This includes any commitment that does not presuppose authority, but it doesn't cover agreements or consensuses in terms of waiving supposed rights over other people ("I'll let you do such and such..." or "I'll let you do this with these specific people"). In this context, these are false transactions premised on the idea that in relationships, people gain authority over each other and lose bodily autonomy. Against this, anarchists insist no one has the right to tell another person what they can do with their body. Thus, boundaries constitute a fundamental element that substantiates another key aspect: consent. This means that vetoes like, "I'll allow you to do this to ME and not that," can and should be brought up.

One way to illustrate this is to imagine that I'm chatting with someone and they ask me to come to an agreement with them about where I should go on a vacation that they're not coming along for. Saying "to come to an agreement" or anything of the sort is clearly absurd. They can offer advice and suggestions, and they may even passionately insist that I go to some wonderful place they adore, but there is nothing to agree on. We generally do not recognize their right or power over my vacation. Of course, I can voluntarily commit to bringing back souvenirs. Curiously, though, in many relationship practices — not only the normative ones — the idea of authority is inherited from hegemonic thought. It isn't surprising for someone to try to negotiate and agree on what another person can or can't do in their private life.

On the other hand, we must recognize that my trip may affect others to different extents; therefore, it seems sensible for them to raise objections and think about its consequences and implications. But then again, this all must be in line with anarchist values and without coercion, which means no manipulation or blackmail.

What if several people are going on this trip? Do we intuitively recognize the power or the right of fellow travelers to decide on the destination? In this case, it doesn't seem unwise to come up with an agreement and decide where we want to go on vacation as a group. Ultimately, we can extrapolate out from this example and conclude that consensus on a shared reality does seem to fit into the anarchist framework of values – unlike an agreement that seeks to grant someone else permission to do something in their own intimate life. In any case, we must remember that the intimate realm fundamentally depends on a subjective, specific assessment of each situation.

I will discuss the general clash between this type of analysis and real experience in the chapter on relationship practices. Logically, if we share a certain level of life together, responsibilities, projects, child-raising, and difficulties, it's not easy to establish a measure of how different actions in your intimate life affect me. Nevertheless, the hypothesis I'll develop in that chapter is that some of what we consider to be agreements are actually instances of the moral approach to mutual aid. That is the classic label in anarchist literature, but the same concept has historically appeared in various cultural, religious, political, and activist contexts under different labels with various nuances: solidarity, care, fraternity, cooperation, commitment, dedication, etc. In other words, the anarchist approach would limit consensus to shared or collective issues, and it would replace authorization and exchange with voluntary, responsible commitment and setting boundaries. All of this would be mediated by supportive reflection, respect, consent, and communication.

Focus on the group

A basic aspect of classical social anarchist thought is the importance of the collective as an active element of the organization and a component that should be protected and cared for (and that should offer protection and care). As a result, relationship anarchy rejects the hegemonic framework of values centered on the reproductive couple in order to establish an alternative, community-centered value structure. This is not done by establishing a new regulation that manages affections, intimacy, projects, or any other activity to turn it into a public experience – far from it; it is accomplished by dismantling a system that maintains a hierarchy where the couple's relationship is placed above all other relationships. These non-privileged relationships, which make it possible to weave a network of affection, care, and solidarity, are subjected to the desires and needs of the couple – desires and needs that are expressed in the form of coercive pacts and consensuses (for the members of the couple itself or others).

The result of the hegemonic framework is an atomized social structure that is easier to condition in an obligatory, centralized way. There's higher sensitivity to advertising campaigns, comparisons, and incentives, as well as higher tendencies toward competition, consumption, and meeting high levels of demand for productive performance. Thus, the proposal is a relational organization that looks to the group, creating a network rather than erecting a pedestal with one main person on it (or a few – the end result is the same). One outcome of this new perspective is that the fundamental tool for ensuring the model's sustainability ceases to be learned coercion (and self-coercion) and becomes communication. This is because normative practices do indeed require mechanisms for control (and self-control), but they don't require making each and every operating criterion explicit since they're given by the cultural canon. We know them well enough, or they may even be automatic. However, non-normative practices require regularly making an effort in communication to establish, assess, and refine every detail of a model that, in being self-managed, is specific, conscious, and flexible.

Personal or political activity?

Like classical anarchism, relationship anarchy today is a radical, dissident approach that requires us to distance ourselves from the point of view we've grown up with, to detach ourselves from unconscious convictions that we've come to by observing our family life, our social environment, cultural manifestations, festive and playful events, games, reading, and a thousand daily normalities. Anarchism has traditionally encouraged direct action as a way to change society in its quest to build a better world. Relationship anarchy is part of what has been called *Radical Lifestyle Politics*[62], which suggests that the best way for each person to contribute to social change now is by orienting their everyday personal behaviors and decisions around the ideals they are striving for.

As I said in the introduction, the possibilities for a true revolution are growing smaller every day. Even the new large-scale forms of association and emancipatory political options seem as though they're being absorbed and neutralized by the system overnight, especially when they reach the institutional sphere. This is why lifestyle politics has been proposed as a complementary option that doesn't require having to abandon big collective struggles. While not new, it does seem more interesting than ever. Once again, the personal is always increasingly political.

2.4 Free love, polyamory, ethical non-monogamies, and affective networks

The anarchist demands that came forth in the 19th century, along with influences from other traditions of thought,[63] catalyzed an emancipatory movement in affective-sexual, political, and social behaviors during the 1960s (combined with the anarcho-feminism mentioned earlier, which first appeared under that name in the 1970s and '80s). New languages, proposals, and styles of relating to one another began to take shape, and they led to an enormously influential change in the mindsets and moral foundations of subsequent generations.

From the sexual revolution to free love

In that decade, Masters and Johnson's pioneering study of human sexual response[64] – initially a scientific work – became a global bestseller. Sex education began to make its way into education systems,

---

62 L. Portwood-Stacer, *Lifestyle Politics and Radical Activism*, op. cit.
63 Dadaists, surrealists, constructivists, liberals, initial countercultural currents...
64 W.H. Masters, V.E. Johnson, *Human sexual response*. Little, Brown and Co., Boston, 1966.

access to contraceptives grew, and rigid taboos around sex started to break down. Sex gradually came to be considered a source of happiness and liberation that shouldn't be subject to the moral restrictions and hypocritical social norms that prevailed in previous decades. Contrary to what still persists as a popular stereotype, the so-called "sexual revolution" didn't symbolically separate sex from love but from marriage, exclusivity, possession, and all other previous normative social patterns.

Charles Fourier's work happened to be published in the same decade. Fourier was a utopian socialist who offered a series of imaginative proposals at the beginning of the 19th century. Some of these were markedly naïve and fanciful, though they were framed in a work that could hardly be defined as banal or dispensable. Some of his writings were so disturbing for his contemporaries (his defense of women's emancipation and his unapologetic attitude towards sex, for instance) that the decision was made not to publish them; they remained unpublished until his complete works were released in France in 1967. The piece *Le Nouveau monde amoureux*[65] (*The New Amorous World*) was included in that edition, right as May 68 was going into full swing. In this work, Fourier proposed a new order of love based on the abolition of marriage, collective child-raising, and community work, as well as a sort of "guaranteed basic income for sexual care" as a universal right.[66]

A few months later, the May 68 revolution took place. The movement took up this curious character as a cultural reference point, along with others like Theodor Adorno, Herbert Marcuse, Wilhelm Reich, Sigmund Freud, and the writings of the SexPol association, the *German association for proletarian sexual politics* that was at the heart of intense activity in the years before World War II.

---

65   C. Fourier (1816), Le Nouveau monde amoureux, Prodinnova, Paris, 2019.
66   According to Fourier, the disappearance of the desperate need for sex among individuals would allow relationships to become truly free. This would require a public service that would offer "amorous nobility" that would fulfill this role, knowing how "to subordinate love to the dictates of honor."

Fourier's contribution to the May 68 movement was probably more along the lines of articulating a provocative discourse with bohemian aesthetics than in a literal or practical sense. According to philosopher Ramón Alcoberro:[67]

> "Fourier brought us the first in-depth analysis of the devastating consequences capitalism has on the emotional realm and human subjectivity. Without him, the role of sexuality in society's transformation and the meaning of concepts such as "mutual aid" or solidarity, which he developed outside of its economic logic, could not be understood. His work, however, had little practical influence. As with all utopians, there is a bit of prophecy and of madness in it (the obsessive attempt to classify all social phenomena) and a lot of profound lucidity in understanding societies as a space of conflict, going far beyond the economic and political contradictions."

But that rhetorical and aesthetic revolution made an important mark. Though the term "free love" had been used in numerous proposals and experiences since the 19th century and even before then, this was the first mass movement invoking that concept to gain global, wide-reaching recognition. The challenge to normativity in sexual and affective relationships was also combined with an entire radical countercultural philosophy that, again – as was the case with anarchism a century before – proposed undermining the unmoving foundations of the system through rebellion against the established order. It went so far as to popularize slogans claiming that having an affective sexual relationship with just one person was contributing to upholding the status quo, or that sexual desire that wasn't continuous, intense, and comprehensive could only stem from puritanical, castrating social repression that had to be overcome.

Today, half a century later, we can recognize these postulates as a necessary rupture, but one that evoked fanaticism and disregard for how people feel. This is only the tip of the iceberg of a markedly

---

[67] R. Alcoberro, *Charles Fourier; el amor y las utopías,* in R. Alcoberro and J. Torres. *Filosofia i pensament* (avail. on alcoberro.info).

simplistic ideological and ethical approach whose faults became clear as its outcomes began to be seen and analyzed.

Outcomes of the sexual liberation movements

There were undoubtedly numerous exceptions that would lead communities and individuals who identified with the free love movement of those years to practices that were valuable, egalitarian, respectful, and enriching. But the most common stories and critiques give the feeling that those who took advantage of this revolutionary current were the most privileged: non-racialized men of a certain cultural and socio-economic status. The words of activist Stokely Carmichael encapsulate this critique: "The only position for women in the movement is 'prone.'" This statement referred to racial and sexual tensions and the therefore limited role that women and minorities were allowed to play.[68]

Indeed, the sexual liberation that did take place in those years didn't improve the situation of women in Western societies. Perhaps it was precisely because of this lack of consideration for the fight against gender oppression that it influenced the emergence of the *Women's Liberation Movement* and the current of radical feminism that identifies patriarchy and the power relations it entails as the root of inequality, oppression, and violence against women in these societies. As a result, it was a part of anarcho-feminism's emergence under that name.

At the movement's core were hippie culture and the so-called *New Left,* both dominated by males. "The position of women was no less foul, no less repressive, no less unliberated, than it had ever

---

[68] In this case, the Student Nonviolent Coordinating Committee and before that, the Lowndes County Freedom Organization, groups that were active in the liberation movements of the 1960s – Carmichael, Stokely and Ekwueme Michael Thelwell, *Ready for Revolution: The Life and Struggles of Stokely Carmichael,* Scribner, New York, 2003.

been," stated the 1967 article *Woman Is a Sometime Thing* by a feminist collective in Chicago[69]. This article aligns with many testimonies where women conveyed the feeling that they were living through a transformation designed by cis heterosexual men to suit their own needs and wants. Recognizing female sexuality and pleasure was undoubtedly a step in the right direction.

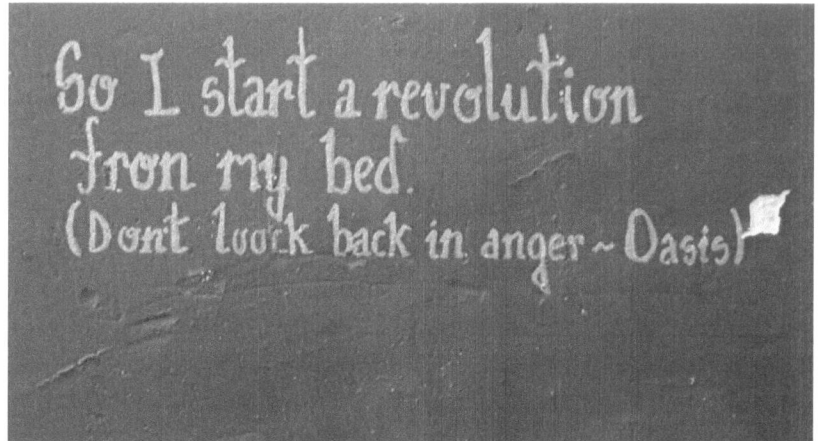

Graffiti on a wall of a cocktail bar. Source: Juan-Carlos Pérez-Cortés

However, it was used as an excuse to build a narrative that spoke of love and sharing but that in the end focused on sexual freedom; the movement showed no concern for the differences between men and women in the cultural construction of desire, expectations, and vulnerabilities. It pursued an ideal of freedom without responsibility, without attention to pre-existing power structures, and without any work on deconstructing the elements that made up the previous relationship model. By reading texts from that moment in history and the analyses that followed, it is immediately apparent that a new normativity was created precisely as a response to a historically

---

69 Brian Alexander, "Free love: Was there a price to pay?", Sexploration column on MSNBC.com, 2013.

rigid, hypocritical moral conception dominated by taboos and prohibitions; liberation and rebellion were mandatory and were themselves valued. Women especially could not renounce that value without risking being considered prudish and old-fashioned. Caught up in the tension between the values they were raised on and this new cultural ideal, women were discouraged from voicing their true desires, reservations, fears, and difficulties. As I've already said, the hippie movement and the countercultural revolution of the '60s forged and spread the popular foundations of many attitudes and conceptions that now seem to be the norm in how familiar and obviously acceptable they are to us. However, this was not the case before that moment. From the normality with which we talk about sex, pacifism, anti-consumerism, environmentalism, a return to nature, spirituality outside of hegemonic religions in the West, to well-established concerns in our culture, such as the critique of imperialism, globalization, the accumulation of wealth and world power in the hands of a few elites, or the lack of control over technological advances in ethical and sustainability terms – these are all new achievements from that era.

The rise of the ethical slut

While the late 20th century was still hung over from the revolutionary experiments that began 20 years before, new social upheavals were already beginning to bud: third-wave feminism and the spread of digital technologies for creation, editing, and communication. In that broad cultural context, a new proposal called polyamory surfaced. Curiously, the first known appearance of the term dates to 1990 is in the article, "A Bouquet of Lovers" in *Green Egg*, a magazine by a California neo-pagan sect (*The Church of All Worlds*) signed by its "High Priestess" Diana Moore under the pseudonym Morning Glory Zell-Ravenheart. One of the goals of this extravagant organization was to produce unicorns by implanting horns in newborn goat kids. Another of its bizarre endeavors was looking for mermaids on the shores of Papua New Guinea. According to its proponents, both projects were completed successfully.[70]

In 1992, Debora Anapol, a psychologist and student of tantric spirituality, published *Love Without Limits – The Quest for Sustainable Intimate Relationships: Responsible Nonmonogamy*[71]. There, she includes the term and outlines the foundations of a responsible alternative to monogamy in how we relate to one another. A revised edition of the work was released in 1997, this time entitled *Polyamory: The New Love Without Limits: Secrets of Sustainable Intimate Relationships*.[72]

That same year, *The Ethical Slut*[73] was published by authors Dossie Easton and Catherine Liszt (a pseudonym used by Janet W. Hardy in the first edition). Despite initially approaching its main theme from a more sexualized perspective, it offers the foundations for a true ethical insurrection based in experience against the hypocrisy that surrounds relationships in our societies, and it does so in experiential and practical terms in the plural first person with a familiar, direct writing style. This book connects with a wider audience to share ideas about an irreverent, emancipatory, feminist expansion of the social perception of affective-sexual relationships during the first decade of the 21st century. I was introduced to these new references at the *Sexo Oral* (*Oral Sex*) colloquia organized by Miguel Vagalume in 2010 at the Consentido bar[74] in Malasaña, Madrid. Miguel has written about *The Ethical Slut*, saying, "One day,

---

70 R. Guiley, *The encyclopedia of witches, witchcraft and wicca*, Facts On File, New York, 2008.
71 D. Anapol, *Love Without Limits: The Quest for Sustainable Intimate Relationships: Responsible Nonmonogamy*, Intinet Resource Center, San Rafael, 1992.
72 D. Anapol, *Polyamory: The New Love Without Limits: Secrets of Sustainable Intimate Relationships*, Intinet Resource Center, San Rafael, 1997.
73 D. Easton, C. Liszt, *The Ethical Slut*, Greenery Press, San Francisco, 1997.
74 Consentido was a unique spot at the end of the '00s. This multipurpose space was dedicated to eroticism, bringing a bar, a boutique, and an art gallery together under the same roof; some of the proceeds went to social projects related to the fight against sexual exploitation. It closed in 2012. Its micro-history can be found in "El placer de lo consentido" ("The pleasure of the consensual") on elmundo.es.

a book exploded in my hands (...) Over time, I learned that the same thing had happened to many others around the world..."[75]

Consentido. A multi-space in Madrid that brought together bar, library, boutique and art gallery, where the "Oral Sex" colloquiums had place.

To finish out this historical tour of the influences and contributions that feed the ideology and rhetoric of polyamory and concluding with its constituent elements, we find contributions from sexual liberation movements, various queer or LGTBIQ+ subcultures, BDSM, kink, sex positivity, and particularly feminisms with more radical, emancipatory discourses.

However, the bibliographic material that seems to have a more significant role in constructing polyamorous identarian sentiment employs an empowering, subversive expressiveness. Its expository model, though, is sometimes more reminiscent of self-help guides than political and social reflection or analyses of oppressions and power structures.

Its instructive style, with examples presented as models of success or failure, and its approach in terms of the objectives and the ultimate meaning of the path to be traveled, which is more reformer than radical, make that move seem at times more like a move from one regulation to another. It could be said that any analysis that proposes real alternatives will end up falling into the same problem,

---

75 Blog Eros from *El País*, Oct. 6, 2013.

but some recognition of that reality – and alerting the reader to it – could be included.

On the other hand, the dialectic of personal development and growth tends to psychologize and particularize social dynamics[76], emphasizing individual autonomy and freedom to the detriment of structural aspects (despite the fact that, as I've said, the narrative style used tends to be against the established cultural order in critical and insurgent terms). The key words are usually communication, caring and self-care, knowing oneself, respect, responsibility, work and personal improvement, deconstruction, drama, jealousy versus "compersion," empathy, and assertiveness. And, above all, management and negotiation, management and agreements, management and consensus... and management and management and management... These notions are set up as a toolbox I can use to overcome the enormous difficulties (a toolbox that often hides an underlying victimizing gaze and semantics of irremediable pain and suffering) of transitioning from monogamy to a new polyamorous identity in an evolution that is often more reminiscent of a rite of initiation or a path of spiritual growth than a process of social opposition.

It is true that there are works and activities where the context is analyzed in political terms; oppressed identities; axes of power; challenging ethnocentrism and elitism; considering the enormous differences between people in terms of gender or material, cultural, social, and geographical conditions, and so on.[77] In practice, though, access to these sources and announcements has, until recently, been reserved for those who have the time and energy to get involved intensely in activist groups.

---

76 See J. Haritaworn, Chin-ju Lin, C. Klesse, "Poly/logue: A Critical Introduction to Polyamory," *Sexualities*, SAGE Publ., 2006.
77 In Spain, examples include the works of Brigitte Vasallo, Miguel Vagalume, Mari Luz Esteban, Giazu Enciso, meetings with several well-defined themes like Eixams and, to a more variable degree, Opencons in Europe and the "RAD unconferences" in the US. I will talk about these meetings in the last chapter.

The most common material is geared toward helping me in the almost arithmetic multiplication of my sexual and affective relationships: communicating more, caring more, knowing myself more, and working more on my insecurities, my jealousies, my fears – all while preserving normative logic and the system of rights and obligations stemming from the hegemonic relationship model – simply adapting it to a new framework of negotiation. Predictably, the end result tends to be quite similar to what can be seen in the trajectory of conventional relationships, just amplified by the difficulty of multiplied expectations and duties to be carried out simultaneously.

Leaving aside relationship anarchy (since, as I've noted on several occasions, I don't consider it to be a proposal that has a place in the historical lineage discussed in this section), the most recent and, in my opinion, the most interesting approaches transcend the semantics associated with terminology and forms such as "poly..." or "non-monogamous..." They stop focusing on the number like some sort of multiplication problem and start focusing on the concept of the affective network, the rhizome.[78] These proposals also explore power relations, as well as symbolic and material violence; they critically examine the cultural colonialism behind the false universalism of some of the new age propositions that stem from the most paradoxical post-modernity (intellectualizing decontextualized Eastern spiritualist elements in Western terms and then applying the pretentious scope of a cosmovision to them).

2.5 Biological and anthropological perspective

When it comes to analyzing and justifying a moral position, principles, ways of proceeding, identarian guidelines, or a normative order, the common, most operable temptation is surely to resort to what's natural or to some universal, absolute values. In both cases, the weight and consistency of a pre-existing, unshakeable element

---

[78] B. Vasallo, *Amores: Redes Afectivas y revoluciones*, Pensaré Cartoneras, Valencia, 2015, and B. Vasallo, *Pensamiento monógamo, terror poliamoroso*, La Oveja Roja, Madrid, 2018.

are valued over the cultural context and the collective will, which are aspects that can be swayed. What's natural and sacred are safe references that are easy to understand. I may or may not like them, but they won't mislead me because they don't change. Giving up anchors carries the risk of finding yourself adrift. Accepting that my individual values and those of society may, over time, be the target of criticism, adjustment, and approval or denunciation and revocation is more complicated than it seems. Hence, the tendency to invoke nature or dogma as defenders of my ethical positions and my daily practices.

The opposite path — maintaining that values, principles, and behaviors are conditioned by dominant ideologies and beliefs, and that what I recognize as common sense is common only in my culture at my time — requires intellectual effort and willpower. This is not thinking that anything goes, that anything could be accepted in certain contextual conditions and that all attitudes are comparable and valid – not at all. Building values, whether these or those, is part of my life's work, my commitment to those around me, and ultimately, my responsibility as a human being. Accepting that my actions are guided by what's natural, sacred, the reason I came to this universe or what destiny has in store for me, what's written in ancient texts or in the stars, or what happened in previous lives and must be restored by a universal spirit of justice and balance... accepting any of those mandates is to renounce that responsibility, that commitment, and that life's work.

In fact, one of the ways that authority and power take root in societies is through the naturalization or sacralization of such ideas and behaviors that serve to perpetuate those same instances of authority and power. When it comes to maintaining the social model, the most important structures and their modes of dominance and control are naturalized or sacralized; they are given as a priori truths that everyone should know and respect because they're universal – obeying them is inescapable.

In the case of naturalization, they are truths that work like laws of physics – gravity or thermodynamics, for instance – imposing restrictions that cannot be argued with or objected to for fear of falling into the void or burning to a crisp. Sacralization works similarly by resorting to beliefs or absolute values, such as the gods' commandments or values and symbols like homelands, flags, or national principles.

One example that's easy to understand is the role historically assigned to women. It's no coincidence that, at different eras in each patriarchal society, the feminine traits that were considered natural have been the most useful for the prevailing system of social organization. The behaviors that the different gods have required in their moral mandates have also always been ideal for maintaining stable patriarchal models of power.

It has been precisely at those times when questions were raised about whether these traits were really inherent in the nature of the oppressed groups, or when faith in the designs of the idolized deities was weakened that the frameworks of power have been destabilized and the greatest social advances have been made. Questions that challenged ideas so normalized they became common sense are what have really allowed revolutions and conquests of thought to triumph.

In the specific case of patterns of cohabitation associated with relationships, there is a vast number of works, hypotheses, and interpretations about what the human being's natural condition and innate tendencies are. Of course, the moral mandates of different religions, philosophies, and ideological doctrines on personal, sexual, and cohabitational relationships make up a significant portion of their normative bodies and repressive codes, featuring impressive catalogs of threats, sanctions, and punishments for violating their precepts.

Interpretations of natural forms of relationship

The first question that could be analyzed is what we mean by natural. One ironic yet very illuminating quip is that what we consider natural is that we can't recall how and when it was imposed. Apart from reflection and historical criticism, a practical characterization could focus on how each individual (human or not) perceives what is natural from birth until they are fully developed. Just as how each creature has to survive in the ecosystem where it emerges and adapt to it as much as its characteristics allow, for each person, the natural environment is the environment where they are born, learn, and grow.

A human being born in a developed urban context during the 21st century encounters a natural environment composed of physical surroundings made of cement, asphalt, steel, walls, glass, fabrics, paper, color touch screens, information flowing in all directions, motorized mobility, mixed physical and virtual socialization starting in childhood, and so on. Much of this environment consists of highly technological elements that we consider artificial[79]; materially, though, that member of the human species has encountered those circumstances and has to develop in them (or die, if they do not succeed).

In any case, if we insist on continuing to analyze interpretations of what supposedly natural forms of behavior would be like, we will have to come to a conventional agreement. The simplest way is to assume that technologies like rudimentary tools made of wood and stone, as well as a primitive language, could be accepted as sufficiently unintrusive so as not to disturb this stereotypical condition of what is "natural." Thus, hunter-gatherer groups of humans prior

---

[79] In the same way that a modern hunter-gatherer in the Amazon would consider the conditions of a first-century Roman house to be completely artificial, with its ceramic technology for pavement and accumulating water in containers, textile and tanning technology for clothing and footwear, cutting tools and more based on metallurgical technology, etc.

to the Neolithic (and more recent populations of a similar technological level) would be a suitable example.

To delve even more specifically into the question studied in this section, let's go over what is known about the relational behavior of people in prehistoric human groups and the level of reliability that can be attributed to that knowledge; throughout this inquiry, we will not cease to insist on the thesis that, even if the data were unequivocal and the conclusions unquestionable, I can grant them limited or no influence as premises and guides for my behavior.

In *Sex at Dawn*,[80] Christopher Ryan and Cacilda Jethá analyze what they call the "Standard Narrative" of paleoanthropology and of evolutionary anthropology and psychology from a critical perspective, using accessible language in a book that is exciting and revealing to read. The main ideas of this narrative, which is widely accepted and cited even in recent decades, are that men and women express very clear innate interests according to a heterosexual monogamous model: males look for signs of youth, fertility, and sexual inexperience in an effort to ensure their "parental investment" in their own offspring and not those of other men; females focus on the candidate's social status and the expectation that he will be faithful and offer sustenance and protection during the young's gestation, lactation, and development.

Both tend to form an exclusive, lasting union (though this exclusivity is admittedly imperfect) as a fundamental trait of the species. After this relationship has formed, females demonstrate an instinct to keep their man away from other women in order to avoid the risk of losing that support in raising offspring, and they show an eventual interest in fleeting relations with other males with outstanding genetic traits. The males instinctively keep their wives safe from intimacy with other men so as not to invest in raising young that does not contain their genetic material; they also show a constant

---

80   C. Ryan and C. Jethá, Sex at Dawn: How We Mate, Why We Stray, and What It Means for Modern Relationships, op. cit.

urge to surreptitiously spread their seed if given the opportunity to perpetuate their genes while investing minimal energy.

Since the fossil record doesn't provide direct information on behavior patterns at this level, the empirical evidence supporting this persuasive account (which gives off the suspicious air of an adapted screenplay) comes from studies on human behavior and interpretations based on knowledge of processes of natural selection. The problem is that the methodology behind these studies, particularly how they are interpreted, shows a clear bias towards a narrative aligned with the morals and values of the day and the society from which those who proposed them came.

Fortunately, ethnocentric bias becomes less obvious as the decades go by. In 1967, Desmond Morris wrote in his influential work *The Naked Ape*:[81]

> "It is interesting that although it still occurs in a number of minor cultures today, all the major societies (which account for the vast majority of the world population of the species) are monogamous. Even in those that permit polygamy, it is not usually practised by more than a small minority of the males concerned. It is intriguing to speculate as to whether its omission from almost all the larger cultures has, in fact, been a major factor in the attainment of their present successful status. We can, at any rate, sum up by saying that, whatever obscure, backward tribal units are doing today, the mainstream of our species expresses its pair-bonding character in its most extreme form, namely long-term monogamous matings."

Like The Naked Ape in its day, fifty years later Yuval Noah Harari's *Sapiens*[82] has become a best-seller. It seems that this last half-century has given rise to a hopeful shift in perspective, moving from disgraceful ethnocentrism to an approach that demonstrates the minimum requirement of intellectual humility:

---

81   Translated into 23 languages and more than 20 million copies sold.
82   20 million copies sold worldwide.

> "The sociopolitical world of the foragers is another area about which we know next to nothing. As explained above, scholars cannot even agree on the basics, such as the existence of private property, nuclear families and monogamous relationships. It's likely that different bands had different structures. Some may have been as hierarchical, tense and violent as the nastiest chimpanzee group, while others were as laid-back, peaceful and lascivious as a bunch of bonobos."

Though Harari's chosen adjectives continue to suggest a degree of what Lawrence W. Levine called "Flintstonizing of the past,"[83] his approach is comparatively refreshing and respectful. The comparison made in the quote is quite notable, given that chimpanzees likely do demonstrate more hierarchical, tense behavior, yet it is no less "lascivious" or distant from the "nuclear family" than that of bonobos.

Recent work that has been scientifically and professionally recognized by therapists, such as Amir Levine and Rachel Heller's *Attached*,[84] has offered a de-pathologizing approach that is critical of individualism, and it is undoubtedly valuable and useful in the current social context. But in this work, interpretations of empirical observations and the focus on the entire analysis fall under the unquestionable axiom of the species' fundamental monogamous union. Looking through that prism leads to such striking conclusions as, "Numerous studies show that once we become attached to someone, the two of us form one physiological unit. Our partner regulates our blood pressure, our heart rate, our breathing, and the levels of hormones in our blood. We are no longer separate entities," (under the heading *The Biological Truth*), or "one of the main messages of this theory is that in romantic situations, we are programmed to act in a predetermined manner."

---

[83] Representation via familiar concepts hinders seeing history as a process that leads to the present. L.W. Levine, *The opening of the American mind: canons, culture, and history*, p. xv, 1996, for the cartoon *The Flintstones*.

[84] A. Levine, R. Heller, *Attached: Are you Anxious, Avoidant or Secure? How the science of adult attachment can help*, Books4pocket, 2016.

From the opposite point of view, Ryan and Jethá's work, which I've cited previously, brings together an enormous amount of evidence about current hunter-gatherer societies from Polynesia to the Amazon. Along with details on behavior compared to the other four species of great apes (the absence of estrous cycles, orgasms, copulatory vocalizations) and reproductive anatomy (breasts, size and location of the testicles, the shape of the penis, and the chemistry of semen), these allow us to conclude that for most of human evolution, the basic sexual unit must have encompassed all or some undefined subset of the nomadic hunting and gathering group; almost everything would have been cooperative, including sex, attachment, mutual care, and caring for offspring.

Therefore, as for how human beings behaved in prehistoric times, we have on one hand the standard narrative with works that complete and qualify it, and which do not fit into the scope of this project. On the other hand are alternatives that offer a completely different vision, suggesting that the great cultures across the planet exhibit behaviors adapted to the social structures and power relations that appeared with sedentarization rather than the environment the species adapted to for 95% of its evolutionary timeline.

As for the second question raised – which part of basic human behavior is innate and which is due to the environment? – developmental and behavioral psychology were shaped by now-classic controversies in the 20th century, notably those among Jean Piaget, Lev. S. Vygotsky, Noam Chomsky, B.F. Skinner, John B. Watson, Ivan Pavlov, Steven Pinker, Stephen Jay Gould, and so on. Theories on development or on the epistemic subject, where behavior is fundamentally shaped by biology; behaviorism, which emphasizes the environment; and the innumerable nuances, arguments, empirical contributions, and subsequent interpretations they offer form a true collage that is fascinating but not very enlightening.

To begin with, we must remember that notions about what is innate, instinctive, or genetic are related, but they don't mean the same thing. Intuitively, we know that we're talking about which part of who we are is independent of where and how we develop, but that definition doesn't help us characterize a specific behavioral trait. Formally, a trait is defined as "innate" when it presents an organized structure by the time it appears, bringing together several coordinated actions without the need for prior training. For instance, on hearing a noise, most vertebrates have a predetermined pattern of turning to look at where it came from – an innate behavior. The concepts of being "genetic" or "hereditary" have to do with how those behaviors are transmitted from one generation to the next. The term "instinctive" refers to the fact that a certain capacity is typical of a particular type or family of organisms that always show it.

From a biological point of view, innate traits and behaviors must be encoded in DNA in such a way that they give rise to an anatomical and biochemical structure that expresses those traits through series of processes. Starting with DNA, proteins are synthesized in the cells of a living being and conditions are fostered so that each cell performs a function; it reproduces itself to create other cells, and together, that entire set works together according to a particular overall design in the organism's program of development and maintenance, which is the genetic code.

Growth gives way to tissues, organs, systems, connections, enzymes, hormones, neurotransmitters, and ultimately, a functional organization of everything that is also highly dependent on very diverse conditions that vary over time. Complex behaviors, both conscious and instinctive, are those of interest here and are fundamentally governed by the central nervous system; the brain is the most important area, and it is significantly influenced by particular biochemical, hormonal, and metabolic parameters.

As is also true of other organs, part of the brain's general structure is directly encoded in DNA: areas with specific types of neurons, as well as specific connections between them, circuits of stimulation, inhibition, firing, ways of passing information on, and acquiring perceptions from the sense organs. Another more detailed level of design develops based on epigenetic mechanisms that complement the development process through interactions between the code and regulatory substances that modify its final expression; they also build different structures based on the same gene sequence. They are also layers – the classical genetic and the epigenetic levels – that intertwine with no defining line between them. It's like how we can cook a slightly different dish every day following the same recipe; it all depends on whether the heat is a little higher or lower, whether we put more or less water, or what extra ingredients we have on hand or are about to go bad.

By turning our hands over, we can find the very clear example of our fingerprints and palm prints in this very moment. These patterns of lines, which can seem like some whimsical, inspired designs, are not encoded as well-defined sketches in our genetic code. The exact patterns of our papillary ridges have no major functional effect and are therefore useless information in terms of genome economics. We have this guide so that it can lead cells to differentiate into ridges and valleys, helping us grasp a branch or a rock or hold something firmly between our fingers; what we don't store are the starting or ending points or the curvature of each line. That is determined by the physical and chemical factors affecting cell growth during embryonic development. Therefore, even two identical twins, univitelline individuals who share the same genetic information, have different fingerprints, though the general design is similar (more so than that of two people who don't share DNA).

The connections between individual neurons are also not coded in advance; this detailed structure of our brain takes on a particular pattern during embryonic growth, just like the lines on the skin of the fingers and hands. To this we must add the enormous plasticity of the circuits established by following the connections between neurons as segments along the path. Plasticity means that they will be developed, enhanced, or inhibited based on sensory, biochemical, and proprioceptive stimuli (proprioceptive senses measure the body's current state) throughout development, learning, and life. These circuits and activation routes for the cells of the central nervous system, which are mediated by neurotransmitters, hormones, and other substances, make up our brain activity. All together, they form the basis for what we are at a conscious level, as well as much of our unconscious behavior.

This is the case with our ability to remember faces, for instance. We can recognize a familiar face out of thousands, even if it has changed significantly since the last time we saw it or is far away, partially hidden, in profile, or with different facial expressions. There is an area of the brain in the infratemporal cortex that is dedicated to this specialized task. We know this because when it's damaged, a cognitive difference called prosopagnosia appears which prevents recognizing faces; when the area is specifically stimulated, facial recognition is affected. However, recent experiments suggest that[85] that area of the brain's innately encoded specialization is only what is strictly necessary to detect and store relevant images efficiently, not faces in particular. Monkeys also have this area of the brain, and when they grow up with all of the stimuli required for their development, including physical contact, hugs, and games but no exposure to any images of faces, they dedicate that area to recognizing other important visual stimuli, such as hands.

Another example is the curious phenomenon of filial imprinting, which occurs in birds, mammals, fish, insects, and other organisms. This is an instinctive trait that leads a newborn animal to recognize and follow what it observes in motion (in the case of visual imprinting). Auditory, olfactory, tactile, and even thermal imprinting – which is related to body heat – decisively sway the ecological behavior of many species, causing them to return to places or reproduce behaviors whose characteristics they perceived during a critical phase in their development.

---

[85] M.J. Arcaro, P.F. Schade, J.L. Vincent, C.R. Ponce, M.S. Livingstone, "Seeing faces is necessary for face-domain formation," *Nature Neuroscience*, 2017.

Sexual imprinting has also been described, and in some species, it can go so far as to be quite unusual. In a moving, nearly lifelong effort to save the whooping crane from extinction, passionate conservationist George Archibald finally got a captive-bred female that was artificially inseminated to lay a clutch (which is required for reproduction) by executing a mating ritual dance that included an imitation of the calls and corresponding movements.[86] The crane, Tex, later died when a raccoon snuck into the facility, but her direct descendants still live on (the average lifespan of cranes is over 20 years). This species is still endangered, and attempts to support its recovery include stimulating migrations where cranes fly following an ultralight aircraft that they've been induced to imprint on visually.

George Archibald executing a mating ritual dance with the crane Tex.
Source: International Crane Foundation

The instinct of attaching to what is perceived during a critical phase of development is likely an efficient way of storing a behavioral pattern in a limited space for code like DNA, much how fingerprint patterns and many other anatomical features are not detailed plans but

---

86 G. Archibald, *My Life with Cranes,* International Crane Foundation, 2016.

primordial outlines. The structure will unfold to form a limb or organ, just as a good jazz performance turns a basic rhythmic and harmonic pattern into exciting artistic improvisation.

Therefore, conscious and complex human behaviors can't really be stored completely and deterministically in the genetic code. There's a limit to the information that can be stored, and the very process of our nervous system's construction and progress over time is conditioned by variable elements, internal and external influences, perceptions, and experiences. There could be basic, predefined psychological tendencies (fear, anger, empathy, etc.), characteristic factors determining susceptibility, and predispositions to develop certain general traits (universal abilities, for instance: the ability to walk, smile or laugh, cry, talk... though on close examination, this always occurs in a differentiated way, giving rise to different ways of walking, smiling, or speaking). None of these, however, are governed by detailed or sophisticated rational guidelines. I think it is highly unlikely that the conscious, detailed articulation of how we relate to one another intimately, sexually, and affectively over the course of our lifetimes is innately conditioned, much less that this conditioning is universal. Nor do I believe this to be the case with cognitive behaviors (beyond reflexes and hormonal issues related to reproductive anatomy) associated with femininity, masculinity, the construction of desire, transformative and subversive potentiality, vocational trends, or life goals in general.

In short, as I've analyzed at the beginning of this section, determining what the natural environment is for the human species is complex and ultimately not very useful. If we set the chronological reference point during the Paleolithic era, evidence about what relational and social behavior was at that time is indirect and controversial; if we try to delimit the traits that are innate and those that are cultural, as discussed in the last few paragraphs, we reach even more speculative results. But going back to the initial argument, even if we could hypothetically come to precise knowledge that gives us absolute confidence about these two questions, what should we do with that knowledge?

Suppose advances made in evolutionary anthropology led us to the conviction that, 30,000 years ago, human beings lived in groups of about 150 individuals, and particular relationships were in some way defined between males, females, and their offspring (a risky assumption). Moreover, say we knew that the strongest males controlled the size of the community by killing young perceived to be descended from other males when food was scarce, even going so far as to feed on them when the lack of nutrients in the environment was prolonged. Suppose that we discover beyond any doubt that this behavior, at that level of complexity, is innate to our species – that we are cannibalistic infanticides. Should this serve as inspiration, support, or an argument for changing our principles and policies on protecting children, for instance? Obviously not.

Therefore, it goes without question that knowledge is a value in itself, and seeking it, improving on it, and refining it as much as possible is a noble, necessary task. What am I, who am I, where do I come from, and how did I get here? I want answers to these questions from a scientific point of view, and I understand that this knowledge can influence my emotions. But I want to act in a political way to decide what I will be, who I will be, where I'm going, and how I can get to where I want to go. I'd like to decide on this as part of a process, a life journey that is collective, and along that way, I want to consider the reality and the emotional process of those who are on that journey with me. I'm talking about how we want to relate to each other in our world, our peculiar ecosystem of concrete, metal, and silicon – not that of a thousand, ten thousand, or a hundred thousand years ago.

Moral and dogmatic models for regulating relationships

In our Western societies today — especially in Europe — a steadily decreasing number of people seem to hold doctrinal religious beliefs. Few claim to believe in the existence of a supernatural being (or a group of them) that is well-defined, eternal, and capable of perception, cognition, intelligence, and will in relation to reality. Even those with more spiritual tendencies are finding it difficult to subscribe to the idea of a corporeal or incorporeal entity that is aware of our behaviors at all times; that can process and evaluate that information to come to conclusions and then use those conclusions to determine courses of action within the framework of a set of moral values; and finally, that has the will to carry out those decisions to modify the real world in a particular way.

Taking this belief literally is increasingly difficult due to the complexities of modern life. Starting in childhood, we are constantly exposed to highly diverse stimuli, people from other cultures and creeds, traveling around the world, empirical descriptions based on observation, analysis and rational decision, technologies that surprise us with their accuracy (orders of magnitude higher than human precision); we receive so much information and go through many experiences that are interesting, motivating, dramatic, and terrible, and whose natural causes are generally clear, even though we still understand that there's much left to learn.

The result is that the dominant spirituality is not based on clear reflection on the existence of one or more omniscient, omnipotent, omnipresent, and omnibenevolent divinities, but on a diffuse cosmovision that answers questions of faith[87] with an imprecise belief in "something out there," or vague references to concepts borrowed from scientific terminology – "forces," "energies," "the universe." The prevailing view is a mystified agnostic stance, which is closer to ontology and metaphysics – two fields that entail wondering what exists and what reality is made of beyond what we can perceive – than

---

87 Questions often asked in mainstream media opinion polls in a markedly uninquisitive way, at least in Southern Europe. Under the guise of simplicity, they avoid delving into the population's level of religiosity by asking questions like, "Do you consider yourself a believer?" instead of, "Do you believe that there is a supernatural being who rewards or punishes people's behavior in this reality and in another life after death?" Surely statistics on the latter, where theological doctrines come into question, would be cause for concern for religious hierarchies.

to religion; in contrast, the latter involves emotions and attitudes consistent with basic dogmas and a faith that is spiritual in origin, and which is lived with conviction in accordance with a sacred doctrine and expressed in daily worship. The exception would be ritual celebrations that kindle fervor, but these are more closely linked to adherence to tradition that has been experienced since childhood and identification with a sociocultural environment than to a conscious religious faith.

In line with all this, the moral mandates associated with religious affiliations and their dogmatic principles are obeyed less and less by those who declare themselves believers. In many countries, this is reflected in divorce rates, the growing use of contraceptives, very low attendance at regular worship services, and many other indicators that reflect the social normalization of conflicting behavior between observed morality and self-designated beliefs. This dissonance is so normalized that it isn't even the subject of debate or controversy. The only thing that is controversial is what is perceived as a frontal attack on collective social rites (whether formally religious or atavistic in nature, such as the ritualization of festivities, pilgrimages, processions of varying degrees of solemnity, etc.).

Therefore, the current reality in our cultures can be synthesized as a generally accepted and self-designated yet diffuse spirituality, an acceptance of prevailing moral norms in eclectic, lax, and relatively fast-evolving terms, and a strident rejection of what is perceived as an attack or threat.

This synthesis, when applied to the hegemonic relationship model, aligns with what we can observe quite accurately. The accepted forms of relationship are constantly expanding, from the rigid, sexist, strongly coercive nuclear family of a century ago to the current diversity. However, it becomes problematic to move from an implicit tolerance of practices like homosexual or non-normative relationships – when not presented in formal terms but as larks and whims – to social acceptance of same-sex marriage or formalized free, open, or multiple relationships.

Accepting that each person relates to whomever however they want, even when their behavior is not in line with the moral principles that I recognize as my own (including the ones I don't faithfully observe) is likely easier for me than modifying those moral principles. Admitting the fragility of my ethical model poses a threat since it is a structure I didn't build but that was given to me; therefore, changing it can seem risky and disturbing.

A story that's often told to illustrate how easily culturally-induced responses are acquired is that of "the five monkeys." The story doesn't seem to be from any one real experiment, but it is inspired by a study carried out in the 1960s by Gordon R. Stephenson – and it leads to similar conclusions.[88]

There is a group of five monkeys and a bunch of bananas hanging from the ceiling, out of reach. They can get to the bananas with a ladder that's there, and the most active animal recognizes this and starts to climb right away. At that moment, everyone is sprayed with cold water. The one who started to climb the ladder comes down immediately, and all five of them are wet and scared... until the temptation of food leads another to try to reach the bananas again. The bothersome stimulus is repeated until the monkeys acquire the behavior of not climbing the ladder. One monkey is then removed from the cage, and a new one is brought in. On seeing the bananas, the new monkey naturally starts to climb towards them, but the rest of the group violently dissuades that new member. Finally, one monkey is replaced after another until none of the ones who were sprayed remain. This group can no longer directly associate the action of climbing the ladder with anything negative, yet they have all learned to hit and dissuade anyone who tries to do so. As such, the

---

88 G.R. Stephenson, "Cultural Acquisition of a Specific Learned Response Among Rhesus Monkeys," comp by D. Starek, R. Schneider, and H.J. Kuhn, in *Progress in Primatology*, Fischer, 1967., pp. 279-288. A similar experiment on human groups in a laboratory simulation was carried out by Robert Jacobs and Donald Cambell (1961), "The perpetuation of an arbitrary tradition through several generations of a laboratory microculture," *J. of Abnormal and Social Psychology*, 62(3), 649-658, 1961.

group is ultimately unable to enjoy the bananas. Cold water is no longer needed for the taboo to be maintained indefinitely.

As I said, when we don't know the origin of our behavioral patterns, challenges to them can be even scarier. We don't have any clues about whether the actions are taboo because of risks we are unaware of rather than merely by convention.

In short, we can conclude that new proposals for relationships and alternative ways of life in general (even though they challenge dominant moral norms) don't pose a threat or set off alarms as long as they remain just that: alternatives. The sensitivities more closely tied to the security offered by tradition go on red alert when these proposals are visibilized and normalized. The same is true when religious sentiment, State symbols like the Crown or the flag, the patriarchy, marriage and the family, festive traditions and rituals, or anything else considered sacred is affronted. When you're hanging out at the bar, you can hear actual blasphemies and irreverent jabs at many of these symbols, but there, they elicit laughter and even complicity. In a public demonstration, especially one that is collective and effective, the same words are certainly cause for alarm.

I believe that this is why visibility and normalization are crucial. We've seen this throughout history with the struggle for the rights of many groups and minorities, most recently the LGBTIQ+ population, and we're starting to see it with the feminist struggle. Widening the scope of these revolutions is precisely what provokes reactionary movements. When we get through the system's hard outer shell and leathery epidermis, making it shudder and roar – that is the time to persevere and insist.

Chapter 3. I relate to others in a different way: labels, models, and practices

> "Conformity requires us to minimize our differences for the greater good. We fear that if we don't conform, we will be abandoned, but there is no loneliness like having people only see you after you've erased yourself."
> Alok Vaid-Menon

Over the last two chapters – quite a few pages already – I've tried to frame the proposal of relationship anarchy in different ethical models, cultural and political traditions, and specific interpretations raised by different communities and from various sensitivities. In this third chapter, I want to offer an initial approach to the experiences of those who developed the proposal and of those of us who have built small realities within this general framework of thought, as well as to the labels for these ideas and practices.

3.1 Labels and models

Descriptive and prescriptive labels

One of the first obstacles you face when you start living life some way different from the norm in your environment (a way of acting that's not properly described with any of the usual categories) is simply knowing what to say when you're asked about it. I don't mean rhetorical questions or inquiries laced with criticism or condemnation, but sincere, well-intentioned questions from those who appreciate you and want to understand you. Of course, the best option – when you have the time, place, and atmosphere that allow for it – is to explain everything from the beginning, with all the background and context clues needed to be understood, satisfying their curiosity and clearing up any questions. That almost always comes with learning a little more about yourself and your circumstances in the process through the reflection needed to explain and from the reactions and opinions of those listening to you.

But those conditions don't always exist. Normally, time is limited, and conversations flow smoothly from one topic to another; the chances that they will listen to you patiently and make an effort to understand are low. Labels are therefore quite convenient for us. However, I have discussed that the words that we all use do not always describe what we do adequately, so we have to resort to neologisms and concepts that aren't widely used. I'll talk about that shortly, but there is a third option. That's just making what I'm not doing clear. This may not sound particularly positive, clarifying, or helpful, but it will at least keep certain conventions from being taken for granted. It's possible that the subject may come up again on a more favorable occasion, and then the details can be discussed at length.

Hence, the title of this chapter. Of all the short, simple answers I know for stereotypical questions like, "Are you a couple?," "How long have you been together?," "Is she just your friend, or more than that?," "Do you have a partner?," " Are you looking for a partner?," "How long have you been single?," "When are you going to settle down?," "Are you thinking about shaking things up your life?," "Are you still together?," "Did you break up?"... and a thousand other inquiries along those lines, the one that I most prefer is the humble, restrained, "I relate to others in a different way."[89]

Simply being able to easily express what your life is like, your way of seeing and living it, where it's at, or even how you're feeling – this constitutes an important privilege. This is a privilege you have to give up when you do things differently, in a way that has no name or where nuances are important (because another characteristic of hegemony, besides making oppressions and prejudices invisible, is digesting and assimilating nuances).

---

[89] I owe this formulation to Sonia Pina.

This is why it's so common to hear or read that relationship anarchy is about getting rid of labels. It might serve as a headline, an introductory simplification, grabbing attention, or piquing curiosity – but no, it isn't that. To begin with, the phrase "relationship anarchy" itself is a label; while some uses of labels cloak very real dangers, that is not, in my opinion, the central or essential piece of the proposal. Much how the renunciation of sexual and affective exclusivity – that is, the monogamous mandate – can occur throughout an experiential development framed in relationship anarchy, getting past labels supposes yet another derivation, but neither of these constitutes the nuclear element.

To analyze the importance of this causal link, it may help to differentiate between two types of labels or identifications: descriptive and prescriptive ones. The former are generally useful tools for communication and thought (especially when they're self-assigned, since a descriptive label can also be applied to another person for perverse purposes). The obstacles I mentioned at the beginning of this section point to the need for this type of label —the self-assigned, descriptive ones— to get around those road blocks, to be able to describe our experiences and our emotions. The second – prescriptive labels – show up when a definition becomes a normative identification – when it becomes a cage. At that moment, what is described becomes a coercive space, a mental or emotional place that it is not comfortable or possible to get out of.[90]

First, as an approach that challenges any form of authority that some people hold over others, relationship anarchy must clearly mention in its proposal the models of domination that underlie these coercive spaces and continuously alert us to them. When, for instance, "you are my love" stops describing and starts chaining and

---

90 Here, as is almost always the case, there is a potential gray area. Descriptive sorts of labels, which are harmless in principle, can become crutches that help us feel more confident; they can become assurances that end up assigning more value to some forms of behavior than to others; finally, they can become fetishes, in the sense of an object to which a supernatural power is attributed, and their captivating effect comes dangerously close to the dimension of the prescriptive.

submitting or, at the other extreme, when "we're open" doesn't tell us what we want to be like but conditions our feelings and embarrasses us when we recognize inevitable vestiges of our upbringing and our fears and insecurities in them. And secondly, as a proposal that proclaims the need for mutual aid, the creation of horizontal networks of personal, affective solidarity, and responsible collective self-management, it must reject exclusive identity labels. Those include any that reinforce hegemonic elements like the nuclear family and clannish self-interest.

In short, relationship anarchy may have as an effect associated with its anti-authoritarian and self-managed approaches the rejection of prescriptive labels and, above all, normative labels – that is, those associated with dominant, culturally established precepts. It is about using a critical eye to examine the universality of the predetermined routes that start out from normative practices, go through taking on conventional labels, and end up generating identifications loaded with stereotyped expectations, idealizations, prerogatives, and obligations.

For example, the concept of queer-platonic relationships has emerged from aromantic communities in the United States and reached a broader scope; the point is to refer to a deep bond while at the same time escaping the closed concept of a couple. In these relationships, the other person is literally called "my zucchini" or any other vegetable (even eggplant – no joke) to make it clear that every bond is different. The idea is to get beyond the conventional labels so as not to pile on the semantic baggage associated with it.[91]

But a critical analysis that simply uses "common sense" – considering that we've grown up under the hegemony of normative ties, that we've not been exposed to anything else, and that common sense is therefore the only thing we see – immediately leads to questions: what's wrong with calling things by their name? Why can't I say "they're my partner" when talking about someone who fills me

---

91 "Queerplatonic Zucchinis: A Short Primer," on rottenzucchinisfiles.files.wordpress .com.

with love, passion, and trust, someone I love spending time or even living with? Can we not go from being friends to being boyfriend or girlfriend, or lovers, or a couple, or saying that we're are together if we fall in love? Why deny that a relationship is over when it's not working anymore? Can't we go from being a couple to being friends if we fall out of love?

Of course we can. Relationship anarchy doesn't prohibit anything, not by any means. Nor does it condemn, disapprove of, or reproach any of these positions. It simply warns us that if we're interested in exploring a relational model based on the principles of anarchism and the ideas I've introduced and repeatedly mentioned in these pages, we must pay attention to the possibility that these labels condition us. They've got baggage. If we're not highly attentive to this, we will bring in authoritarian behaviors, automatic rights over others, the expectation that they behave "like they should" with me – how "everyone knows" they should, as someone who accepts that recipe for a pre-cooked plate of rights and obligations. The problem arises when we let that word define our behavior by default, when it is no longer necessary to reflect, share, and discuss how we want to live – when this word, this label that marks us and defines us is a seal that says it all.

Since the sign we attach to our adventure also determines how things should be and gives us the security of a shared identity, a beautiful sealed case with letterhead, it suddenly acquires enormous value. Something so precious – almost a luxury – can't be treated lightly. We must be sure as to whether we have it in our possession or not. It must be well-defined in time. Celebrate it and shout it from the rooftops when it comes (and celebrating can be nice when there are no misunderstandings, doubts, different points of view, idealizations…), but ascertain and define the precise moment it ends. And even in the best of cases, that is not a pleasant process. It can mean months or years of heartbreak. It might precede months or years of doubt, grief, trying it again… And worst of all, part of that discomfort and uncertainty is useless, brought on only by the need to name, delimit, and close off.

It makes sense to be sad that another person, someone I love, doesn't feel like doing certain things with me, that they don't share emotions we used to feel together, that they don't agree with basic aspects of my life in the present... But that's not what we end up talking about all the time. Rather, it's the pennant, the name defining our bond. A "couple" with a seal of approval and designation of origin, which doesn't allow for half measures. It's all or nothing. We are or we aren't. What are we?

This is exactly why I like the thought behind "I relate to others in a different way." There are no tricks, no resorting to keywords that might be making headlines in the most fashionable magazines and blogs; it simply frees us from hegemonic normativity and leaves us enough room so as not to fall into other normativities to the best of our abilities.

In other words, I suggest moving away from the "Relationship Anarchist" brand as a label for identity, just as the meaning of those two words, and which I'm dedicating all these pages to, suggests moving away from all these brands with a seal of approval: "Couple," "Boyfriends," "Girlfriends," "Friends," "Partners," "Lovers," "MyGuy," "MyGirl"... I propose understanding each other without coercing each other, taking care of each other without recipes, letting approaches like relationship anarchy show not how things should be, but how they could be. What could they be like if we could live according to near-utopian principles that, if we like, are there to seduce us. They will seduce us only if we let ourselves be seduced, only as much as we let ourselves be seduced, and only until when we stop letting ourselves be seduced.

Models and self-management

If labels enclose complexities and dangers, I think that managing models is even more difficult and risky. The term "model" encompasses a wide range of concepts, from an example to follow to an abstract or numerical representation of a phenomenon and including a mold, a guide, an inspiration, something we want to copy, someone who lends their body to a design so that it can be appreciated, a miniature made to scale, a diagram or blueprint, and even an adjective used to describe a prison. A certain lyricism and poetic irony can be found in each of these meanings when we look at them in the context of relationships and bonds. However, I'll focus on one relatively simple meaning of this word: a set of thoughts, norms, and guidelines that make up a pattern of behavior.

Exploring the axis that goes from the individual to the universal, the first thing we find are the models that each person self-imposes as their own: my patterns of behavior, those I'd like to follow, the ones I actually follow (from the intersubjective point of view – the behaviors seen by those close to me), and those I think I follow as per my own perception of my behavior. Other models are more collective: they're shared with small social circles, such as the people you live with, or wider circles, such as your professional environment or arenas of activism, leisure, or social class. On the other side of that axis are the basic cultural norms: first, the explicit ones, such as the level of physical contact that's acceptable when greeting someone you don't know or whether or not to burp after a big meal. Finally, at the far end are the hegemonic norms, those that are so naturalized that we don't notice them, but they govern my behavior from the deepest depths.

On the other hand, the extent to which these models – personal, shared, or culturally normative – are monitored can also vary. In some cases, my behavior conforms 100% to a certain model; in others, I might apply it more loosely. Sometimes, it is just a set of general standards that serve as a guide. This depends on the circumstances, learning, and the degree of emancipation that are developed over the course of one's life.

The fact is that if I pay enough attention, I can identify a set of patterns in my thoughts and behavior that are rooted and followed at different levels in my daily practices. Specifically in terms of the relationships we have with other people, the hegemonic model is combined with personal and group aspects that set up a scaffolding we move on when interacting.

One advantage that models of relational behavior offer with this shared cultural basis is that they allow us to establish connections in a relatively simple way, knowing how others expect me to behave and how they're expected to behave. Even so, conflicts can arise when there are differences in how these generalized guidelines are interpreted; after all, at no time is it necessary to discuss or validate them explicitly. The subject of assumptions and expectations and that of communication are important, and I will discuss them later on.

But the problem that interests me most regarding relationship models is that of how to shift from a normative model to a dynamic of collective self-management channeled through a network of bonds. Sometimes, it can seem like I'm abandoning a model that has clear rules – even though they don't quite work and we haven't personally developed and worked on them – to move towards an uncertain space where I don't know what I'm going to find. Other times, I might feel like I've left one model behind simply to fall into another one that seems more modern and emancipating, but which is still a pre-cooked dish after all. The third possible perception of these processes arises when I don't want to go somewhere else but instead change what's happening right where I am: to stir up a little revolution. In that case, I must be aware of the fact that I'll have to disassemble the very structure I'm living in, and with great care so as not to fall into the void.

The first of these options, leaving the norm for something whose final form is unknown to me, poses a series of problems, and it could end up leading to the second path (moving from one norm to another). The main difficulties may be my own limitations when it comes to renouncing clichés and privileges and overcoming insecurities and doubts, or when trying to align my capacity for change to the rhythm of the network of bonds I want to move with. I'll talk about these problems in the fifth chapter, as well.

The same obstacles that keep me from leaving normativity behind to build something new may end up leading me to other models where I can find more space, a certain feeling of liberation, and other advantages without having to face something that's completely unknown. It's also possible that I may want to keep some of my sense of security and thus choose an alternative with clear rules straight away, which seems less risky than pure self-management for relationships. One important aspect which I think must be kept in mind when analyzing this situation is the tendency to judge the coercive components of control in these new models with a much less critical eye than I would when evaluating the model I'm coming from. I'll go over an entire catalog of paradigms that offer an alternative to the hegemonic model, and I'll try to point out this bias in the last part of this chapter.

Finally, the option of deconstructing or dismantling the cultural scaffolding that governs how I manage bonds also requires precise pacing alongside the deconstruction that other members of my network of relationships are undertaking. The different individual diachronies can lead to personal suffering and imbalances in the model being dismantled and transformed. This often leads to a painful evolution that's full of setbacks, one that's very slow and is ultimately abandoned. Keep in mind, you can be against the system, but from the outset and surely over a long period of time, you can't avoid being in the system. I can't blame myself for starting out where I was put, or for having been left there without a map or a compass to know which direction to go.

But perhaps the important thing is not where I get to, but daring to challenge the tyranny of an order that I perceive as being imposed. As I try to reconstruct something different over the hegemonic structure, it's one thing to encounter obstacles that are impossible to overcome or require an effort that's too painful or exhausting; it's another to think that the dominant model is the only one that's possible, the one that represents the essence of how we relate to one another as human beings. The mere fact of realizing this and how ingrained these ideas are, how much it takes to sway them, is a victory.

3.2 The relationship escalator

In her shows, the feminist playwright, theater director, and actress Patricia Sornosa delivers a gag in the form of a personal anecdote that graphically reflects not only the naturalness with which we experience patriarchy in everyday life, but also the incremental and progressive nature of the processes that sustain it and its relationship with the economic system. The joke is part of the family's "romantic love story:" Sornosa says that her father and mother met because she used to clean his house. "They fell in love, they started living together, and... she stopped charging by the hour."

The "progress" experienced by the woman in this story constitutes a naturalized step in any normative relationship. Couples meet, fall in love, get to know each other more, decide to combine their life projects, and share more and more things. Without this obligatory evolution, the normative account would rate the bond to be unsatisfactory, immature, insubstantial, low-quality. It is echoed in a highly successful parallel by American journalist Amy Gahran, under the pseudonym Aggie Sez, in a blog post on solopoly.net from November 2012 titled Riding the Relationship Escalator, or Not?. The resulting interest in this analogy, which is cited in many other articles and used at workshops and talks, led Gahran to publish the book Stepping Off the Relationship Escalator: Uncommon Love and Life in February 2017.

Steps and their unrelenting ascent

According to Gahran, in our culture (it can vary slightly depending on social groups and the passage of time), the relationship escalator is essentially set up for exactly two people, no more, who will follow these steps:

Making contact: They meet at a common social space or go on any sort of date. From there, they go out to get to know each other; at some point, they may have sexual encounters.

Initiation: A romantic language and rituals are established according to the narrative of falling in love and emotional involvement. At this point, sexual encounters are already the general rule, with exceptions in the case of highly traditional or religious sectors.

Claiming and defining: The romantic relationship is publicly recognized; they decide to introduce themselves as a couple and take on the corresponding labels of "my boyfriend or girlfriend," "my partner," etc.

Establishment: They adjust their lifestyles to each other on a permanent basis. An effort is made and required to spend time together and to exhibit stereotypical behaviors that reinforce the bond in accordance with the norm, such as having dinner at the other person's house, having sex, sleeping in the same bed, talking or messaging each other every day.

Commitment: You get to know the other person's family and make plans for a future together. This is when the right to know everything about the other person appears, the implicit obligation for each of them to say where they are going and what they're doing at all times.

Merging: The decision is made to share a home, whether renting or buying, a mortgage, basic goods like furniture, vehicles, etc., and in some cases, preparing for a civil or religious union.

Conclusion: Some sort of ritual of union is carried out, or the basic procedures are carried out to give the bond legal and social value. Now, the relationship has reached its culmination, and the goal becomes maintaining this until the death of one of the people (or both, if they so happen to die at the same time).

This is what is expected to happen, what constantly guides the actions and defines the rights and obligations of those who have climbed that escalator. Scrupulous adherence to that sequence is the measure of success throughout the entire process. As Frank Sinatra sings:[92]

> "Love and marriage, love and marriage,
> Go together like a horse and carriage.
> This I tell ya, brother, you can't have one without the other.
> Love and marriage, love and marriage,
> It's an institute you can't disparage.
> Ask the local gentry and they will say it's elementary."

There are a few more elements that can add quality and validity to the whole, such as responding to the heteronormative standard, having children, prospering financially, and projecting an image of happiness throughout life. The absence of any of these doesn't invalidate the outcome, but it does make it less complete and categorical.

Breakdowns and flaws in the mechanism

On the other hand, there is an explicit social acceptance that something can go wrong along this itinerary, and the trip can be interrupted at any time. In fact, in the last decades, the idea that many relationships that have reached the conclusion stage will only last a few years has become naturalized. In that case, there is a grieving process that may be shorter or longer, as well as a potential expansive stage of exploration where meeting other people is sometimes inscribed in a different dynamic, a lesser scope that is limited to the first few steps.

But that stage is "temporary." To assume the opposite – which could respond to different ways of relating to others with varying degrees of satisfaction but no expiration date – would be to cast doubt on the model. I have to "rebuild my life" and "settle down" again, phrases that are clearly loaded with normativity and control. The escalator may stop, take a rest, and start over at times. It may temporarily break down, but we cannot let it stand still indefinitely.

---

[92] Song lyrics: "Love and Marriage" by Sammy Cahn (music by Jimmy Van Heusen)

On the other hand, another factor of imperfection whose existence and social prevalence is widely recognized – even assumed – is infidelity. According to a survey at the end of 2018,[93] 31% of adults in Spain admit to having been unfaithful; 27% are certain that they have been victims of infidelity, and 13% suspect they have. Older studies show similar, sometimes higher, values in other Western countries. In the U.S., Los Angeles private investigators[94] say that 30% to 60% of all married individuals will engage in infidelity at some point during a marriage, and 74% of men and 68% of women say they would have an affair if they knew they would never get caught.

On an improvised axis of infamy, it's hard to pinpoint whether the social perception of infidelity locates this reality closer to the framework of hooligan mischief, a minor understandable indecency, socially reprehensible misconduct, worrying moral corruption, or intolerable depravity. But I'm convinced that the results would be notable if we asked whether infidelity is closer to mischief or depravity (the extremes of the proposed axis) and where a non-normative lifestyle would fall if it had no obligations or explicit control over aspects like affective sexual exclusivity or waiving the right to personal privacy. There is little doubt in my mind that the former (infidelity) would be judged less harshly than the latter (relational diversity).

Indeed, we live in societies that judge lying and thus breaking a valuable pact for the person we share the most with, including love and personal projects, more leniently than adopting a different way of relating to others. Of course, both assessments depend on gender and other axes of oppression; they are much more severe and punitive when directed at people who are not cis-hetero men or who are racialized; those of low socio-economic status or advanced age; those

---

93 Sample of 1003 adults taken in Spain from October 23 to 25, 2018; "Radiografía de los cuernos en España," on huffingtonpost.es.
94 laintelligence.com.

with functional diversity, and generally speaking, those who have less erotic and relational capital.

I believe that the reasons justifying this paradoxical scenario, which is incoherent with society's own set of moral principles, have more to do with the perception of a threat than with moral judgment. News of infidelity, or even a statistical increase in its rate, is more of an anecdote than a feeling of risk or unease. It's an improper, unpleasant story, not a challenging pattern that might lead me to uncomfortable reflection or bring those close to me to reconsider our relationship, for instance. I have to say, based on personal experience and so many stories that I've heard and shared, it's not really an unwarranted fear. Facing your own doubts or embarrassment and unpredictable desires for change from the other person I'm on this journey with isn't easy. Relating to others in a different way, even just thinking about it, isn't easy at all.

The escalator is what I've internalized as a model of success my entire life. So if I consider a different way of approaching others, the first difficulty I have to face is the continuous feeling that I'm not doing it right. Often, even if my desires are clear and quite present, I still feel like I'm not getting anywhere. The successes or moments of fulfillment always seem transitory; the mistakes, misunderstandings, moments of pain or loneliness, those seem like confirmation from the deepest parts of myself that I'm doing a terrible job. Abandoning the hegemonic paradigm means losing the main emotional crutch, giving up the most effective excuse, the perfect alibi to justify adverse situations with the comfort that "that's the way things are, what can I do about it."

The price of dissent

But apart from these hardships – separation and infidelity, which are set up as failures and require starting the journey over again with another person – there are alternatives or dissidences that are beginning to be partially accepted by the most avant-garde social and cultural sectors. The first of these is the conscious, thoughtful decision not to have children. It's the least disruptive and is accepted as an option, but it often involves questions, expressions of surprise, and hints of condescension for years. It is a decision that entails a questioning directed above all to the woman in a potentially reproductive, heterosexual couple and that, therefore, once again has the gender axis as one of the conditioning factors added to the main one: the normativity of the reproductive component as visa and seal of approval for successfully ascending the relationship escalator.

The heterodoxy that would come next in order of cultural admissibility contradicts the sixth step: merging. Not taking the step of cohabitation if you are able, not simply postponing or waiting for a better time, but knowing that living separately is my preferred long-term alternative will stir up suspicions in your surroundings that the relationship isn't really working well, and this will lower your social value. It will never be as valuable and authentic as a relationship where those involved live together and share income, expenses, assets, and debts (or are fighting hard against the system to make that possible). Interestingly, if cohabitation and that economic family unit take place among more than two unrelated adults (a community of cohabitation of any sort), its social approval and value will once again plummet. The norm strictly legitimizes one number: two.

The third irregularity, now entering the field of head-on ethical rejection and the feeling of generalized threat in traditional settings, is taking on agreements at any stage of the escalator to open the couple up to the possibility of external sexual relations and affective ties. Purely sexual openness comes in multiple variations, but the most common ones are "tolerating" erotic adventures outside the couple (with more or less transparency, but under the agreement that it is "allowed"), and the possibility of carrying out joint sexual games with other people, couples, or groups. The first option is usually called an open relationship, and the second is swinging. If openness includes accepting affective-sexual bonds, understood as external relationships that are not only sexually but emotionally involved, it is often referred to as hierarchical polyamory.

Finally, a more extreme form of dissent – still without leaving the framework of the relationship escalator – entails increasing the number of people who are on it with me. In this case, we're talking about non-hierarchical polyamory. However, replacing the number two with a larger number doesn't essentially alter the character of the process. If we go over the phases that appear above in this regard, we'll only find the difference of another difficulty to overcome at the third step: "Claiming and Defining." The resistance from the social and family environment that can be expected often generates the need to avoid or delay communicating a new relationship when one already exists. In analogy with the classic problem of publicly declaring one's sexual orientation, this is called "coming out of the closet."

The other steps on the escalator stay the same with slight nuances, yet always preserving the basic features of normativity and expectations of progress that characterize the demand for the situation to progress along a defined course of more and more involvement. An additional peculiarity is that we find ourselves on the same escalator with several people ascending to different steps at the same time. As experience shows, this scenario is almost always more complex and delicate due to the lack of reference points and insecurities, jealousy, comparisons, and doubts showing up. Polyamory is a coherent ethical response to having to choose and give up one person to get closer to another, but it is still a response within the framework of the relationship escalator. Like every other solution, without exception (including relationship anarchy, which is located outside this framework), this poses many difficulties. So many that it may not make sense to understand them as solutions but rather as exciting adventures that are filled with uncertainty.

3.3 Queer theory

Relationship anarchy offers an interesting perspective from queer theory: challenging sexual, gender, identity, orientation, and expression binarisms, and more, would be extrapolated to relationships between people, in this case to the dichotomy "intimate/non-intimate relationship." These lines of reasoning start out from similar bases: rejecting essentialism, which is based on the reproductive condition of the intimate heterosexual union and extends to all other bonds considered to be intimate, and the normativity that establishes how we should behave depending on how the relationship is assigned (assigned or labeled, internally or externally, which aren't necessarily the same). Given the importance of these affinities and connections, I find it relevant at this point to briefly go over the key aspects of queer theory.

Background

The word queer originally meant different, strange, or peculiar. It evolved into a slur and began to be applied pejoratively to effeminate men and homosexuals. It was from this offensive use that the LGBTIQ+ community decided to reclaim the word in order to promote that prohibited signifier. That strategy led to the positive interpretation we can attribute to it today; in many cases, it is actually interchangeable with the community's acronym. "Queer" may have its downsides, but it is certainly a more intuitive lexeme than the sequence of initials, which is hard to remember and pronounce (and never quite represents everyone it should).

From this resignification, the concept of queer activisms was born. Those, in turn, cross-pollinate with the academic field, where the different manifestations of queer theory emerge. Despite the fact that these perspectives and interpretations that constitute what is known today as queer theory are marked by diversity, criticism, and constant dissent, as could only be the case, I'll focus on the basic elements that are common to all of them.

First, though, I'll go over the origins of contemporary thought that led to what would later become queer theory, according to the excellent and accessible book by Meg-John Barker and Julia Scheele, *Queer: A Graphic History*.[95]

The existentialist current that starts up at the end of the 19th century and develops over the first half of the 20th century puts existence before essence. In Spain, Ortega and Unamuno represented this trend at its start, but it was Sartre and Simone de Beauvoir who developed the ideas that have the most subsequent influence in this field. They introduced concepts such as self-deception, which makes us think that we are what society says we should be, and freedom as a space limited and restricted by what we know, by the references given to us.

Another relevant school of thought is not philosophical but a scientific one. In biology, researchers like pioneer Alfred Kinsey and those who followed him described human sexual behavior in much more objective and open terms than what was the norm up to that time, finding that homosexual attractions and practices, masturbation, and other behaviors are much more frequent than was assumed, and that they don't follow stereotypes but vary and are distributed across a spectrum of experiences and feelings, not in fixed, unalterable categories.

Feminisms and homosexual rights

Feminist movements took the lead in the 1970s, particularly black feminists in the United States. They developed the first political analyses taking to the streets and studying the intersections between axes of oppression such as race, social class, gender, and sexuality. Intersectionality was proposed later on based on Kimberlé Crenshaw's analyses. Verifying the existence of those identities that intersect, exclude groups, and sustain vectors of privilege, subjugation, and exploitation gave support and more foundation to the ideas that crystallized in activism and queer theory soon after.

The homosexual community's fight for recognition also hit a turning point during New York's Stonewall riots in 1969. From that

---

95 M.J. Barker, J. Scheele, *Queer: A Graphic History*, Icon Books, London, 2016.

moment on, the strategy of overcoming stigmas and feelings of guilt by claiming pride for being homosexual took stronger hold. This reinforced the identity, the search for recognition as a minority with rights comparable to those of the majority, and assimilation into the system. This is exactly where radical criticisms of that process meet with the postulates of queer theory, redirecting the focus on essentialism: moving from "being homosexual" as an identity to "practicing homosexual acts" as normality; highlighting the fact that oppressed identities are diverse and are oppressed based on race, origin, gender, beliefs, socioeconomic status, and so on, with queer as an umbrella term for all these realities.

It was also at that time that alternative forms of queer activism also emerged, such as queeruption, a queercore current (a punk subculture with special emphasis on the LGBTIQ+ perspective) that contributes to developing the anarcha-queer or queer anarchist movement; among other things, it is defined as anti-assimilationist, anti-capitalist, anti-authoritarian, radical queer, and trans-identified.[96]

Poststructuralism, sexuality, and identity subversion

The most recent and direct philosophical precedent for queer theory is the poststructuralism of Derrida, Lacan, Foucault, Deleuze, Butler, Habermas, and De Lauretis. It supposes a critique or a revaluation of structuralism, the reductionism that it implies, and the dichotomies that give shape to its conceptual structures. It places knowledge in the space of cultural constructions and the axes of power that exist in societies, preventing knowledge from being deemed natural and an absolute value. The stories we construct based on reality, including our identities and the mental models we use to represent the people and phenomena that surround us, are subjective, diverse, and variable, and they inherit the social and cultural production of our thinking and our personalities. This means

---

96 See queerfist.blogspot.com.

that our identities are subject to our internal and external circumstances. The specific works that most influenced queer theory's formation were those of Michel Foucault and Judith Butler, specifically Foucault's *Histoire de la sexualité* and *Butler's Gender Trouble: Feminism And the Subversion of Identity*, which definitively outlines the basic aspects of the queer hypothesis. The term "queer theory" is credited to scholars Gloria Anzaldúa and Teresa de Lauretis. The latter helped spread this expression when she gave a conference rejecting the accepted analyses up to that point that considered standard heterosexual sexuality as normal and defined all the other options in relation to it. She also stressed the importance of sexual subjectivity and its interactions with all other social factors, such as race and gender.

Queer theory in five points

As I've said, the codes that currently articulate this theory are expressed from different perspectives containing a high level of diversity and dissent, but they do have some basic aspects in common that are generally accepted:

1. The idea that power is no longer just a vector that emanates from kings, palaces, leaders, and armies out to the masses, subjected by armed forces. This simple configuration has given way to a more complex one that has multiple axes of power acting through different foci of hegemony: social, functional, racial, sexual, economic, religious, cultural... It has gone from a projection of authority that went from ruler to ruled to other projections that act between innumerable points of intersection, forming networks of privilege and submission, supremacy and dependence, all in a society where some of us monitor others.

   The security forces are now only used on special occasions – sometimes irresponsibly and with serious consequences, as we mustn't forget – but by taking advantage of the generalized need for acceptance, the daily weapons of containment have become cultural hegemony and a common sense instilled from the elites through generally insidious messages with well-defined objectives. The "normal/abnormal" or "inside/outside" binarism is what dominates societies today. We're obliged to build our lives and our thinking to be "normal," or we will be the object of marginalization and exclusion.

In the Philippines, a popular expression attributed to the feminist writer Ninotchka Rosca describes these concepts quite graphically: "having a crab in a bucket mentality." This phrase refers to the fact that, though crabs climb easily, the containers they're kept in at stores can be left open: when one crab tries to get out, the others grab onto it and hold it back. The crabs monitor and restrain each other.

2. The notion of normality in bodies, practices, and behaviors is a form of control that aims to instill in people these docile, insecure identities that require recognition and validation from the environment, in accordance with supposedly universal models. Hegemonic schemes are established, spread, and sustained in a heavily centralized way by influential minorities with specific interests. This gives rise to a social dynamic of submission and dependence, a far cry from the horizontal interdependence that brings with it mechanisms of approval, solidarity, support, and consideration among equals in networks that don't have to be based on the dominant models, much less accept them as indisputable patterns.

3. The performativity of gender and its influence on identity, preferences, attractions, desires, and behaviors is recognized. In opposition to the essentialist view, Butler writes that gender is what you do, not who you are. In this sense, gender can be disputed by resisting the obligation to label yourself according to stereotypes. By rejecting binarism,

which requires designating each person as a man or a woman, the concept of non-binary or genderqueer identity emerges.

4. As for the claims made and forms of protest, the need not to base struggles in defining affinities and exacerbating differences that may end up binarizing and labeling specific identities is recognized: workers, homosexuals, women, etc., because that actually means urban, domestic, cis male workers; homosexuals with social capital and financial capacity; middle-class white women, and so on. Sometimes, as a tactical exception, the idea of a strategic essentialism is defended; as a dialectical and activist tool, this allows attention and claims to be focused on a specific objective in particular moments and circumstances.

5. Stemming from a literal interpretation of Judith Butler's idea that gender is a social construct, radical trans exclusivist feminist perspectives crop up blaming transgender people for wanting to choose their gender assignment. Butler opposes this interpretation on the grounds that the fact that something is a construction doesn't mean that it does not exist and that it has no influence on people's lives. This is important in this context and many others related to the issues dealt with in this book.

Other tensions between certain manifestations of feminism and queer activism surface regarding kink culture, sex work, and the very basis of challenges to gender; in some ways, those challenges can dissolve the collective identity considered necessary for an effective fight (these loose ends are what strategic essentialism aims to address). However, the number of activists and researchers who consider themselves feminist and queer at the same time minimizes these tensions in light of shared elements.

JUAN-CARLOS PÉREZ-CORTÉS

Five parallels with relationship anarchy

A 21st-century anarchist proposal that has relationships as a leitmotif and is put forward by people who declare themselves non-binary (at least in the case of Andie Nordgren, as mentioned) will inevitably have many influences from queer theory. Any queer perspective on reality stems from confronting essentialist ideas, such as sexual and gender identities being inherent to each individual and established at birth. As we've seen, this also entails confronting the idea that some types of affective sexual desire or practices are "normal" and others are not. These critical approaches give rise to questioning the very foundation of categorizing people and the binarisms of identity and orientation, in the same way that relationship anarchy questions categorizing relationships and the binarisms of amatonormativity and allosexism (relationships with or without romantic love and relationships with or without sex). Similarly, there is a strong parallel between the analysis of conflict and power relations arising from identities, as queer theory examines, and from relationship categories, per relationship anarchy's approach. Going into specific details, the key aspects I've listed in the previous section could translate in these ways when moving from focusing on people and their categorization to the realm of relationships:

1. The critical intersections of power that have come to operate among people within the social fabric and the idea that some people monitor others, giving rise to threats of exclusion and rejection, don't only work among individuals. An important element of this mechanism is the nuclear family as the prominent node of these intersections of control. The "bubbles" formed by reproductive heteronormative couples are most active in this process of vigilance and homogenization. If these "bubbles" were replaced by broader networks, ideally one single network consisting of connections among different types of non-competing relationships that would not

challenge and nullify each other, as happens in the amatonormative model, the structure of this moral, normalizing policing would lose a fundamental prop. It would only be a small jump from thinking of a social fabric made up of clusters of normative, family self-centeredness to a rhizome-like mesh where the bonds it contains act in a horizontal, solidary way.

2. A model of recognition and validation in relationships that's not centralized in culturally prescribed normality would contribute to the development of identities that are less docile and less subject to social mandates. This contribution would be quite significant simply because it relies on the existence of a broad network of backing and support, a network built on diversity and clear interdependence that is only limited by boundaries set by personal consent and responsible autonomy.

3. The question of gender would be paralleled by the proposal for networked relationships as an alternative to the normative heterosexual couple. Much like gender, relationships would not be defined by what they are but by what is done in them. The concepts of gender, orientation, identity, etc., are the equivalent of stereotyped categories of bonds. Relationship anarchy would correlate to this central idea of queer theory by shifting from individuals to relationships.

4. The approach that leads to resistances that don't isolate the struggles of the various axes of oppression corresponds to one of the important aspects of relationship anarchy: how diversity fits into affective networks that link people with different backgrounds and tendencies that could hardly be connected directly in a traditional structure of bonds.

5. Finally, from within relationship anarchy, it must be stressed that challenging the categories of bonds does not mean that these categories aren't present in all areas of so-

ciety or in our feelings, since we've grown up with those emotional constructs. This is a point that must be reiterated and understood. This is why it is essential to make both things compatible and concern ourselves with the real problems people face without abandoning this utopia.

Recently, Roma de las Heras proposed a perspective that frames relationship anarchy from the queer feminist perspective as a political philosophy that rethinks work related to caretaking and family relationships; it is in the same line of thought as Judith Butler and Kath Weston, with the emotional, personal, and social value that friendships have for queer people, according to Saha Roseneil. According to Roma, the political perspective gives shape to an instrument that can build alternatives to a hegemonic structure that revolves around the nuclear family and which uses compulsory monogamy and heterosexuality as behavioral cases of the sex-gender system.

3.4 Axes of a multidimensional relational space

Relationship anarchy is not the only approach that is proposing alternative models to the dominant way of establishing relationships in our culture. Most of these models are strongly ethnocentric and are inevitably expressed with more or less explicit streaks of amatonormativity, ableism, authoritarianism, capitalism, binarism, homophobia, sexism, allosexism, ageism, xenophobia, and racism. Relationship anarchy itself, when approached from our cultural construct, will inevitably incur all of these to some extent. One of the objectives that I think we cannot stop pursuing is gradually filing those edges off as we identify them, while simultaneously preventing the addition of new ones. Socialization has introduced these vectors of domination and privilege into our thinking and our subconscious behavior. We're constantly falling into sexism, even if we identify as women and believe we're aware of gender issues; into racism, even if our environment reads us as racialized; into xenophobia, even if we come from other places; into aporophobia and collusion with capitalism, even if we are poor... and we'll be ageist until we turn 100.

With this recognition as a perpetual word of warning, I'm going to try to define the relational models I think are most significant due to their current or possible future reach. I'll determine this according to various criteria and, of course, from the perspective of relationship anarchy as the starting point. The first of these axes, which shape a multidimensional space, is precisely the main theme of a previous section: the relationship escalator as a dynamic representation of the basic pattern of normativity in relationships.

The axis of normative progress, or the escalator

In going through the possible derivations of relationship escalator, I mentioned swingers, open couples, hierarchical polyamory, and nonhierarchical polyamory as forms of departure that aren't actually so at heart. In the first three cases, there are, in order of appearance, models of open relationships that range from the purely sexual shared experience to non-shared ones and permitting each member of the relationship's emotional involvement with other people. The rest of the path remains intact, allowing only partial access to the escalator. Those who are higher up are often seen as in their right to set limits on the height that those who have arrived later or stayed at lower echelons are allowed to reach. The concept of consensus, pact, or explicit agreement presiding over the ethical arguments in which these paradigms are supposedly founded only work from the top down. The agreements made at higher levels define the limitations established for the lower echelons.

In non-hierarchical polyamory, the number of people riding the escalator at the same time is what changes from the traditional model. They are still not necessarily all on the same step, but there are no predetermined limits, and the agreements are made in an egalitarian fashion – though they often still take the format of commercial transactions. The escalator moves the same way; the steps are quite similar, as are the consequences in every way, though multiplied by the number of bonds.

Relationship anarchy confronts the normative scheme symbolized by the escalator head-on because the latter is an imposed, naturalized structure. Just as the Church, religion, or the State impose their authority through adhesion contracts that must be "signed" and executed under pain of punishment, whether in hell or on earth, the model instituted by the cultural canon in the field of relationships also works as a normative code. Therefore, the perspective of relationship anarchy would propose reviewing each and every one of the elements that describe this model and critically evaluating them, preventing them from being understood as the natural way of evolving and from being established as automatic obligations, rights, and expectations.

Wishes, decisions, and behaviors are not questioned. This assessment doesn't get into whether they're similar to, the same as, or the opposite of their hegemonic counterparts, nor whether they have a lot or nothing in common (as long as they don't mask forms of violence and oppression). It instead discourages resorting to "common sense," the claim that "this is what's normal," or "this is what everybody does/expects."

Rather, what is "done/expected" is what each person involved in a relationship explicitly values while considering others (those that are already there and those that may join later) and taking their critical judgments into account at the same level. We must keep in mind that this is very complicated: automatic behaviors, subconscious reactions, and involuntary thoughts will always coincide with the predominant cultural construct. Therefore, these will lead to normative dynamics and practices without even thinking about it. I can only keep this at bay if I have a deep-seated conviction and enough motivation to be on guard at all times.

If my direct or indirect experiences have persuaded me that I don't like these hegemonic dynamics or where they lead to, it is possible for this alertness to end up becoming part of my behavior, replacing the automatic cultural responses. This is not easy – nor is it impossible. To a large extent, it is my personal situation and that of many others who live in highly diverse configurations in terms of the number of relationships (single, a couple, in a network...) in terms of the number of bonds of cohabitation (including communal assets, mortgages, raising children, etc.), of our level of involvement, identities, affective sexual orientations, the length of our experiences within and outside the norm, in terms of our feelings of comfort or discomfort, the consistency of our convictions, and even diverse combinations of relationships that are more or less normative in the same networks.

The axis of normative labeling or the sense of security

If I've managed to get across the idea that it isn't strictly the relationship configuration in quantitative terms that determines whether we are living in a more or less normative or self-managed way, it will be easier to explain why I understand relationship anarchy as questioning certain labels when these are used for the purpose of feeling protected and a false sense of security. Most relationship models rely on a binary notion of "we have X bond or we don't." If we have that type of bond, we act one way; if not, we act another way.

In models like serial monogamy, free love, polyamory, traditional polygamies, swinging, open relationships, and many others, there are more or less possible configurations, ideals of solidarity and consideration, moral nuances, shades of gray, degrees of rebellion, ethical implications, obligations, freedoms, individualistic fictions, or identarian utopias; however, there are very few paradigms that include questioning the idea that there must be definite, well-defined transitions and statuses in relationships. I believe that managing transitions is precisely one of the key elements in relational practices. But before getting into this issue, I want to go back to the analysis outlined in previous chapters of how we get to questioning the binarism of bonds from the anarchist principles of collective self-management and non-coercion.

First, the dichotomy "we are a couple" / "we're not a couple," or any other dualism with different words that pushes us to decide whether or not we're subject to some description of our relationship, is an effective tool for identifying with a specific thought, practices, expectations, and dynamics for evolving. Even when I make an effort for my expression not to go beyond explaining a reality in a concise way, a performative effect is produced that puts me on one of the two sides of the duality, and the communicative tool goes from being an instrument to a frame of reference, from an indicative marker to a delimiting border. Therefore, even after putting all the effort in the world into defining what we want to be without falling into stereotypes, without paying attention to how people read our relationship or what they expect of it, without compromising on accepting the social rituals assigned to us... Even so, the cumbersome baggage with that label ends up weighing us down and affecting us little by little.

This baggage eats away at our work in self-management. If it doesn't manage to impose anything on it as we uphold our subversive convictions, it does inspire, influence, show us the way when there's something that's not been established and agreed on in advance. In the end, the norm rears its head, filling in spaces and making a place for itself in our grid of resistance practices. The title of our bond may end up operating as a loophole that the cultural pattern (or alternative model) can take advantage of to exert its coercion on our reality.

But is that really so important, so serious? Do we have to avoid it at all costs? How can it affect my day-to-day life, my well-being, and that of those around me? These are highly important questions.

Naturally, I don't think that the importance of delimiting and naming types of relationships has to do with principles that prohibit it or some childish identity marker: "I'm a relationship anarchist, and I don't label bonds." Of course, that isn't the approach I intend to convey from here. But the significance of this idea does reside in its value as a tool and as an alarm signal. If I'm aware that labels are double-edged swords, that I have to pay special attention when using most tools to avoid hurting myself or someone else, I will be able to identify those dangers and avoid them to the extent that I deem appropriate at different times: perhaps today, I'll risk using a chainsaw, because I need it now and the danger is worth it, even though I know I can hurt myself if I'm not on guard.

The problem of managing transitions, as I've said, stems from the existence of demarcations and borders between relational territories. This brings about the need to cross those frontiers and unleashes a series of consequences. On the one hand, it provides a sense of security and control. It's common to hear people say things like, "I need to be clear on where we're at," or "Decide whether we're together or not." Naming is associated with committing. In the same way that showing a property title gives us rights, stating who we are evokes the same feeling. It isn't, of course, a real security, nor does the trust that comes from a cultural stamp ensure a special level of reliability, commitment, or compliance, but that is how we perceive it: as a refuge. Whoever can afford to buy devices, vehicles, or food from a well-known commercial brand will do so because they offer peace of mind based on the idea of reputation; similarly, the prestige of hegemonic badges is persuasive and convincing.

On the other hand, though, choosing to join a category that's sealed with a bow of legitimacy and commitment on top has one effect that's potentially very negative and can be seen everywhere – or at least, I see it around me all the time: the emotional toll of handling the loss when moving from a higher-ranking status to a lower one in the hierarchy of relationships. This possibility generates a sustained feeling of fear, and thus dependence. When it happens, it can lead to a period of loss, frustration, sadness, and various feelings of pain: the process of grief.

Changes are probably inevitable, but the more defined and identifying the statuses I go through are, the more dramatic the consequences seem to me. When each situation is assessed and strictly associated with specific, often everyday practices, I have to decide whether or not I'm in a certain state to manage whether or not I do certain things. This need, which seeks to offer clarity, actually sows disorientation; it leads to the confusion between feelings and practices, between attachments and behaviors, between affection, solidarity, support, passion, cohabitation, loyalty, desires... The obligation to take on an entire set of these or detach from it and embrace a different one is surely incompatible with having a calm attitude towards others or lucid, liberating, introspective analysis. At least, that's my experience and what I discern in a thousand stories I've heard. Those stories are full of confusion and feelings of frustration over not knowing how to fit emotions and feelings into a rigid, uncompromising reality. So, the question is, what if we don't need to fit into anything? What if we look at people and not the boxes? We'll talk more about this.

The axis of the number of relationships or exclusivity

Most of the relationship approaches that appear in this section – dedicated precisely to comparing relationship anarchy with other models – are framed within the scope of what is usually called "ethical non-monogamies." The first particle of the substantive in this syntactic formula is "non," therefore constituting a notion marked by alterity opposed to another element: the hegemonic device of monogamy.

Indeed, the hegemonic construction of meaning that prevails in each region of the world is a genuine social device that has evolved to establish itself and endure over the centuries, one that has continually adapted to the changes resulting from intellectual and geopolitical progress and by technological advances. It is the set of these belief systems and behaviors that these "non-monogamies" aim to confront. They've taken their name in opposition to what they call a monogamous system because, according to most cultural norms, there is a strict prohibition on having several affective sexual relationships at one time.[97]

But the hegemonic system of relationships is much more complex and encompasses many more facets than the word monogamy suggests. Therefore, I insist that questioning only (or focusing specifically) on this relationship trait is insufficient, and it doesn't lead to any fundamental change in the bonds, nor does it help transform how we relate to each other socially and politically.

Of course, forced affective and sexual exclusivity is a vector of coercion. If it weren't, if it constituted a natural feature of the species, as I've already noted, it wouldn't require punishment, vigilance, and threats of purgatories and hells in the same way that "potential customs" like not eating rocks or not sleeping hanging from your feet: these just don't happen (the extravagance of the examples is intentional). Of course, as a coercive guideline, it collides head-on with the approaches of relationship anarchy. But all the other elements that appear as axes of comparison in this section also collide with relationship anarchy – to name a few: normative labeling; outwardly directed affective and sexual limits; identities as mechanisms of control; exemption from commitments, responsibilities, consideration; the normativities associated with communication and transparency. Therefore, relationship anarchy would be

---

97 There are traditions such as the Mormon church, some interpretations of the Koran, and other cultures that don't share this general prohibition. The ethnocentric temptation (framed by axes of oppression like racism and xenophobia) occasionally rears its head to point out these exceptions in order to highlight the fact that *our model is different: it's modern, secular, and* rebellious – *not like theirs, which is traditional, sexist, and backward,* while, in fact, all the hegemonic systems, including "ours," pile up and exhibit many traits of domination and violence. For example, Kim TallBear's work on *settler sexualities,* which I cited in the first chapter, illustrates the violence of cultural colonization on Native American peoples' non-monogamous forms of relationship: K. TallBear, "Making Love and Relations Beyond Settler Sex and Family" *in* A.E. Clarke and D. Haraway, *Making Kin Not Population,* Prickly Paradigm Press, Chicago, 2018.

both an "ethical non-monogamy" as well as an "ethical non-labelity," an "ethical non-limitivity," an "ethical non-identifyity," an "ethical non-exemptivity," and an "ethically non-normativity."

In short, I believe that relationship anarchy is not an approach that fits into the category of "non-monogamies," nor can it be included under the umbrella term of "polyamory" since it doesn't focus on refuting affective sexual exclusivity. Instead, it centers on challenging the whole set of authoritarian, normative, individualistic, and coercive attributes of the dominant culture in terms of relationships. Throughout these years of practice and activism, my impression is that the form these expressions take and their reference to numbers (both "non-monogamous" and "poly" make plurality explicit) are not irrelevant. This conditions many who are interested in new relationship formats, pointing them in a specific direction: to change how many people I interact with ("I'm poly"), not how I relate.

The axis of love and affection

One of the workhorses for some proposals that seek to offer an alternative to the relationship system is dismantling the myths of romantic love. Sometimes, though, the very concept of affectivity is presented as a scapegoat. It's as if, behind all the dogmas that are culturally imposed, there weren't a set of axes of power and privilege, interests in perpetuating an unjust status quo, and convenient structures of social organization. Love will always take the blame because it's what is closest at hand; power is almost always at more of a distance, and it is scarier to question it. But let's go over the axiomatic beliefs that, according to the definition of a myth, represent imaginary assumptions that alter the true qualities of something, giving it more value than it actually has.

According to researchers Tomasa Luengo and Carmen Rodríguez,[98] these beliefs are:

---

[98] T. Luengo Rodríguez and C. Rodríguez Sumaza, "El mito de la fusión romántica: sus efectos en el vínculo de la pareja," *Anuario de Sexología*, 2010.

1. The person we love was the only possible choice: the one predestined for us (the myth of our better half).
2. The heterosexual couple is natural and universal, and deviating from that norm will necessarily be problematic (the myth of pairing up).
3. It's impossible to truly love two people at the same time (the myth of exclusivity).
4. Desires must be satisfied exclusively with one's partner (the myth of fidelity).
5. Jealousy is a sign of love, even the indispensable requirement of true love (the myth of jealousy).
6. If a person stops being passionately in love, it's because they no longer love their partner (the myth of equivalence between falling in love, passion, and love).
7. If it is true love, that's enough to solve any problem because "love can do everything" (the myth of omnipotence).
8. Feelings of love are intimate and aren't influenced by social, biological, and cultural factors (the myth of free will).
9. Passionate romantic love must lead to the couple's stable union and become the only basis for cohabitation (the myth of marriage).
10. Passionate romantic love can and should last after years of living together (the myth of eternal passion).

Other ideas cited in the same regard are that true love is irrational and involves unbridled feelings; that if we love each other, we have to spend all our time together; that if you love someone, they have to give up all their privacy and there can be no secrets; that love means forgiving everything and that if there is no forgiveness, there was no love; that suffering is always part of amorous relationships because there's passion; that the other person will change; that the two people have to become one in a process of depersonalization and merging; that couples argue and that it's normal and healthy; that opposites attract; that happiness is given to me by the other person;

and that there must be complete surrender without expecting reciprocity because love is unconditional.

In stereotypical terms, this is embodied in a heterosexual couple with reproductive intent, a construct that supports a structure of vectors of domination and spaces of privilege that seek to perpetuate themselves by upholding a regulated, easily governable social order. It is therefore a model that must be rejected by anarchist logic. But, as I was saying, it doesn't make sense to question love, affection, or attachment, but rather the device of mythification that idealizes these and turns them into cutting, obsequious mechanisms.

Some approaches take affection itself (not its idealization) as their target of criticism or establish its expression as a relational taboo. They function as an intellectualization of the classic emotional or affective individualism, just enriched with avant-garde terminology. This phenomenon is problematized by different authors such as Brigitte Vasallo, Renata Grossi, David West, Begonya Enguix, and Jordi Roca.[99] Mari Luz Esteban's work, which has already been referenced,[100] focuses on love from a critical perspective while providing theoretical and ethnographic work with a very wide coverage of references and valuable methodological soundness. In fact, her conclusions reinforce many of the outcomes of the principles contained in relationship anarchy and, in my opinion, they fit harmoniously with it:

> "Any initiative that aims to improve the characteristics and conditions of the different spaces and contexts where we establish our communal relations (whether domestic, neighborly, work, leisure…); any project that intends to ensure basic rights and needs; any action that seeks mutual commitment and respect, promoting autonomy… will have a positive effect on bonds, on exchanges. It will reinvent them, even though they may be limited spaces and

---

99 B. Vasallo, "Romper la monogamia como apuesta política," *Pikara Magazine*, 2013. R. Grossi, D. West, *The Radicalism of Romantic Love. Critical Perspectives*, Routledge, London, 2017. B. Enguix, J. Roca, *Rethinking Romantic Love: Discussions, Imaginaries and Practices*, Cambridge Scholars Publishing, Cambridge, 2015.
100 M.L. Esteban, *Crítica del pensamiento amoroso*, op. cit.

times. Even better if they are. The people who have participated in this study have reaffirmed the idea that thinking and specifying the limits of human relationships is always positive.

In these webs of bonds of recognition, reciprocity, and redistribution, there will also be amorous feelings, there will be affection – how could it be otherwise? And there will be more or less stable commitments, which may or may not overcome reciprocities in the strictest sense. It's also likely that certain situations, such as raising kids, require stable unions more than others, commitments that, in any case, should always be temporary.

But affection, love is only one of the ingredients of human relationships. It's just one component of several that are all basic and fundamental: mutual respect, justice, solidarity, autonomy, freedom..."

The axis of physical intimacy

Socially, bonds are considered to be more valuable (deeper, more serious, or more sacred, depending on the angle) when they include sexual intimacy in addition to emotional connection. This is called allosexism. It's common to hear those who are exploring different relationship paths testifying that – after explaining to someone close how comfortable we feel with someone we've met, how many things we have in common, that we learn and have a good time in their company – we end up facing the same question: "But are you fucking?" It isn't always morbid curiosity or malicious gossip, but a sincere desire to understand how far the relationship has progressed. If it has started to be important or if they're "just" friends.

Based on the different elaborations I've been developing, relationship anarchy would question allosexism as a normative axis and would once again propose a call to self-management of shared sexuality without a priori guidelines or expectations. In this sense, a relationship that includes physical closeness of any kind would be as valuable as one where that closeness doesn't develop – but not as an initial or intermediate stage, nor as an element to be problematized, or even as a prelude to an extinction of the bond, but as a possibility in itself that's as valid as any other, at any time for any duration.

The obligatory nature of traits such as eroticism, sensuality, or genital or non-genital bodily contact functions as yet another vector of normative violence. When I've talked about asexual people's interpretation of relationship anarchy, I've stressed how important it is for someone who doesn't feel sexual desire, or someone who experiences erotic desire differently than what is classified as normal, to be able to develop such deep, passionate bonds with as much tenderness, dedication, and love as anyone else. Getting rid of the dominant allosexism would mean freeing our relationship model from the violence that these limitations represent and which entails devalued social recognition of the connections that don't meet the requirements of a reproductive union. Homosexual unions have achieved a certain degree of social acceptance but are deemed less valuable than heterosexual relationships; openly asexual unions are assigned even less value: socially, it's "just" friendship.

In other approaches like polyamory or ethical non-monogamies, the interest is specifically in the non-exclusivity of relationships that are intimate, amorous or sexual, romantic, or in a couple (for instance, Wikipedia entries on polyamory in Asturian, Catalan, English, Italian, and Portuguese refer to "intimacy;" Castilian Spanish and Basque speak of "loving or sexual" relationships, while in German, only "loving;" in French, it is "romantic," and in Galician, relationships "analogous to those of a couple").

And the question is focused on "non-exclusivity" because these are precisely the types of bonds where the hegemonic order demands affective sexual exclusivity. This is particularly because they include sex (intimacy) as an important ingredient. In the standard narrative, it isn't very noteworthy for someone to say that they really love someone other than their partner. This is because that feeling of love is nuanced, blurred, and diluted in the social flow of friendship or family kinship without making anything more of it. It would be something else entirely for you to say that you enjoy sex with someone other than your spouse.

Thus, there is an unavoidable allosexist bias in the focus on monogamy and its otherness expressed in the prefixes "non-mono" and "poly." It is a bias of normative authority, one that the theoretical formulation of relationship anarchy must be opposed to by complete coherence with the outcomes of the principles that inspire it. I believe that hegemonic normativity is being applied, for instance, when a relationship is expected to include sex or not include sex, when there is an expectation or pressure of any sort, or when there's automatic appreciation or depreciation. However, if there is no default behavior that's expected, I'll call it self-management. In any case, the procedures in all their forms must always be carried out with consideration and respect, considering the opinions of everyone involved.

The axis of communication and transparency

The so-called "ethical non-monogamies" fundamentally attribute the moral qualification of their "ethical" label to the fact that there is no cheating. Hence, another of the most widespread phrases is "consensual non-monogamies." Undoubtedly, the fact that the behaviors that involve lying and pretending crop up so frequently in the hegemonic monogamous system – and which elicit such universal moral objection – makes the dichotomy of hypocrisy and sincerity a logical outcome that plays an important role. It is undeniable that, for the vast majority of moral constructs that are admissible from our cultural perspective, honesty and truth are preferable to deception and lies, at least from an analysis of deontological or virtue ethics. But the exercise of sincerity, like that of freedom, may not always have fair outcomes when playing in a field with steep gradients of privilege, power, abilities, and control.

As the saying goes, "forewarned is forearmed" – but the one who brings that warning may be selfish, irresponsible, authoritarian, disrespectful, and even abusive and cruel. There are many nuances in every single aspect of communication in relationships, and these often lead to vectors of abuse, violence, lack of consideration, and passing responsibility on to others. Let's consider a relationship where one of the parties intensely experiences some sort of dependency or asymmetry, whether it's economic, emotional, tied to insecurity, etc. – take, for instance, the situation of a migrant woman who is racialized and unemployed, doesn't have a network of contacts, much less one of affections, and has a history of abuse. The idea of sincerely offering her a set of proposals and reaching a consensus seems discursively perfect, but this can cloak a reality that's much less innocent. Simply put, a power dynamic that gradually gives rise to agreements that are more in line with the will of one of the parties than another can lead those who are less assertive to end up in a situation that is far from reasonably comfortable or fair.

In short, a relationship based on lies and imposition is objectionable, but a relationship where sincerity and consensus reign (with a seal of approval and guarantee) will not always be positive for everyone involved. Only constant attention that accounts for situations of marked inequality or asymmetry to prevent invisible processes of coercion can serve to uphold any bonds that fit into a non-authoritarian framework. On the other hand, the opposite way of thinking is also open to examination through the lens of relationship anarchy. I specifically mean that, with the understanding that sincerity is not enough to guarantee a fair relationship, the complementary question is whether complete transparency is necessary or desirable in general. Again, in most of the non-monogamous approaches adopted as a basis in activist circles, conversations, books, articles, talks, and workshops, the "obligation" of maximum transparency in relationships is an almost inviolable axiom. It's a requirement of any relationship that seeks to adhere to ethical non-monogamy, according to the most common standards. The basic questions on which the analysis was founded would once again be the same: does the normative obligation (poly-normative or non-monogamous-ethical-normative, in this case) to renounce personal privacy fit into a model of self-management for relationships? And can a possible vector of authority or power be derived from this demand?

The first question is easy to answer: unless we include the imperative to share personal acts or make them known (even thoughts) in the set of anarchism's basic principles, establishing that behavior as a mandate is consistent with a normative approach, not collective self-management. In other words, the limits of privacy must be open to discussion and explicit commitment since, in anarchist thought, association is not an extension of the individual and does not nullify their sovereignty. As for the second question, the influence of the playing field, along with its axes of power and its asymmetries, appears once again: an agreement that entails more transparency will generally benefit those who are in a dominant position, who have greater security, and who perceive a lesser feeling of dependency. For the person with a lower level of security and confidence, communicating will require more effort; it will entail a higher degree of self-censorship (I prefer not to do certain things if I'm obligated to report them); and it will involve more fear, given the consequences that may arise (reproach, reprisal, abandonment...).

Therefore, if the objective is to study how a communicative model fits within the framework of relationship anarchy (as always, in order to try to build a consistent reference point through reflection, which I can later take on, omit, or adjust to my circumstances), it is necessary to distinguish different levels of visibility and consider what the consequences may be if the balance between privacy and exposure is modulated in one way or another. At the most normative extreme, there would be complete transparency: a relationship (whether monogamous or not) would have the seal of approval only with a significant renunciation of individuality, but with that renunciation being understood not as a commitment to mutual care and support but as an identity. You have to shift from being two to one (in the case of non-monogamy, with each relationship) and share even your most intimate thoughts with the person or people you love.

At the other extreme, there would be an absolute lack of transparency; curiously enough, that also ends up being deeply normative. One of its consequences would be the need to follow each and every one of the cultural mandates: if there is no communication, it's taken for granted that we'll do what is expected of us. Any variation from that would actually be cheating.

Between the normativities of what's absolutely explicit and what's rigorously tacit, we would have to find a space to share and take care of ourselves without renouncing our autonomy and without canceling ourselves out by watering down a mythologized bond. Organizations dedicated to defending civil rights are constantly denouncing the loss of privacy that's stemmed from the revolution in communications and information technology; there are laws proposed to limit and regulate the use of personal data; global players in the field of technology are looked at with reasonable suspicion; we're alerted to the dangers of losing control over our most essential private information. However, we assume that transparency in the realm of relationships would never be dangerous – a definite sign we've fallen into the trap of the myths around romantic love.

On the other hand, it's also obvious that we need to know what's at stake in any relationship or network of relationships. This means that there is a set of elements we have to share, especially — once again — if we don't want the hegemonic cultural guidelines to be taken for granted. A dynamic of collective self-management —and in this case, as in the rest of the book, "collective" starts at and includes the number two, and even one in some way when projected towards the potentiality of a network— requires communally defining, or at least going over each and every one of the guidelines (not the specific behaviors and practices) and sharing everything that may have consequences for those participating in this dynamic or who are affected by it. This is the minimum. Defining the optimal level is much more difficult. Surely, balanced practices could be based on trusting that others will tell me anything that's important, that really affects us deeply, and so I don't need to know anything else. In the chapter on keys to relationships, I'll talk about proposals, ideas, and feelings about how the desires to share develop organically when there is no explicit obligation, when telling each other things gradually becomes an experience received not with judgments, reproaches, or anger but with support, happiness, and mutual understanding.[101]

The axis of identity

In 2006, Andie Nordgren, the most recognized figure from the Swedish anarchist community that gave rise to the concept of relationship anarchy, was running a blog called Dr Andie. Below is the translation of one of the first entries:

> "There's a new movement growing in this country. They call themselves "poly," with or without different endings, such as "-gam" and "-amorous." It's something like an identity, and how people choose to live according to it is discussed on mailing lists and forums. Some perceive it as an "orientation" that they've discovered as an alternative to life in a couple. Others approach it as an ideological proposal that's based on different considerations about monogamy as a supporting structure for patriarchy, for instance. Some are faithful within their polyamorous networks; others have primary and secondary relationships that give structure to spouses, boyfriends, and girlfriends. For me, this approach is too focused on the number of people they relate to and how these are organized.
>
> I'm interested in following those discussions because they're about questioning the same type of norms that I also want to dismantle. The way I live could also be called polyamorous, but that doesn't seem like the right name to me. Why? In addition to the recurring reason that "I'm more complex than a label," it's because the fundamental "poly" concept doesn't fit with my way of relating to others. Polyamory focuses on having multiple loves, and this

---

[101] The word *compersion* is often used in literature on non-monogamies to refer to the happiness and satisfaction that comes from seeing that someone you love is happy as a result of their relationship with another person.

has become the defining aspect of the polyamorous identity. Discussions about this concept focus on that specific issue. A common definition of polyamory is that someone can love several people at the same time, which implicitly means that "love" is used in the sense of "amorous or romantic love," because no one questions that you can love multiple friends, parents, or children at the same time. "I'm poly" is the same as saying, "I want to have multiple partners."

But even if we no longer distinguish between the relationships of the typical couple and other types, it's strange to build an identity based on the fact that I can enjoy more than one of those relationships. Of course, no question about it! With relationship anarchy, I've instead tried to define an approach where the aim of all my relationships is to create a community based on voluntary participation, affection, communication, and non-obligation. I don't want anyone to do anything they don't want to do or for them to stop doing something they want to do because of my explicit or implicit demands. I want the relationship to be limited to our will to interact with each other. I don't want to make any demands or be subject to them. I believe that this is the only way to have meaningful relationships with another person when both are two humans with similar degrees of freedom to act (a parent-child relationship is one exception: a child has little freedom to act with regard to their parents, so they must therefore be able to demand certain things from them).

From this point of view, I cannot ask someone else to refrain from love, tenderness, closeness, and intimacy with others. This leads to relationships that can be called polyamorous, but the difference is that the starting point is not the desire to have multiple partners: it's the desire to have relationships without demands and with communication. The definition of "poly" offers a good starting point for relationships that defy social norms and an identity that can be used to amplify those ideas. However, I see a big difference between that concept and my thoughts, and that shows why I'm sometimes uncomfortable with the norms of the poly label often seem so inadequate to me.

> Relationship anarchy doesn't focus on multiplying relationships. It focuses on new ways of relating and communicating, not the number of partners. "Poly" is just another outcome!!

It's been 17 years since these reflections were posted, where A. Nordgren recognized an emerging identity in society in Sweden (and presumably in neighboring countries): the "poly" identity. This identity worked and continues to work as an umbrella term that includes the various ways of questioning the predominant normative system when it comes to relating to others. However, relationship anarchy didn't – and in my opinion, still doesn't – fit in it very well. There are groups that organize talks, events, discuss books, and so on; they usually include people who are interested in any alternative way of relating to others, so there is intense interaction between those forms. In a 2015 post on her blog Emotional Mutation, American activist R. Foxtale recounted this experience that took place at a meeting for a polyamorous group:

> "... Older poly dude was kind of nodding along indulgently to this, when I chimed in and added that "Relationship Anarchy" is actually a framework that was originally developed by anarchists, not by polyamorists, and that its primary focus is ultimately on not making relationship agreements e.g., on not laying down explicit rules and expectations for any of the interpersonal relationships in your life. At this, older poly dude started to look really uncomfortable, younger poly queer kid looked really excited, poly queer kid's until-now quiet boyfriend squeaked, "Oh wow, that sounds really scary!" and poly queer kid turned to comfort him with, "Yeah...yeah, that really doesn't sound like something I'd be ready for, um, yet."

Indeed, it seems like people who are exploring polyamory experience it as a process of identity, and they sometimes perceive relationship anarchy as a step that's further down the road. Just as it doesn't make sense for me to define the paths taken in life here, nor is it up to me to reject them. This is an understandable way to get your head around a fascinating, and at the same time overwhelming, experiential adventure like challenging the status quo in a space as intimate as that of relationships. Building a collective identity as a place for welcoming, reference, and socialization isn't objectionable. That challenge does have something quite in common with many of the proposals I'm looking at here. After all, one of the most effective ingredients for constructing identity is in contrast to another or several others. In that sense, relationship anarchy seems to confront that other – the dominant identity – in a more intense, comprehensive way. It might therefore seem like another step, a bolder aim.

In my opinion, this more radical appearance is only partially correct. It's true that there is a greater political, revolutionary implication of contestation and social change. But on the other hand, a certain form of transversality is more evident in relationship anarchy than in other non-monogamous approaches for precisely that reason: it doesn't confront monogamy as a limitation or as a practice, though it does challenge it as a cultural guideline or mandate and the sole reference point available. On close examination, polyamory does not challenge the behaviors freely chosen by each person; its primary objective is instead to overcome affective sexual exclusivity, and that ends up becoming its basic identifying feature. An essential attribute of a supposed relationship anarchist identity would be pursuing self-management of bonds and leveling them — in terms of privileges, not emotional importance — as an alternative to normativity. But the number of bonds that anyone recognizes is already generally greater than one. When we don't position some relationships as higher than others in terms of status, we don't need to allow ourselves to have several: we already do.

The axis of commitment

Relationship anarchy's hypothesis on commitment is that coercion is not necessary (or convenient) for supporting the most important commitments that appear in the development of relationships when they are governed by principles of self-management, solidarity, and horizontality. If shared life commitments, child-raising, caretaking, affection, and responsibility can be conceived between people who identify their relationship as friendship, this conception can be extrapolated out to any other relationship simply by reconstructing the configuration we give to the system of bonds.

It's the tendency we have to privilege formal, recognized affective sexual bonds that sometimes leads us to consider the commitments taken on in these contexts to be more valuable than those we acquire in the framework of relationships that don't meet that criterion. Or not to establish such commitments at all because there is no guiding expectation for us in that regard.

According to Andie Nordgren, relationship anarchy doesn't ever suggest avoiding commitment; rather, it suggests that you can design your own commitments with the people around you according to the circumstances, affinities, and the very course of events. For example, we can try to build networks of intimacy and commitment with different expectations: intensity, sustainability, permanence, flux, or no expectations at all.

In principle, the different consensual non-monogamies approach the notion of commitment similarly, albeit limited to relationships that are labeled as intimate. The perspective of relationship anarchy is broader and more horizontal, but as a result, it can be more demanding. After all, it requires considering how we are building bonds when it comes to long-term commitments in order to prevent the obligation to fulfill them from affecting others – in other words, to prevent the appearance of structures of domination and situations of privilege.

The axis of individualism, consideration, and responsibility

In the documentary "The Swedish Theory of Love," which has achieved some reach and recognition in intellectual circles throughout Europe in recent years, Italian director Erik Gandini criticizes – in my opinion, from a patriarchal and normative perspective disguised as a countercultural, paradigmatic heir of new age thought

— a supposed epidemic of loneliness in northern European societies. He especially focuses on Sweden, the cradle of relationship anarchy, and makes the argument that its system of social protection, redistribution of wealth, and universal access to equal education ends up creating loneliness and unhappiness. He sets it up against the incredible discursive counterpoint of the situation in Ethiopia, no less, through the cooperative efforts of a Swedish surgeon in that country who does a commendable job of saving lives. Through images showing that medical activity, he emphasizes fraternity and solidary support networks that allow the population to survive in a place where violence, death, and misery abound.

Its conclusion, along the lines of the terrible argument that "rich people have problems too", is that "we're better off in the south." It seems that it's not a question of rights, means to attend to health, education, dependency, precarity, inequalities, or oppressions like sexism or homophobia. No. The point is that they live too well there and are therefore — because they can be — too independent. Curiously, neither individualism nor selfishness is explicitly: it's independence in the sense of functional autonomy, a right that has been fought for over decades, something that only a few states in the entire world are capable of offering to some extent to young people, the elderly, those with functional diversity in workplace integration, etc. Loneliness is also condemned, or rather, life outside a normative family (the statistics cited don't look at other forms of association, support networks, affection, or trust). The fact that women don't want to be mothers or want to be mothers without a man is condemned because the traditional family is a source of happiness. That knowledge is only held by those of us in this wonderful south where – I must resort to irony – the egalitarian, liberating solidarity of the family shines like the sun.

Under the hypothesis that dependence is from the outset a situation to be problematized – at least in terms of lack, not inevitable interdependence – the logic on which the different models of ethical non-monogamy are built is that of somehow balancing the need to attend to one's own needs, especially affective sexual freedom, with consideration for others who are involved.

At the most normative level, that of open relationships, this consideration translates into maintaining the basic ingredients of the monogamous couple with the added freedom to start other relationships that don't go past a certain level of commitment – usually limited to physical aspects – and have as little influence as possible on the strength of the couple, often including the "don't ask, don't tell" norm. As for polyamorous relationships in networks or groups, this translates into large doses of communication, adjustment, management, patience, and generosity, all within one or more models that are collectively developed and which establish guidelines that define the relationships and behaviors. Amatonormative privilege is usually upheld; in other words, an attempt is made to define when a relationship includes love and when it doesn't, prioritizing the former and even avoiding using the word "relationship" for the latter: this word is reserved for affective relationships or even only affective sexual ones (allosexist privilege).

In *More Than Two*,[102] one of the books considered to be a reference in the field of ethical non-monogamies, relationship anarchy is portrayed as the extreme end of personal autonomy, compared to community-oriented forms of polyamory and the interconnection of their relationships. On a quick read, it is shocking that a proposal like relationship anarchy, which is founded on the basic tenets of collective self-management and mutual aid, would be presented in opposition to the more communal models under the umbrella of polyamory. But the rationale behind the categorization presented by Veaux and Rickert is explicitly directed at the analysis of personal agency, of decision-making processes. In the case of relationship anarchy, when establishing new relationships, there would not be a demand for explicit authorization and management of potential con-

---

102   F. Veaux, E Rickert, *More Than Two*, Thorntree Press, Tampa, 2018

flict from the community's members. This is like how, when we traditionally "meet someone," we don't think about how this new connection of camaraderie will affect each of the people we're already friends with – much less do we meet with each of them to manage it.

This does not mean that relationship anarchy limits the maximum depth of personal interactions to the level we normally assign to friendship. It means that it doesn't associate the intensity of a bond or the commitment or dedication to it with a limitation on personal sovereignty, nor does that level of intensity entail a reduction in our compliance with fulfilling collective commitments, which are established and respected in voluntary, horizontal, non-authoritarian terms. Dependency is limited as a transfer of agency and sovereignty, and solidarity and care for voluntary interdependence between people, arising from the very approach of a collective organization, is maintained.

The axis of hierarchy and authority

Some of the most widespread interpretations of relationship anarchy present it as a response to the hierarchies that exist in polyamory. Hierarchies do exist almost inevitably in any model, but they're hard to square with an ethical view of relationships. The fact that relationship anarchy comes from a tradition of thought that rejects authority, hierarchy, and privileges leads to an emphasis on this exact aspect before others like communication, transparency, commitment, stability, the joining of objectives and interests, or the preservation of a bond and its development in order to reach the highest levels of intensity and union possible.

It is not that these ethical objectives are necessarily contradictory; in fact, they're probably all desirable, but the practices that can arise from them often vary depending on the main focus and the priorities assigned to each of these aspects from the start. When the basic aspiration is to ensure that several relationships work in a healthy, satisfactory way for everyone involved, yet there is no critical perspective with the relationship model or with the fact that it inherits many hierarchical features of the hegemonic relationship model, the efforts made are focused on defining frameworks for negotiation, communication, and empathy that make it possible to maintain a relationship with sexual or affective sexual openness, or to manage several amorous relationships at once.

When, on the other hand, the motivation is oriented around changing how I relate to others to do so without coercion, objectification, possession, or hierarchies, the prevailing difficulties are instead the need to maintain constant alertness to attitudes of control that appear without me realizing it, the temptation to set limits on the agency of others (when mine isn't directly affected), and to exchange these vetoes for concessions.

An additional difficulty that occurs at both extremes of this axis and every shade of gray between, shades that will inevitably emerge and are quite relevant, is reconciling these objectives with managing the network of affections that includes the ambition of mutual aid and collective management. The desire to protect sincere, lasting relationships, on the one hand, and absolute respect for horizontality on the other can complicate the task of building and maintaining a network of support, care, and shared well-being: a network with a calling for continuity, freedom held in common, and collective consideration. Our deepest sentiments are unique to each person and are generally fragile. When many feelings are at stake in delicate and complex dynamics, the probability that not everyone will be satisfied and that someone will get hurt increases.

In the case of relationship anarchy, the difficult task of balancing the approach based in principles and the necessary adaptation to who we are – people with limitations raised in a cultural environment with ownership and control – requires taking a whole set of criteria into account. At least, it's necessary to avoid a priori behaviors that impose unacceptable restrictions, that try to enforce horizontality without accounting for who has put more on the line (including more time), that confuse the levels of importance, enthusiasm, dedication, or hope in relationships with hierarchies or normativities. In short, avoiding rigid positions that don't allow adapting the theoretical principles to each individual's limits and diversities.

The political axis

Relationship anarchy is an individual political position that sets up its collective scope only through networks of bonds. It is not a field of study that's part of the coursework in political science departments; it doesn't include administrative or governmental approaches; it doesn't propose large-scale social regimes of coexistence or management models for public power. But it is a political stance. It can't be understood in any other way, with its origin rooted in anarchist thought, the environment where it is proposed and developed, anarchist activism, and its ideological foundation based in subversive principles of collective transcendence that are transformers of reality.

It is about replacing the normative principles, which are focused on the configuration of a couple (one or several), with affective networks that function on the organizational foundations of self-management. It is about replacing amatonormativity — the prevalence of the construct of "coupled love (or loves)" over other forms of relationship — with a more horizontal configuration of bonds, minimizing practices that involve authority and coercion in its broadest sense or, in other words, seeking to eradicate violence in relationships.

Generally all states – and particularly those that are patriarchal and capitalist, since they hit closer to home – tend to foster stereotyped bonds through the cultural hegemonies built onto societies for several reasons: if those bonds encompass smaller groups (the couple), these are more susceptible to prevailing influences; if they are more homogeneous (heterosexual and normalized), it is easier for them to fit the needs of the state and the market; if they are reproductive, they feed the machinery that sustains the system; and if they are amatonormative, they uphold a very powerful fiction that disassociates community from the emotional realm and deactivates many possibilities for self-organization. It turns out to be very useful for a system that is inclined to perpetuate itself to place friendship and companionship as far as possible from the recognized forms of organizing a life project. In a recent article, Maialen Lizarralde concludes:[103]

> "Everything that the couple offers can be achieved through many types of bonds. That's right: we don't need a partner. What we need are valuable, safe, reciprocal bonds, relationships based on care, empathy, reciprocity. Special people, if you want. And these can be friends, lovers, relatives, neighbors, colleagues from work or adventures (listen to Mari Luz Esteban).
>
> The fetishization of "that something" that we attribute to the couple is neither universal nor innate: it is a cultural fiction (a quite recent one, by the way), like so many others. And like any human institution, it has its function, its light and dark, its precursors, and its dissent. It's important to situate it in the profane, earthly realm to be able to dissect it and evolve into forms of organization that we want to make emerge.
>
> On a social level, the isolation generated by something designed to bring us together is paradoxical. Society is a kind of archipelago of couples. They tend to isolate themselves in their intimate republic, and their social bonds diminish."

Obviously, one can have an interest in relating to others in a different way without political awareness, and even while rejecting that concept. But that can only have two interpretations: either the indifference and opposition are purely nominal, the result of apathy or disenchantment with the public sphere and community, or it's

---

103 "Soltera, no sola," on ctxt.es.

directly addressing the transition to another model based in acceptance and service to the system, with its injustices and its axes of authoritarianism and oppression, which include heteropatriarchy, the freedom to exploitation granted to those who have capital in economic, high-profile, social, or relational terms, and so on. Whatever that model is, (and this is a subjective value judgment that I'm convinced of) it doesn't deserve the name "relationship anarchy."

An approach that does not include a position that's decidedly opposed to sexism; economic or social privilege; the authoritarianism of the traditional nuclear family; the religious moral authority; homophobia, transphobia, xenophobia, aporophobia, racism; shaming sexual, passionate, amorous activity in any consensual form; discrediting sovereignty over one's own body; dishonoring internationally recognized human rights, and other forms of reactionary and conservative thought, cannot in any way be identified with relationship anarchy. As The Thinking Aro powerfully states:[104]

> "So don't tell me that you're entitled to call your polyamory or your casual sex "relationship anarchy," as you conduct your social life with anti-anarchism principles and the same amatonormativity that all the coupled-up monogamists preach and believe in. Don't tell me you're a "relationship anarchist" when you don't give a fuck about friendship or community or political resistance, just sex and romance and your freedom to be non-monogamous. Relationship anarchy is not a cover for fuckboys. And it is not nonhierarchical polyamory."

We must also consider the other side of the coin: that non-normative practices carry a continuous risk of exclusion and censorship, especially in certain environments and for those in underprivileged communities. Those who face danger with highly negative social consequences need to avoid the conflict and not to seem like a threat by

---

[104] "Relationship Anarchy is Not About Sex or Polyamory," on thethinkingasexual.wordpress.com.

any means possible. They already do, simply due to the fact that they don't fit into social mandates.

From its angle of activism that confronts the status quo and seeks to change society from the ground up, relationship anarchy is opposed to the compulsory heteropatriarchal and monogamous model, marriage and the nuclear family as the only reference points for relationships, the normativity that invades every single cultural and social manifestation. It must be an active force for profound criticism and debate. It must be precisely what part of the polyamorous movement (especially in the English-speaking world) has spent years trying to convince everyone that it is not: a threat to the system.

As I mentioned a moment ago, trying to do what is socially done behind closed doors openly isn't easy, and it can lead to the temptation to whitewash proposals as much as possible – artificially moving away from any political implication or appearance of perversion or fanaticism and, worse yet, often resorting to xenophobic and racist messages in an attempt to distance themselves from other cultures, to keep the proposals for non-normative practices from being identified with those of traditions or societies that are presented as morally backward. That is a serious mistake. This is not about comparing moral traditions: it's about building something new.

In any case, the slogan "the personal is political" is a valuable and exciting banner, but it is essential to strike a certain balance between the intention to apply my principles to the emotional reality of my daily life, on the one hand, and on the other, my ability to control these emotions. Working on and managing my feelings, inclinations, shortcomings, and desires so that they align with my convictions is interesting. However, subordinating everything to that goal and turning my daily life into a fight against my own emotions, at the cost of continual bouts of suffering and frustration, and a feeling of constant anguish — that certainly doesn't seem sensible. It isn't easy to define what that balance is, nor is it easy to achieve.

But, as is almost always the case, remembering that we're not superhuman is a good idea.

To wrap up about this axis, I think it's important to recognize the value of so many pioneering people and communities that have never needed to adopt or identify with a new category such as relationship anarchy, but who have already been applying anarchist principles in their daily lives and relationships. This ranges from the first experiments of the 19th century, as mentioned in the first chapter, to the most recent proposals of the last few decades.[105]

The axis of the monogamy/non-monogamy binary

From a heavily academic perspective that includes an extensive bibliography, J. Ferrer[106] illustrates numerous criticisms of the binary conception of the monogamous/non-monogamous system, which he considers to be wrong. This is part of his attempt to characterize this binary and to overcome it through three itineraries that are defined, respectively, by the notions of fluidity, hybridization, and transcendence. Using the way that the transgender rights movement has used to deconstruct and overcome the gender binary as an example, he proposes a new term: nougamy or transbinary relational modes. This term seeks to break down this dichotomous model by opening a space to situate and understand ways of relating to others that we see today with a more universal and inclusive vision.

Although the "cold" academic gaze can't help but give the unpleasant sensation that we're being analyzed under a microscope, like so many protozoa swimming around in a petri dish, flailing our cilia and flagella without a purpose or a destination, it does offer the

---

105 For example, Mae Bee's 2004 proposal ("A Green Anarchist Project on Freedom and Love," on theanarchistlibrary.org), those of Jamie Heckert ("Love without borders? Intimacy, identity and the state of compulsory monogamy," in M.J. Barker, D. Langdridge, *Understanding Non-Monogamies*, Routledge, New York, 2010), that of ReLOVEution (on reloveutionnow.wordpress.com) or the more "explosive" example by Clémence X. Clémentine and Associates from the Infinite Venom Girl Gang ("Against the Couple-Form," on liesjournal.net).
106 J. N. Ferrer, "Beyond the non/monogamy system: fluidity, hybridity, and transcendence in intimate relationships," *Psychology & Sexuality*, 2018.

benefits of rigorous, disciplined analysis. As for relationship anarchy, he places it on the "anti-categorical path of the transcendence mode." Of course, one undeniably useful part of this specification is boasting at any soirée where moderate levels of alcohol have been consumed.

In all seriousness, though, the valuable dissection that Ferrer offers us corroborates the hypothesis that most of the approaches and practices that fall under the umbrella of consensual non-monogamies constitute extensions – in a broad sense, and as variants that he calls neo-categorical, anti-categorical, and trans-categorical – of the same line of thought. Each of these variants can be reached through the itineraries mentioned: fluidity, hybridization, and transcendence. Simply put, we can draw a map that contains all the different ways we can relate to others, showing that none of them is really separate from the hegemonic model. Relationship anarchy rejects (transcends) the authoritarian, objectifying, possessive vision of the orthodox model of the couple, and it challenges the categorization that that model imposes on relationships.

3.5 From amorous thought to non-normative practices

Any attempt to create change, whether in the intellectual realm of thought or in the field of behavior and everyday social practices, entails a critical judgment of the previous model – here, particularly of the culturally dominant scheme – and a process of transition and adaptation. Giazú Enciso et al. have studied[107] the theoretical difficulties involved in this process, framing it within the concept of liminality. In their work, they analyze the practical outcomes in the specific case of non-normative, polyamorous-style relationships, but

---

107 Enciso Domínguez, Giazú; Pujol, Juan; Motzkau, Johanna F.; and Popper, Miroslav, "Suspended transitions and affective orderings: From troubled monogamy to liminal polyamory," *Theory and Psychology,* 2017.

their conclusions can possibly be extrapolated to other transitions, such as those that relationship anarchy entails.

They carry out a detailed examination of the liminal state that occurs at the moment when one considers abandoning a position that's well-established through the social norm, legality, custom, convention, and the conglomeration of daily social ceremonies. This decision to leave presents enormous difficulties that prevent a clean transition to the model that one has considered and wants to move to. This isn't so much because it's more or less utopian, but because there are elements from the initial context that one continues to adhere to and uncertainties around how to fit in and support oneself in the new context. In fact, there is a situation of liminality because the feeling that often arises is one of having taken a failed jump and landing somewhere in between, in a no man's land.

This scenario, often a ritual of deep crisis, tends to be marked by episodes of fierce criticism from one's surroundings, where there is talk of betrayal and cheating on "official" relationships (spouses, family members, etc., because, from the outside and with no knowledge of the process, this is what others suppose has happened), emotional destabilization, guilt, and very complicated struggles within and without. Moreover, this situation of a liminal stage doesn't have an easy resolution: the destination isn't clearly defined under cultural norms and conventions, and it can create an entrenched feeling of indeterminacy, the sensation of never feeling like I've gotten to where I want to go because I don't know what that place is like. It seems like I'm always looking for it and not enjoying where I've gotten so far.

The fact that a constant collective effort is being made to learn more about these new models and improve them also makes them moving targets that are even harder to reach. Sometimes, there is a phenomenon of oscillation where identification swings back and forth between the origin and the destination, or there's even the feeling of being in both identities or models at the same time.

In any case, the proposal is to analyze the initial space and make it explicit since its hegemonic status makes it invisible to a gaze that doesn't have strong contrast staining and the effort to isolate and analyze what it's seeking to highlight. The next step is presenting which alternatives could confront the features that have been detected and detailed. Those would be a potential destination to try to jump to. The better I can sketch it out, the more hope I'll have of making a clear jump, if it's really what I want and is truly possible in terms of my circumstances and my abilities.

I've previously mentioned the metaphor of crabs in a bucket when discussing how surveillance occurs between individuals in society (or rather, between bubbles as small family clans) in response to the procedures of an ideological hegemony that certain elites usually set up. In Meg-John Barker's book *Rewriting the Rules*,[108] the metaphor is extended to a beach where different people who are fishing each have a bucket of crabs beside them. When one of those crustaceans somehow manages to get out of one of the buckets, they find themselves alone in the sand, far from the water, out in the full light of day, and at the mercy of the seagulls... so they go off to look for another bucket where they can at least have some company and aren't such an easy target for their predators. The buckets, of course, are the different forms of normativity. They trap you, and your own environment keeps you from getting out, but if you can manage to escape, you end up looking for another one where the same thing will happen to you. This is a danger to be aware of.

Romantic, monogamous, amorous – Disney – thinking

In her wonderful *Crítica del pensamiento amoroso*[109] (Critique of Amorous Thought) Mari Luz Esteban defines the concept that gives her work its name as:

> "(...) an absolutely dominant way of conceiving the human and representing the bonds between people (...): an articulated set of

---

108 M-J. Barker, *Rewriting the Rules*, Routledge, Oxfordshire, 2012.
109 M. L. Esteban, *Crítica del pensamiento amoroso*, op. cit.

symbols, notions, and theories around love, which permeates all social spaces, including institutional ones, and directly influences people's practices, structuring unequal gender, class, and ethnic relations, and a specific, heterosexual way of understanding desire, identity, and ultimately, the subject. An absolutely hypertrophied way of thinking whose inspection and transformation is, in my view, a *sine qua non* for a world that can be sustained by fertile webs of symbolic and material redistributions, reciprocities, and recognition.

(...) understood as the most genuine, the most sublime, absolute, transcendent, the solution to that supposed lack that the human being would have for the mere fact of being such... an absolutely cultural and Western reading that makes love into the natural basis for this organization of society, family, and kinship. It isn't the only possible one, nor is it by any means the fairest one."

In her book *Revolutions of the Heart*[110], Wendy Langford also addresses the question of romantic love's association with the idea of freedom, rebellion, and redemption when it actually hides a sugar-coated mechanism to reproduce the relations of power oppression that are present in society, especially in relation to gender. The work draws a parallel between romantic love and a form of "government by love." Indeed, today's mechanisms of power aren't limited to Montesquieu's classic "legislative, executive, and judicial" branches; they arise in society as multiple gradients of domination, some of which are more subtle while others are more explicit. In this sense, Langford writes:

"It is true that the tendency to form relationships through attraction and emotional attachment is a universal one, and that attachment love needs to have a positive place within any human society. But this does not mean that it is a good thing for such relationships, entered into for their own sake, to determine the course of our lives or be the foundation of our social being. This does not result in a society determined by equity and humanity at

---

[110] W. Langford, *Revolutions of the Heart: Gender, Power and the Delusions of Love*, Routledge, New York, 1999.

all, but one in which the individual is either subject to the insidious regulation of 'government by love' or cast aside like a piece of flotsam upon the whim of love's unruly passions."

Other authors like Coral Herrera and Brigitte Vasallo have analyzed the consequences of this omnipresent, dominant paradigm under names such as "romantic love"[111] or "monogamous thinking."[112] In this sense, Vasallo suggests avoiding the ambiguity that appears when we use the word "romantic" to refer to the normative, fairytale model of love. Instead, she suggests using "Disney love"[113] to refer to the effective dissemination of cultural stereotypes of the languid damsel – rescued by the brave, courageous Prince Charming, who she will live happily ever after with – that has been carried out for decades in the films of the Disney factory. The term "romantic," on the other hand, brings to mind images of tenderness, caresses, pampering, dining in front of a fireplace or on the beach in the moonlight. There's nothing wrong with that. In fact, the only bad thing about it is that we don't do it enough.

Alternatives to hegemonic thinking

We can fall into the temptation of thinking that hegemony is like a fashion, and that we can escape it simply by demonstrating some sympathetic rebellion, using those "wide margins of freedom offered to us by the liberal democratic state and law." This is not the case. Freedom — in this context — is the faculty that allows us to choose between the things we know through cultural references or those we imagine through inquiry and our own creation. We rarely come up with options outside of the semantic fields and referential realms we've culturally had access to. That is a possibility, but it is certainly a rare and anecdotal one. The hegemonic position is invisible and naturalized. For example, thinking that I have certain privileges over someone I have an established affective sexual bond with,

---

111   Coral Herrera Gómez, *La construcción sociocultural del amor romántico*, Fundamentos, Madrid, 2011.
112   Brigitte Vasallo, *Pensamiento monógamo, terror poliamoroso*, op. cit.
113   "OccupyLove: por una revolución de los afectos," on diagonalperiodico.net.

someone I can negotiate rules with by offering not to get angry in exchange (because I have the right to get angry if we don't come to an agreement), is reasoning based in dominant thought. This means that if I ask someone, without specifying what I mean, whether they exercise some kind of control over other people in their daily life, they may answer honestly and with conviction that they do not; however, they will continue to behave just as before, in a "natural" way, without realizing it – in other words, claiming their right to be the privileged party that the other person has to come to an agreement regarding their own conduct with. The idea that affective sexual relationships grant special privileges to those parties over any other relationship is one of the notions of hegemonic thought that relationship anarchy questions. Other notions that fall into the same category include:

1. The guideline that a relationship must be affective and romantic and have a sexual component for the most important commitments, such as sharing a home or property, or having children, to be considered socially serious and binding.
2. The idea that the moral imperative of mutual aid has an essentially different character depending on the type of bond.
3. The notion that "important" (affective sexual) relationships must be clearly delimited. They have to have a well-defined beginning and end. They can start and stop as many times as necessary, but it must be clear what stage we're in – "on" or "off." Otherwise, we might have inappropriate thoughts or behaviors, those that don't correspond to what the norm has established for that type of relationship.
4. The conviction that commitment involves being able to negotiate, "among equals," someone else's agency, what they can do with their body, their time, and their circumstances, in exchange for granting concessions with respect to our own agency. This is accepting dimensions of authority and coercion while assuming an initial balance of power that's neutral (which is rarely true). So, this generally means that this

authority is not balanced and can lead to violence and practices of domination.
5. The renunciation of personal privacy, since a "real relationship" is necessarily assumed to involve a high degree of transparency. Trust, sincerity, and respect are not enough. I have the right to ask you to share everything with me. On the contrary, I have the right to share everything with you, without consideration for the fact that when when somebody demands explanations, it isn't always to listen and understand, nor is the decision to share something always made to inform or facilitate management or participation in decision-making; it can be done to shift responsibilities or shirk blame.

All these standards function as invisible mandates. Challenging them is not only difficult because of their ability to camouflage themselves among what we consider logical reasoning, but because by seeking autonomy of thought, we can fall into opposition and antagonism. Benjamin Prado said that "The opposite of accepting orders isn't giving them, but disobeying."[114] It's not about looking for a new doctrinal body or normative model; it's about seeking a space of thoughtful rebellion nourished by principles that have crystallized through decades of anarchist thought. In this regard, some possible alternatives to the elements of the hegemonic model that I've just identified and listed would be:
1. Giving up couple privilege, trying to internalize the idea that the other bonds someone has, no matter how important that person is in my life, have the same right as our relationship to be defined, built, and evolve according to the wishes and circumstances of those directly involved. Avoiding imposing a pattern of amatonormativity that associates

---

114 "Ser novelista es conocer una historia...," on pradobenjamin.blogspot.com.

my love, my commitment, or my dedication with the format, label, and rank in the social hierarchy of each relationship.
2. Not assessing commitments based on a relationship's normative status. All commitments must be voluntary, conscious, responsible, loyal, freely made, and reciprocal in these basic aspects (not necessarily reciprocal in general). The principles of mutual aid and solidarity do not have to depend on the type of relationship. The levels of intensity, frequency, attention, concern, and dedication will inevitably be different since each bond is different, but it is important to escape the same old cinematographic idea that "family always comes first" in relation to any sort of hierarchical organization of relationships, not only that of the nuclear family, blood relations, or clan.
3. Considering the origin of the need to establish relationship milestones, to define and make it publicly known when the different forms of the bonds I have with each person begin and end. It is often a matter of feeling more secure knowing where I'm at (because the label specifies this well enough on its own, so I don't need to communicate wishes, concerns, demands, and expectations), or making it clear to others what situation they're in and what situation I'm (often in terms of free or taken, or even objectifying parallels that allude to one's availability "on the market").
6. If labeling myself or someone else helps provide a feeling of calm, it may be useful; however, we must recognize that this security is more imagined than real. It takes time and energy, and it generates an infinite number of conflicts that are likely unnecessary.
4. Evaluating how ethical it is in terms of my moral principles – whether they're close to anarchism's not – to negotiate aspects that go beyond my body, my presence, and my direct interaction. Assessing whether it is an exchange between equals or coercion, as well as assessing whether everyone

who may be affected now and in the future are represented in the negotiation. Since it is practically impossible for those who will be affected in the future to participate in coming up with the agreement, assessing whether it is really ethical to include elements besides those involved only in the interaction at hand – that is, whether it's ethical to negotiate what can or cannot be done outside of shared spaces and times.

7. It is also very important to ask oneself whether the transactions can be carried out under true conditions of equality or if there is some element of asymmetry and subordination, and whether the agreements negotiated deal with reasonable needs that are the result of reflection, or whether they're whims that are put on the table because they're considered to be part of "my property rights," according to cultural norms.

8. In practice, I find it difficult to come to the conviction that I'm not overlooking respect for other people's agency and that I'm paying enough attention to assessing their position so that they aren't forced to accept agreements (assuming it's truly possible to assess someone else's position, or even my own, in this context). This is why I suggest that a negotiation shouldn't take place in commercial or transactional terms — except in the most commonplace aspects, such as logistical ones. Instead, *a)* voluntary, conscious, responsible commitments should be proposed, and *b)* personal limits that are circumscribed to my space, my body, and respect for my dignity and my agency should be established.

5. Clearly distinguishing between sincerity and transparency. Because hiding important aspects of my ethical, political, or relational approaches is not acceptable; however, that doesn't mean assuming the conventional idea that when a bond is important and valuable, you should restrict the ways out and everything, down to wishes, every last detail, every thought has to be held in common. Sincerity, understood as

the need to share what's important – everything that involves those in a relationship – is a value. But the coercive imposition of a regime of transparency in the sphere of the relationship entails the obligation to renounce sovereignty and personal privacy.
9. Clearly, demanding "the daily report" and striving to share because the amorous union "with a seal of approval" requires it is not the same as developing a high level of trust through the dynamics of the relationship. That trust is gained when the interaction is rewarding, when it reflects and creates well-being. When communicating wishes and satisfaction leads to smiles and mutual understanding, and when relaying concerns and hardships leads to support and attention.

A final aspect that appears when analyzing the connections between communication and normativity is the unpleasant feeling that the hegemonic structure does not need to be addressed and non-normative ones do (precisely because the context, the label, and the standard logic delineate one thing in detail and not the other). When a relationship is taking shape, it sometimes seems like it isn't enough for everyone involved to have laid out their principles, approaches, and limits: the behaviors they accept and the ones they do not. The feeling of guilt surfaces if one isn't explicit about what is not aligned with hegemonic practices. From the angle of communication, this makes sense: it's logical for the default expectation about the forms of acting, the ways of relating, and the assessments of others to follow the normative orthodoxy. Anything that gets out of line with that model is therefore important to communicate because it will be unexpected.

But on the other hand, by following this criterion, we are implicitly accepting — and somehow validating — the fact that hegemonic normativity is the reference point, the only genuine geodesic vertex around which any communicative discourse must be configured.

This is a variant of what Miranda Fricker[115] has called epistemic, hermeneutical injustice: a type of submission that appears when there are no widely shared terms and meanings that represent the different features that characterize a subaltern status.

I don't have a solution to this dichotomy. I tend to choose effective communication over this particular form of rebellion because sincerity is only authentic when you confirm that the message has arrived and been understood. I believe that deception is a departure from any acceptable ethical principle. Besides, in practice, it's never a good ally.

---

115 M. Fricker, *Epistemic Injustice: Power and the Ethics of Knowing*, Oxford U. Press, Oxford, 2007.

Chapter 4. The revolution that starts with bonds: ethical, collective keys

"Resistance is the secret of Joy."

— Alice Walker

There is a disturbing paradox that those who actively oppose the status quo in an organized way on a wide range of fronts are often precisely people who are, or could be, on the privileged side: those who have had access to formal or self-taught education; those who have resources in the form of social, relational, cultural, or (sometimes) economic capital; those who have the option of deciding to rebel against the established order because they have grown up in a context that facilitated the development of their own agency and of a social and ethical conscience. The irony, I must say, is that these people are usually among the potential beneficiaries of some of the privileges they're fighting against.

4.1 Privileges and resistance practices

By honing in on the question that this book examines, not everyone can consider having relationships in a non-normative way in our societies – for example, according to relationship anarchy's approaches. Outside of a progressive, urban, first-world environment, outside of subcultures that practice collective support and care, without minimum essential needs being assured, or without access to communication, mobility, and socialization, etc., it's hard to challenge the standard relationship model (or to challenge anything other than constant threats to one's own survival).

So, in the end, there is a very significant bias in any formulation of lifestyle activism. This bias entails a bourgeois, white perspective, even when promoting an anti-racist, inclusive project meant for all people. Of course, this bias can be combatted if – first – it is recognized and accepted as such, and – second – integrating the most groups possible is pursued in the work of generating ideas and taking stances. It's necessary to prevent the dynamics of privilege that exist and are socially normalized from recurring in activist movements, in the people who shape them, and in their proposals.

On the other hand, as Alberto Melucci explains very well[116]:

> "(...) All these forms of collective action challenge the dominant logic on a symbolic ground. They question definition of codes, nomination of reality. They don't ask, they offer. They offer by their own existence other ways of defining the meaning of individual and collective action. They don't separate individual change from collective action, they translate ageneral appeal in the here and now of individual experience. They act as new media: they enlighten what every system doesn't say of itself, the amount of silence, violence, irrationality which is always hidden in dominant codes.
>
> At the same time, through what they do, or rather through how they do it, movements announce to society that something "else" is possible."

And that could be the goal. I think we can't aspire to much more than that. Certainly not to purity and perfection, much less to exemplarity through sacrifice. Our strengths and abilities are the diversity of identities of resistance and the desire to articulate nonnormative disagreements, knowledges, life lessons, views, and experiences. We have the will to confront the violence of a system that must cease to be the only reference point, the only imaginable model. We must take advantage of the new possibilities stemming from the knowledge and abilities to communicate in order to propose alternatives that don't slip through in the margins, alternatives that offer possibilities to improve the lives of the majority and which

---

116 A. Melucci, "The Symbolic Challenge of Contemporary Movements," *Social Research*, 1985.

aren't co-opted and swallowed up by that very system. As the memorable Carmen Alborch said when receiving the Medal of the University of Valencia shortly before her death, "Every day, I'm more convinced that the deep secret of joy is resistance."

Knowledges, truths, and submission

Maite Larrauri[117] studies how Michel Foucault's work in the '70s gave rise to a new approach for understanding the forms that power takes and their relationship to knowledges and forms of resistance. For Foucault, all the interactions that take place between people are mediated by power relations. When this power is adapted to the circumstances and context, it is recognizable and, to some extent, controllable; it's just another element to deal with in everyday reality. But when it becomes chronic as a substantial part of the interaction – a part that's difficult to challenge, invulnerable, and gradually invisible and automated – the relationship becomes one of domination. A stable, self-supporting structure is created.

The knowledges that function culturally as obligatory truths provide a basis that sustains and gives structural stability to certain power relations, turning them into relations of domination. Larrauri finds in Foucault's proposals an understanding of the need for a kind of epistemological anarchism (Foucauldian *anarcheology*) that would aim to distinguish between the intellectual acceptance of certain truths and the submission we derive from them in a direct, automated way. In other words, it is not a question of refuting or contradicting more or less established teachings and knowledges; rather, it's a question of preventing these from becoming a source of truth and authority instead of knowledge.

In this sense, anarcheology is an anarchist position that interprets the truths considered to be scientific in the field of the humanities as a consequence of cultural configurations, symbolic interpretations related to the dominant cognitive and linguistic structure,

---

117 M. Larrauri, *Anarqueología: Foucault y la verdad como campo de batalla*, Enclave de Libros, Madrid, 2018.

and the result of the interaction between the thought we have access to and the practices that define our reality. We configure our identity in accordance with these cultural truths; that, in turn, shapes our personal narrative throughout life.

Foucault's interpretation of power establishes a change in the direction of the gaze, a change that had been gradually taking shape in the history of recent thought. It is no longer a question of challenging institutions or states (this made revolutions more conceivable in previous centuries, when battering rams could be aimed at a palace, when the walls of a castle or a fortress could be scaled) because true power is no longer there: it's in a social field of forces that is manifested in human relationships, and which defines our perception of everyday reality, of what is possible, what is acceptable, and what we want. This, freely extrapolated to the current context of relationship activism, is what I have been calling hegemonic thinking and normativity.

Foucault distinguishes between legal norms, the legal system, and their development and execution by State authorities, on the one hand, and social, daily, generalized practices, on the other. The latter are what make up the true field of forces, while the former represent points where there is a greater density of power. However, these are not the points of origin or generation but terminal forms, areas where causes and effects converge as a result of a complex game. In other words, social practices and formal rules interrelate and influence each other, but a characteristic of these regions that was highlighted by Foucault – one that is becoming more and more prophetic – is that terminal forms take advantage of, use, and modify the forces present, intensifying some of them and softening others so that the net result is some sectors' domination over others. The system doesn't generate the winds or the tides; it takes advantage of them by directing them and extracting their energy to benefit the spheres of power.

Proposals like relationship anarchy could constitute a first approach that, even in a very partial, modest way, may contribute to adapting revolutionary paradigms that have aged poorly in the face of this new distributed conception of power and authority. In short, as Foucault wrote, "Where there is power, there is resistance."[118]

Power, relationships, and gender

A fundamental power gradient, especially in the realm of relationships, is the one determined by gender. Since the 19th century, anarchism and anarcho-feminism have been analyzing this model of domination and putting it on the agenda of revolutionary struggles. In 1905, anarchist Teresa Claramunt wrote[119]:

> "Woman cries out of habit, just as men have made her do. Her only weapon of defense is tears, artifice, slyness. But as I said before, it is not she who is responsible for her condition. It cannot be her: she has lived under the constant tyranny of man, and it is known that every state of tyranny must necessarily produce cunning, hypocrisy, and lies. Degradation is the logical outcome of the humiliating state of inferiority.
>
> The prohibition of expressing the feelings of love purely and spontaneously weighs on womankind. She must hide her feelings of love carefully, as one would hide a crime. She cannot choose: she has to wait for the man to ask, and to answer, she needs the permission of the family court. She must contain all the natural impulses, as their manifestation would constitute an inexcusable shame, and the good name of the family would be in danger.
>
> It is more chaste, healthier, according to the morality of our times, to resign oneself to being the flesh of pleasure for the first upstart who cloaks his lust with the base pleat woven from prudishness, being a piece of luxury furniture, matter to be used, descending to the category as a prostitute, with or without modesty. These acts of prostitution simply have to be legalized so as not to

---

118 But there is also the risk of romanticizing resistance and turning it into a self-justifying way of life. I find it necessary to vindicate the nobility of so many invisible everyday heroisms, but also to recognize that they are sometimes mythologized and turned into real life dynamics with a tendency for constant epic drama.
119 Teresa Claramunt, "La mujer: consideraciones generales sobre su estado ante las prerrogativas del hombre," Biblioteca "El porvenir del obrero," 1905.

upset any pretense of modesty. Man, with his vices and his clumsy vanity, plays a miserable role, accepting what is merely routine, selfishness, and speculation as manifestations of sincere love."

In the same text, Claramunt reflects on the difference between the structural and the anecdotal with a lucidity that is at once exciting and depressing, considering that more than a century has passed and still so many people, especially many men, still do not understand:

> "I think that it is quite appropriate to see to it that each individual has the right to glorify what they find to be good, but in the field of reality, the general takes precedence over the particular. I speak here of real life without specifics, and I leave exceptions to whoever thinks it necessary to make them. If those who read my writings know how to let go of all suspicion and reflect on my words impartially, they will come to realize the disastrous development that the aforementioned prejudices can take on and the vices they introduce in raising families, inevitably accumulating in social life. It is enough to look at household customs to be convinced of the seriousness of this evil. Woman, being subordinate to the dominion of man, imposes that same dominion to the other weaker beings around her, intending to inspire fear in them. This is how she is taught; this is how she then teaches. Obedience is irrationally imposed on her, and she imposes it in the same way on her children."

Around that same time, the idea of the multiplication of oppressions was already surfacing with texts that referred to women as "slaves of the male slave, objects of pleasure that suffered the onslaught of the master, the priests, and their infamous husbands."[120]

Different currents of thought have led postcolonial feminism to develop this idea incorporating dimensions of power such as class, racialization, geographical origin, sexual identities and orientations, age, etc. to account for the sum of the effects of all these oppressions and to recognize that these imbalances also operate within

---

120   Laura Fernández Cordero, *Amor y anarquismo*, Siglo XXI, Buenos Aires, 2017.

the community of women and feminist struggles. Thus, the most recent proposals focus on overcoming not only attitudes of ethnocentric colonialism and racial and cultural hierarchy, but also moralisms, stigmatization and victimization, moral instruction, and remote-controlled liberations from the alleged mud and barbarism (which are never seen or heard).

Analysis by key feminist authors like Judith Butler and Teresa de Lauretis has been crucial in advancing the understanding of how power permeates representations and behaviors in the realm of relationships. Butler speaks of "the psychic life of power" to show how complex, unconscious emotional dynamics surface from the axes of power. These ideas are very important in combatting the tendency to attribute the different features of relationship practices to a natural, essential character of man and woman. These authors understand gender as a device in which mechanisms of identity and power are at work. This allows us to think in political terms: we can act on that device; we don't have to settle for resigning to accept the best-selling self-help book's terrifying stereotype that "men are from Mars and women are from Venus."

Our societies are plagued by these essentialist ideas, and in their imaginaries, men and women are polar opposites. They possess determinant biological and hormonal configurations, desires, feelings, and inclinations that are different and virtually fixed and unchanging. Men are autonomous and rational and have just a few basic needs. Women are dependent and emotional, and they need to bond with a man who completes them. Hundreds of works in a range of fields (psychology, sociology, anthropology, biology, neurosciences...) operate under this hypothesis and offer – as one might expect – very clear results that corroborate it.

Those behavioral ideals are reproduced, repeated, chiseled into the stone supports of culture. They're amplified through the mythological process of love and romantic passion, placing each of the figures on a different level; that leads to the development of unequal behaviors and expectations, and — in extreme, though not infrequent, cases — abuse and mistreatment.[121]

But this is not just a role that's available for us to choose whether we act it out or not. Starting in childhood, there is a real, systematic ritualization of practices of conformity that spans everything from the corporal to the cognitive, including the sensorial. This identity modeling relies on imitation but also on games, outfits, colors, activities, teasing, alliances between those who are better integrated, and the marginalization of those who resist, in social interactions, conversations, television, cinema, advertising, songs, books... All because this division of roles is essential in maintaining a particular family configuration and canon of social organization. Women support the entire framework of the reproductive and caretaking system. In order for there to be a genuine, vocational dedication to this role – a role that has no economic reward or social consideration, nor is necessarily a fertile source of pleasure and satisfaction – from birth, women are taken along on a path of assimilating the myths and beliefs like that of romantic love – which can do everything, is cosmic in scope and essentially good – the myth of our better half, Prince Charming...

According to these canons, for women, the reproductive relationship (one that is, therefore, heterosexual, with a man) must become the center of their social existence. Their family of origin and the one chosen up to that moment, bonds of friendship, affection, and support created before the couple is formed... all this moves into second place, losing almost all its value. Both attention and sexuality are focused on that reproductive entity, and they cannot escape that realm. It has to deflect the subversive attacks that other men will deploy, even while some of them are in a couple, because that is the role they're made for. The aim is for this repression and resistance to be backed by a lofty, epic foundation. That feature is amorous

---

121 "A significant majority of girls think that love is enough to deal with aggressive behavior from a boy within the couple." Irantzu Fernández, cit. in M.L. Esteban, *Crítica del pensamiento amoroso*, op. cit., p. 83).

passion, which justifies and provides plenty of strength for that purpose and much more. But this is probably the weak point of the social construct since passion will die out; over the years, the framework may collapse due to this significant weakening.

Graffiti in a wall in Valencia (Spain)

But even in the most favorable sociocultural contexts, those where women have heard the affected slogan of "sexual liberation" for several decades, when they try this out – even timidly – they still run the risk of being judged as promiscuous, superficial, fickle, bad mothers, and above all, they are still receiving a continuous wash of conditioning aimed at building a neuroskeleton of conscious and unconscious self-blame from childhood on. Only within the framework of a relationship of possessive love, on the man's part, can they express that liberation and be respected (or rather, "recognized" in their role of responsible submission to the norm).

As Mari Luz Esteban writes, quoting Kate Millett and Shulamith Firestone:[122]

> ""Love has been the opium of women, as religion has been the opium of the masses. While we loved, men ruled. Perhaps it is not that love itself is bad, but the way it was used to cajole women and make them dependent, in every sense. Between free beings it's something else." (...) "A book on radical feminism that did not deal with love would be a political failure. For love, perhaps even more than childbearing, is the pivot of women's oppression today," and she argues that the very study of love and women, as regards basic pillars of culture, constitutes a threat; she analyzes how masculine supremacy and the stereotypes around women are upheld through women being turned into objects solely for love, the personalization of sex, and the "Beauty Ideal," "Romanticism is a cultural tool of male power to keep women from knowing their conditions.""

Normative enforcement and emancipatory practices

The norm specifies how things are to be: normal or normalized. But anything that doesn't present a certain tendency opposing the norm, a certain resistance to the norm, is not normalized. In a previous chapter, in going over the topic of human beings' supposed "natural" predispositions, I used the example of it not being necessary to forbid eating stones. We don't need some rule to know not to do that. There is no tendency to counteract or disorder to fix. We generally don't like to eat stones as food. Or, as Eduardo Galeano writes in hopeful poetry in his book *Walking Words*:[123]

> "On a tavern wall in Madrid, there's a sign that says: No singing allowed. On an airport wall in Rio de Janeiro, there's a sign that says: No playing with luggage trolleys allowed. In other words: there are still people who sing, there are still people who play."

---

122 Ibid., p. 143.
123 E. Galeano, *Las palabras andantes*, Siglo XXI, Buenos Aires, 2003.

Therefore, the rule only makes sense when it entails some degree of coercion, a demand to change something that occurs or tends to occur. In some way, the existence of anomalies is what gives rise to the norm, what justifies its emergence. On the other hand, its goal is for what's abnormal to disappear and become normal, but it doesn't work like laws and legal procedures do, through well-defined sanctions, punishments, and exclusions for offenders. Instead, normativity creates the spaces where it's safe to walk; it gives them visibility, reputation, prestige, and approval. The non-normative doesn't exist; it has no voice; it falls outside of the well-lit space of normality that sometimes widens a little to subsume and co-opt the most normal part of the abnormal – the most tolerable version or fraction.

This normative space generates a set of gradients of power and privilege that span from the center to the margins. Because being within the bounds of what's normal grants prerogatives that vanish on leaving those limits. Being in the margins is harder. But, as Foucault shows us, the playing field that establishes the norm is not a circle or any simple, regular shape. It is an area that's full of holes and recesses where these gradients give rise to lines and heterogeneous configurations, thanks to the multiple forces, alliances, and bonds that emerge and change in it all the time. That is, to challenge normativity, it's not enough to direct the gaze to a central point and move forward; it requires dealing with those complex forms and arrangements.

That's why one way to start to take power – the portion within our reach – is by defining our own rules and our own identities, or better yet, our own particular sensibility. One of the most interesting nooks of the normative territory is precisely that: the paradox that there is more power when you explicitly decide on and agree to your own rules collectively than when you accept that they are imposed on you. Shouldering the hegemonic mandates is delegating power. Manifesting and stating desires and limitations — and developing them collectively to come to a self-managed operation — is to build a realm of power. A territory that will obviously not automatically remain visible and normalized, but one that becomes one of those complex capillary forces of Foucauldian power, one of those energies of the microphysics of power.

In this regard, relationship anarchy would fit into the dynamic proposed by the French philosopher; in that dynamic, neither class conflict nor storming the winter palace are devices capable of changing the world. That device is the idea that power is not a good; power is a practice. Coming up with our own rules to determine our relationship behaviors freely is an example of a lifestyle policy that, according to Laura Portwood-Stacer, reflects:[124]

> "(...) the whole cultural formation around individuals 'use of everyday choices as a legitimate site of political expression (...) When individuals' lifestyle practices are mobilized toward the goal of "making a difference" in the direction of a strategic political project, we can say that lifestyle choices are functioning as lifestyle tactics, which are collectively and repeatedly wielded for resistant ends."

Power imbalances

I've already discussed the pretense of the idea of freedom when operating in uneven conditions. The same could be said of notions like commitment, responsibility, expectations, agreements, wishes, care, consideration, hope, sincerity, and consent. These concepts don't mean the same thing or have the same impact or scope when experienced and enunciated by someone with a broad ability for choice, decision, and agency, someone with high levels of security, empowerment, and self-esteem who is in a position to manage their emotions and their fears, as when they affect someone who is not in that position.

Therefore, each time these questions appear in a formula, the axes of inequality that are at play must be included in the analysis. The commitments that one person can face are not identical to those

---

124   L. Portwood-Stacer, *Lifestyle Politics and Radical Activism*, op. cit.

that another person can face; the same is true of responsibilities, as these are related to power. The expectations that someone in a position of vulnerability has are a far cry from those of someone with power and autonomy, as are the wishes and attitudes towards the proposal of an agreement or the ability to deny consent when fragility and a low assertive disposition coincide in the same individual. It's easier to communicate and empathize at the pinnacle of privilege than when looking up at that summit. It's also easier to offer sincerity, connection, sweetness, and generosity from a position of power that's safe and stable – and more oppressive to demand them.

It is often argued that these skills are the product of personal emotional work. It is true that these can be developed, and only by breaking away from the comfort of the conventional, through conviction, deconstruction, unlearning, and ultimately, effort, is it possible to relate to others in another way. But these tasks, which aren't easy for anyone, are much more strenuous when one is simultaneously fighting against a thousand obstacles, hindrances, and forms of violence in a hostile environment, when the cultural construct has affected you in a more traumatic way, or when life circumstances have particularly impacted you or placed you in a marginal, subaltern, or dependent condition. Forcing everyone to do that work at the same rate I want is another form of violence.

One very clear example of this issue is when the idea of avoiding labels in relationships is insisted upon and one of the people involved has a personal traumatic history of being denied value, a name, or the importance of a bond. If you have been denied recognition as a mechanism of power in the context of an abusive relationship, you will experience that desire not to name as a violent memory rather than a safeguard against repeating relationships of control and possessiveness. You will understand this as minimizing its significance rather than preventing the imposition of a predetermined format, identified by a label, in establishing how the bond will be set up and evolve.

Therefore, if I'm going to develop a relationship with someone with less power than me on some axis – in terms of finances, social recognition, professional status, age, nationality or racialization, gender, personal history, maturity, need for affection, or something else, or a combination of several dimensions – I must pay special attention and try to act with deep sensitivity and consideration.

There are aspects that are difficult to generalize about, but I have to take these into account to assess the level of imbalance. If it is quite significant, I have to consider the extent to which it is possible to manage it, or perhaps I should limit the depth or intimacy of the relationship. I also have to feel out to what extent it is helpful to make those circumstances explicit and handle them openly, without this being counterproductive. In conclusion, I should ensure that we can maintain a dynamic where the other person's vulnerabilities are compensated in an effective, sustainable way, considering that other sources of conflict may arise beyond the mechanisms of power.

On the other hand, if I'm the one who recognizes an imbalance in favor of the other person, I must try to be aware of it and also assess whether I want to share it explicitly and, in that case, how to address it. Above all, I have to consider that every acceptance, resignation, and lack of assertiveness inevitably accumulates in a sort of long-term "IOU," which isn't good for anyone. I'm not capable of proposing a resolution framework that's general enough to overcome the obstacles imposed by these situations, as the circumstances can be very different in each case. However, I believe that knowing, sharing (if the decision is made to do so), and admitting the significance of these imbalances is essential to making sure that their impact is not as awful as it could be.

In this regard, in a recent 2018 article Andie Nordgren said:[125]

"We always knew it would be more work to have relationships like this – to define them ourself, with those in them with us, ra-

---

[125] Andie Nordgren, "The road to relationship anarchy," *Melk* ["Amor"], n° 6, Kjærlighet, 2018.

ther than falling back on the norm. Today, I also see the importance of acknowledging the power dynamics within anarchistic relationships. And to push for relationships that start with skewed power dynamics, to be aware of this. The cost of making a completely custom relationship agreement can look very different for different people, and the tyranny of 'structurelessness' must be considered – where too little structure can turn into power and benefit for those who already possess it. Relationship Anarchy must be equipped with this power analysis, and be open for declaring structure to relationships when it's needed to protect individuals from each other."

Thirdly, a somewhat less obvious reflection is that from both positions, one can overcompensate and enter into undesirable dynamics of condescension towards others or oneself, of self-protection and emotional armoring, self-censorship, blackmail, and manipulation. Another element that should also be included is that all this analysis is applicable to any type of relationship. As I'm proposing throughout the text, one important aspect that sets the thinking behind relationship anarchy apart is that bonds build community. They are all bonds – that is, these reflections are valid for a relationship of any degree of intimacy, friendship, family, work, etc.

Anarchism, reason, and religion

I have already quoted Kate Millett and her idea that "Love has been the opium of women, as religion has been the opium of the masses." Indeed, the notion that religion constitutes one of the most effective forms of domination over the majorities by the elites has been linked to anarchism from its inception. One of the anarchist banners has traditionally been freedom of thought and its total, absolute disapproval of irrationalism, particularly its institutionalized and dogmatized forms. From the perspective of freedom of thought and anarchism, religions have always been considered antagonists of progress, reason, and knowledge. Since Bakunin, humankind's emancipation from power has been seen as a confrontation with religion as the supreme power in the field of the supernatural and metaphysical, and the State as the supreme power in the physical world. In *God and the State,* Bakunin also emphasizes the fact that religion individualizes the person as a mechanism to control them more effectively:[126]

> "All the other commandments are only addressed to the individual: you shall not kill (except in the very frequent cases where I order it myself, he should have added; you shall not steal, either property, not the wife of another, (also considered in some sense as a property); you shall respect they parents. But above all you will worship me, the jealous, selfish, vain and terrible God, and if you do not want to incur my wrath you will sing my praises and you will prostrate yourself eternally before me."

Well into the 20th century, in the Second Spanish Republic of 1931, the power of religious institutions was considered so decisive that lawyer and representative Clara Campoamor (women could be elected as representatives but could not vote) had to face a section of the parliamentary left in the left's fight for women's right to vote, which was ultimately won. Despite having egalitarian ideals, the left considered women to be so influenced by the Church that they would vote for the right – or even against the Republic as a form of government. Victoria Kent, MP for the Republican Left, dramatically foregrounded this controversy during debate on October 1, 1931, with these impassioned arguments:[127]

> "I think that this is not the time to grant the vote to Spanish women. This from a woman who, at the critical time of saying it, renounces an ideal. (...) If Spanish women had already gone through university studies and were liberated in their conscience, I would rise today in front of the entire Chamber to ask for the female vote. (...) But today, honorable representatives, it is dangerous to grant women the vote."

---

126 Mijail Bakunin (1882), *God and the State,* CreateSpace Independent Publishing Platform, 2017.
127 Victoria Kent, *Discurso ante las Cortes sobre el voto femenino,* 1931.

Unfortunately, neither that liberation of women's conscience – or men's – would come about in the following decades in Spain. The ideas of freedom of thought, rationalist and egalitarian education, ideological pluralism, freedom of expression, academic freedom – all crushed. That immense historical tragedy did not originate in the women's vote, but it became a reality in the form of an armed rebellion and a war that ended with a totalitarian military dictatorship under the Church's mantle, followed by the restoration of the Bourbon monarchs decades later. They were men. Violent men who were armed and supported by the bourgeoisie, the aristocracy, the Church, and the fascist states of a Europe that didn't know how to spot the looming threat in time. In the rest of the continent and the world, fascism did not triumph.

The history of thought kept its pace up and continued its progress, with its waves of unpredictability, its uneven reach, and that irregular diffusion that has always found its way to communities and peoples, yet with fundamental findings and contributions without which today would be much less interesting. One of the most influential figures of twentieth-century thought (whom I have already mentioned when speaking of political anarchism, and here I must confess that I let myself shamelessly get carried away by a personal weakness) was the mathematician, philosopher, Nobel Prize winner in literature[128], and activist Bertrand Russell. His well-known defense of free thought accompanied him throughout a long and prolific life. He was one of the creators of analytic philosophy; he made exceptional contributions to classical logic, mathematical logic, and applications of logical analysis to other areas of thought, such as the philosophy of language, epistemology, and metaphysics. He also contributed to the advancement of mathematics with contributions to set theory and helped lay the foundations of cognitive science, artificial intelligence, and theoretical computing.

---

[128] In 1950. According to the Swedish Academy: "In recognition of his varied and significant writings in which he champions humanitarian ideals and freedom of thought."

His political activism, which landed him in jail during World War I, centered on fighting imperialism and wars and favoring internationalism. After World War II, one of the first international expressions that swayed public opinion against nuclear proliferation was the Russell-Einstein Manifesto; it preceded the Pugwash Conferences, which in turn received the Nobel Peace Prize 40 years later. In his 1944 essay, *The Value of Free Thought*,[129] Russell presents a series of highly valuable considerations related to power, freedom of reason, essentialism, and revolutions:

> "When superstition is needed to promote tyranny, free thought is likely to cause revolution. But when the population has been accustomed to irrational reverence, it is likely to transfer its reverence to the leader of a successful revolution. (…)
>
> If a population is to escape tyranny, it must have a free-thinking attitude towards its government and the theories upon which its government is based, that is to say, it must demand that the government shall act in the general interest, and must not be deceived by a superstitious theology into the belief that what is in fact only the interest of the governing clique is identical with the general interest. For obedience to a tolerable government there are abundant rational motives, but when obedience is given for irrational reasons the resulting "lavishness encourages the government to become tyrannical. Ever since the Reformation, the State has increasingly replaced the Church as the object of superstitious reverence."

As concerns freedom of thought versus superstition, Russell goes on:

> "The universe is what it is, not what I choose that it should be. If it is indifferent to human desires, as it seems to be; if human life is a passing episode, hardly noticeable in the vastness of cosmic processes; if there is no superhuman purpose, and no hope of ultimate salvation, it is better to know and acknowledge this truth

---

[129] Bertrand Russell, *The value of free thought: how to become a truth-seeker and break the chains of mental slavery*, Haldeman-Julius, Girard, KS, 1944.

than to endeavor, in futile self-assertion, to order the universe to be what we find comfortable.

Towards facts, submission is the only rational attitude, but in the realm of ideals there is nothing to which to submit. The universe is neither hostile nor friendly; it neither favors our ideals nor refutes them. Our individual life is brief, and perhaps the whole life of mankind will be brief if measured on an astronomical scale. But that is no reason for not living it as seems best to us. The things that seem to us good are none the less good for not being eternal, and we should not ask of the universe an external approval of our own ethical standards.

The freethinker's universe may seem bleak and cold to those who have been accustomed to the comfortable indoor warmth of the Christian cosmology. But to those who have grown accustomed to it, it has its own sublimity, and confers its own joys. In learning to think freely we have learnt to thrust fear out of our thoughts, and this lesson, once learnt, brings a kind of peace which is impossible to the slave of hesitant and uncertain credulity."

Now in the second half of the 20th century, there is a definite trend of institutionalized religions losing the power to inspire conviction, and they're starting to have problems persuading the population to follow their dogmatically imposed moral guidelines. But this does not mean that younger generations are abandoning those dogmas and facing reality from a strictly rational point of view, at least, not generally speaking. Freedom of thought as a radical intellectual practice has merged with freedom of worship, which is a fundamental right of the modern liberal democratic state. The system appears once again, ominously adapting to these changes in order to perpetuate itself. This fusion manifests in a sort of syncretism of globalized modernity[130] made up of a mosaic of rational attitudes that are hedonistic in nature with cultural traits, traditions, and beliefs from various origins, especially those that are most exotic and farthest

---

[130] With roots that can be recognized in proposals from the late nineteenth century, such as Rudolf Steiner's *Anthroposophy*, Madame Blavatsky's *Theosophy*, or William James's *New Thought*.

from one's own: eastern, Hindu, shamanic (from Siberia and Mongolia), from African tribal cults, Native American peoples, and so on. This is the counterculture's version of the saying, "The grass is always greener on the other side." Astrology, the occult, and a renewed theosophy are also mystical knowledges that fill the void left by monotheistic religions.

The modern spiritual cosmovision has its most recent origin in the New Age movement, which takes the idea of astrological ages from Greek mythology and its divinatory traditions. The new age, the age of Aquarius, would begin when the Sun is at the vernal equinox and enters that constellation on its path through the sky, a path determined by the gyroscopic wobbling of the earth's axis (the effect we see in a spinning top when it begins to lose rotational speed); this is where the astronomical phenomenon of the precession of the equinoxes comes from. The planet's precessional rotation — which is retrograde, meaning in the opposite direction from the orbital movement that gives rise to the sequence of zodiac signs, and is thus why the age of Aquarius follows rather than precedes that of Pisces— has an average period of approximately 25,776 years[131] which; when divided between the 12 signs of the zodiac, that means that each age lasts 2,148 years. The 20 centuries that have elapsed since the birth of Christ, which is said to have taken place during the shift from the age of Aries to that of Pisces, means that[132] we're periodically faced with a cosmic change that is supposedly significant from an astrological point of view.

---

[131] Another curious effect of this oscillation of Earth's axis is that the star that best shows which way is north keeps changing. Now, it's Polaris in the constellation of Ursa Minor; in 2017, the star reached the point closest to the line projected by Earth's axis of rotation. Five thousand years ago, the Egyptians used Thuban, in the constellation of Draco, as a north star; in twelve thousand years, it will be Vega in the constellation of Lyra.

[132] As the constellations' shapes are conventionally defined in astronomical terms, the previous change occurred around the year 500, and the next one will take place in the 27th century.

The rite of passage that sets the stage for this transition is the liberation of the mind and spirit from the dominance of religious institutions. While there are no longer any sacred writings or prophets, there are plenty of authors (mostly men – that hasn't changed) whose best-selling works speak of new forms of consciousness. There is the idea of something supernatural within us (no longer in the traditional heavens or paradises, which at least are held in common, not individually), of "energies" more similar to the notion of the "soul" in various theologies than to the physical concept of energy. These energies differ in the fact that they challenge intersubjective knowledge: they're neither observable nor susceptible to measurement, verification, or refutation.

These notions particularly penetrated what is now popular tradition during the countercultural movements of the 1960s. New beliefs and tools are emerging and growing in popularity, starting with this transition that promises liberation from the classical doctrines. They are presented in terms that tend to merge the problems of the body and the soul, or the internal orders or energies, and they axiomatically propose (as a principle that must be accepted to apply them or even to benefit from them) that there is a mental, emotional, or energetic power capable of acting highly efficiently to control and determine the state and functioning of the body and all its systems and processes. Another fundamental dogma of this structure of beliefs and practices is that the way to achieve all these forms of fulfillment inevitably incorporates a conviction around the brain's capacity (presented as a mysteriously underused organ) and the will to overcome any obstacle: "It's all in your mind."

Life is considered a spiritual path, an inner search for the authentic self, personal liberation supported by a commercial network of gurus (called "personal coaching professionals" in the most pretentious environments) who advertise their willingness to offer me advice for a modest financial contribution. This scheme is quite useful to maintaining the system. Living in a culture where protecting the community, solidarity, mutual aid, the distribution of wealth, caretaking, and recognizing the inherent dignity of people are all dismissed; this canon has convinced many that the anxiety, uncertainty, and all kinds of precarity they're experiencing is all due to some problem with their attitude. The problem comes from the fact that they're not doing their part, they don't see life optimistically or with positivity, that they don't pursue personal growth or self-knowledge, that they don't look inside themselves, that they don't do enough.

We come face to face with a modern outfit designed to dress the new holy men, bishops, and priests, heirs of the same old regime. In this postmodern reincarnation, they make you believe everything is personally your fault, but at the same time, they will help you, give you advice, prepare you – they will sell you the secret recipe so that you can accept the world for what it is and (for a short time) feel like you're on the path of happiness. And they live off of that, just like always. Throughout every age in history, guilds of snake oil salesmen have flourished on finding the path, or rather, the shortcut, to their own happiness at the expense of desperate individuals.

Today, beliefs without institutionalized religion are the fastest growing mindsets in the West and in the world at large. According to the *Research Center's Religion and Public Life Project,* believers who had no particular religion were at 18% in Europe in 2010. Across the world, 31.4% of people belonged to the Christian faith, Muslims at 23.2%, and believers without a religion were at 16.4%.

Godless spirituality has an emotional intensity similar to that of traditional religiosity; as I've mentioned, it also has very broad commercial and cultural infrastructure support in the form of bibliographic, ornamental, ritual, therapeutic, and specialized business material. The emotional experience – which is, in this case, unlike traditional religions – is intensely psychologized, both in terms of the beliefs themselves and in their expression and their forms of circulation. Another important difference with respect to conventional congregations is the insertion of "the experience" as a fundamental element of the journey towards consciousness and personal development. The common search for experiencing powerful moments isn't strange: these hunts may involve psychotropic substances, fasting, ascetic or initiatory travel, living in environments that include all or part of the above, etc.

The globalized present, which is shaped by syncretic tendencies, self-help, and self-knowledge (and here, unlike in anarchist "self-management," "self-" refers to the individual: it generally does not have a collective scope or calling), revolves around the individual sphere. Institutionalized religions' daily rites that are carried in community are looked on as a thing of the past; salvation becomes overcoming, and it isn't a path towards a shared eternity with a god or common deities that is agreed on by those who profess the same faith.

The process is now adaptable, composed of different options that aren't declared to be incompatible with each other (fortunately, religious wars and hells for the infidels haven't been carried over). Above all, though, it is quite often a personal, individual process. The souls or different transcendent versions of human beings connect with each other in other dimensions to form a harmonious whole, but to reach that level of perfection, I have to concentrate within myself. After all, my problems come from my lack of conviction, spiritual development, faith in my abilities... It isn't the world, its injustices, inequalities, privileges, oppressions, and violence that are keeping me from developing. Nor can I be saved by a tangible, collective connection between people in this real universe that's right at hand, nor by solidarity or the fight for justice.

The consequences of this drifting are perfectly captured by Mónica Cornejo and Maribel Blázquez:[133]

---

[133] M. Cornejo Valle and M. Blázquez Rodríguez, "De la mortificación a la new age: genealogía y política de las espiritualidades terapéuticas contemporáneas. Nómadas," *Critical Journal of Social and Juridical Sciences*, 2016, and their references: E. Illouz, *La salvación del alma moderna: terapia, emociones y la cultura de la autoayuda*. Katz, Madrid, 2010; V Papalini, "Recetas para sobrevivir a las exigencias del neocapitalismo (o de cómo la autoayuda se volvió parte de nuestro sentido común)"

"As Eva Illouz (2010) has pointed out in *La salvación del alma moderna*, "the therapeutic culture of self-help, contemporary therapeutic spirituality has become the ideological reservoir as well as that of the logics of capitalism, penetrating fluidly in business policies, for those for whom meditation (especially in the form of mindfulness) is an effective (profitable) proposal when facing problems with stress and burn-out among workers (to the detriment of improvements being made in working conditions)." Vanina Papalini (2013) gestures in a similar direction, stating that, "In terms of social action, collective mobilization or union demands, this type of text has a disempowering effect."

The 1990s were a time when the rhetoric of self-help converged with the generalization of a therapeutic culture that is a necessary condition for a neo-prudentialist socio-political model, which delegates the obligation of self-control and supporting oneself to the subject. In their *Selling Spirituality: the silent takeover of religion*, Jeremy Carrette and Richard King (2005) show us how new age thinking fits especially well into business circles: it's eclectic and flexible; its emphasis on personal development goes hand in hand with the boom in soft skills like leadership, intuition, vision, etc. Moreover, the idea of personal transformation (which is central to new age thinking) also fits in with the business needs of adapting the workforce to the market's changing demands. Hence, these authors go so far as to say, "Spirituality becomes in this instance a GMR – a Genetically Modified Religion – the tasty food additive that makes neoliberalism more palatable."

The idea that "you can do anything you set your mind to" blames anyone who internalizes this message, subjecting them to an obscene, unnecessary anguish when they have to face the reality that chance, misfortune, and one's personal, socioeconomic, and political context play a leading role in existence. Then, by that logic, if you haven't attained the goals you were pursuing or your life hasn't turned out as you planned, it's your fault alone. That message also

---

Nueva Sociedad, 2013 and J. R. Carrette, R. King, *Selling spirituality: The silent takeover of religion.* Routledge, London, 2005.

constitutes the basis of an ideology and a true financial system of domination: it is the key element of the "American dream." Noam Chomsky dissects this myth in *Requiem for the American Dream*,[134] which I highly recommend; the myth is based on the relative prosperity achieved by European families and migrants who arrived in the United States in the 19th century, compared to the misery and lack of freedom they experienced in their home countries. For the first time in history, that allowed many people of humble origins to reach higher socio-economic strata in a society that had as little security and protection as the one they left behind, though there were more opportunities.

But those favorable circumstances disappeared a century ago. The social mobility of North American citizens is now very low, even more so than that of European societies. The inequality is atrocious. A disproportionate percentage of economic resources, especially the means of production, is concentrated in the hands of the very few. But to keep the myth, the dream alive – which, by the way, was exported to much of the world – there is a mechanism of propaganda operating at every level. *New age* ideas on personal growth and self-knowledge, while legitimate and emancipatory in their original iterations, were soon aligned with that need of the system and have been tailored to the changes it has undergone. Today, with the social transformations that are associated with the hyper-globalized digital age, the mechanisms that have appeared are even more terrifying and uncontrollable, and they're especially relevant here because they have to do with communication and interpersonal relationships. As Chomsky reflects:[135]

> "There is popular mobilization and activism, but in very self-destructive directions. It's taking the form of unfocused anger, attacks on one another, and on vulnerable targets – that's what happens in cases like this. It is corrosive of social relations, but that's

---

134 N. Chomsky, *Requiem for the American Dream: The 10 Principles of Concentration of Wealth & Power,* Seven Stories Press, New York, 2017.
135 Ibid., p. 75.

the point. The point is to make people hate and fear each other, and look out only for themselves, and don't do anything for anyone else."

Thus, at the level of relationships, the implications likely run along the same lines. Placing the focus of potentiality and essential development (and, when expectations are not met, of guilt) on the individual or on oneself leads to models of attachment that perfectly cover the needs of adapting supply to demand, needs that question not power relations but individual capacities – in short, approaches where the people who connect and merge in a relationship have to be "authentic," have to "flow." The problem is that things always flow in the same direction. Everything flows from top to bottom. Nothing has ever flowed the other way.

From mysticism and dogma to witches and poetry

But the esoteric, individualistic, globalized mysticism of new age thought, despite having undoubtedly triumphed in Western societies, is not the only path besides rationalism that has been opened up by human thought. One of the figures that has recently been re-read in an emancipating, associative, powerful manner is that of the witch. Selin Yasar writes:[136]

> "Witches don't need a prince to rescue them; the power of their spells and magic will do. And, when needed, they can also rely on their sisters. Many witches decide to gather in covens, which are like a second family, a circle of trust that creates not only powerful magic but also a strong community. Others decide not to join a coven but will meet up with other witches socially, engage on forums, or attend workshops. Despite being a mysterious religion, witchcraft welcomes everybody regardless of race, gender, or sexual orientation. Commitment is the only thing required."

This paradigm, which focuses on women as a group subjected to the pressure of patriarchy, is halfway between symbolic mischief and radical vindication. It aims to contribute to overcoming oppressive

---

[136] S. Yasar, "The rise of the witch," *Medium*, 2018.

factors like physical and gender stereotypes, exclusions, the obligation to adapt to expectations, isolation, and competition among equals:

> "While a princess is typically born into privilege, a witch undergoes different challenges and proves herself in order to shape her life. (...) What defines a witch the most is probably her determination to follow her own will—a trait that can make her a target because she challenges the status quo and triggers the insecurities of some men. "Witches were stoned; witches were hanged; they were prosecuted; they were on the edge of society. So to say 'I'm a witch' is to say 'I have the courage to stand on the edge.'"[137]

Other intellectual routes that aim to go beyond the strictly rational, observable realm are metaphysics and poetry. These aren't very popular forms; this is surely because they don't deal with simple referents and aren't easy to express through short, self-contained messages. Consider the idea that the beauty of the physical universe and our world of shared emotions resides in how we can discover them from a basis of humility and intellectual honesty. It isn't easy to capture all that in the headlines of glossy magazine covers or boil it down into captivating snippets in an eye-catching paperback.

Because aesthetics, poetic inspiration, the search for being, the exploration of consciousness, the fascination of observing and inhaling the distilled essence of the feelings that unite us, the emotions that shake us to our cores and make us love each other... all that is the soul. The spirituality that I understand is that where mysticism is poetry; where the divine comes from inspiration, not from revelation; where thought merges with passion and philosophy with art; where paradise isn't carved up into plots and put up for sale, nor where show homes are listed with karma and transcendent energies.

However, that look beyond the empirical, which complements and enriches it, has remained on the margins of modernity. This is

---

137 Ibid.

the point from which I can reclaim those other windows, which are open to infinity. Nothing stops us from flying, but let's fly high, helping each other to find our way south, in flocks or in disarray, flapping or gliding, but not in formation or timid, low flight. And we don't have to invent everything: there is transcendent thought beyond the Bible, the Tanakh, the Buddhist Canons, the Koran, and the Vedas, beyond Coelho, Osho, Jodorowsky, Bucay, and Chopra.

Astrophysicist and great communicator Carl Sagan wrote:[138]

> "One of the great commandments of science is, "Mistrust arguments from authority." (Scientists, being primates, and thus given to dominance hierarchies, of course do not always follow this commandment.) Too many such arguments have proved too painfully wrong. Authorities must prove their contentions like everybody else. This independence of science, its occasional unwillingness to accept conventional wisdom, makes it dangerous to doctrines less self-critical, or with pretensions to certitude. (...) "Spirit" comes from the Latin word "to breathe." What we breathe is air, which is certainly matter, however thin. Despite usage to the contrary, there is no necessary implication in the word "spiritual" that we are talking of anything other than matter (including the matter of which the brain is made), or anything outside the realm of science. (...)
>
> Science is not only compatible with spirituality; it is a profound source of spirituality. When we recognize our place in an immensity of light-years and in the passage of ages, when we grasp the intricacy, beauty, and subtlety of life, then that soaring feeling, that sense of elation and humility combined, is surely spiritual. So are our emotions in the presence of great art or music or literature, or of acts of exemplary selfless courage such as those of Mohandas Gandhi or Martin Luther King, Jr. The notion that science and spirituality are somehow mutually exclusive does a disservice to both."

---

[138] C. Sagan, *The Demon-Haunted World: Science as a Candle in the Dark*, Ballantine Books, New York, 1997.

Richard P. Feynman, a Nobel laureate in physics and a brilliant genius with a surprising life story, wrote in a similar vein:[139]

"The same thrill, the same awe and mystery, comes again and again when we look at any question deeply enough. With more knowledge comes a deeper, more wonderful mystery, luring one on to penetrate deeper still. Never concerned that the answer may prove disappointing, with pleasure and confidence we turn over each new stone to find unimagined strangeness leading on to more wonderful questions and mysteries – certainly a grand adventure!

It is true that few unscientific people have this particular type of religious experience. Our poets do not write about it; our artists do not try to portray this remarkable thing. I don't know why. Is nobody inspired by our present picture of the universe? This value of science remains unsung by singers. You are reduced to hearing not a song or a poem, but an evening lecture about it. (...)

Perhaps one of the reasons is that you have to know how to read the music. For instance, the scientific article says, perhaps, something like this: "The radioactive phosphorous content of the cerebrum of the rat decreases to one-half in a period of two weeks." Now what does that mean? It means that phosphorus that is in the brain of a rat (and also in mine, and yours is not the same phosphorus as it was two weeks ago, but that all of the atoms that are in the brain are being replaced, and the ones that were there before have gone away. So what is this mind, what are these atoms with consciousness? Last week's potatoes! That is what now can remember what was going on in my mind a year ago – a mind which has long ago been replaced.

That is what it means when one discovers how long it takes for the atoms of the brain to be replaced by other atoms, to note that the thing which I call my individuality is only a pattern or dance. The atoms come into my brain, dance a dance, then go out always new atoms but always doing the same dance, remembering what the dance was yesterday."

---

[139] R. P. Feynman (1988), *What Do You Care What Other People Think?": Further Adventures of a Curious Character*, W. W. Norton & Company, New York, 2001.

Shelley was expelled from Oxford in 1811 for his work *The Necessity of Atheism* and was known for poetic writings like *The Masque of Anarchy*, which was not published during his lifetime and which contains probably the first modern expression of the idea of non-violent resistance. The English romantic poet wrote lines like the following in his *Hymn to Intellectual Beauty*, where he shows that fascination does not have to transcend the human realm to be captivating and poetic:

> "No voice from some sublimer world hath ever
>   To sage or poet these responses given:
>   Therefore the names of Demon, Ghost, and Heaven,
> Remain the records of their vain endeavour:
> Frail spells whose utter'd charm might not avail to sever,
>   From all we hear and all we see,
>   Doubt, chance and mutability.
> Thy light alone like mist o'er mountains driven,
>   Or music by the night-wind sent
>   Through strings of some still instrument,
>   Or moonlight on a midnight stream,
> Gives grace and truth to life's unquiet dream."

Finally, few perspectives have showered poetry with spirituality and spirituality with poetry like that of the great Eduardo Galeano, who did so without losing solid footing, always at the ready. Wonderful examples of this magical anarchist thinking can be found in his book, *The Walking Words*[140]:

> "It was Christmas, and a Swiss man had given his son a Swiss watch. The boy took the clock apart on his bed. And he was playing with the needles, the spring, the glass, the crown, and the other little cogs when his father found him and gave him a tremendous beating. Before that, Nicole Rouan and her brother had been enemies. From that Christmas on, the first Christmas she remembers, the two were fast friends. That day, Nicole knew that she too

---

140   Eduardo Galeano, *Las palabras andantes*, op. cit.

would be punished throughout the years because instead of asking the time of the world's clocks, she was going to ask them what they were like on the inside."

"Religion says: The body is a sin. Science says: The body is a machine. Advertising says: The body is a business. The body says: I am a party."

4.2 Identities and sensibilities

Identity is a proposal that seems to exist in all cultures, in both its individual and collective components. I define who I am through a name that identifies me; I define what I am through a cultural set of tools and raw materials that I use to build that character, that fiction, the construction that I recognize myself in. Compared to other elements of personality and social relationships – such as roles, tendencies, orientations, behaviors, or expressing our thoughts in the form of daily practices – identity is not limited to defining interactions or desires; it establishes a meaning, a symbolic identification of what I am, what I want to be, and what the aim of my actions should be.

Identity is not unique, although there may be a hierarchy among the identities by which a person or a community feels represented: for instance, a primary identity and other secondary ones. Specifically, according to influential sociologist Manuel Castells:[141]

> "By identity, as it refers to social actors, I understand the process of construction of meaning on the basis of a cultural attribute, or a related set of cultural attributes, that is given priority over

---

141 M. Castells, *The Power of Identity*, Wiley Blackwell, Oxford, 2010, from the trilogy *The Information Age: Economy, Society, and Culture* (Castells is also the author of an extensive work that connects with this book, as it examines the contemporary processes that lead to "the network society." His conclusions indicate that vertical hierarchical structures have been preeminent until now because the network structure had material conditions to overcome. These conditions have changed thanks to technology, leading to the emergence of new horizontal, anarchist movements shaping the emancipation of certain groups versus institutions and large corporations, diversity versus homogenization, minority rights, the common good, environmentalism, feminism, etc.).

other sources of meaning. For a given individual, or for a collective actor, there may be a plurality of identities. Yet, such a plurality is a source of stress and contradiction in both self-representation and social action."

As for the places I occupy in society and the tasks that I take on or which are assigned to me, roles are the result of the confrontation that takes place between my will, my desires, my possibilities, and my needs and the real world: they are functional. They don't have to be completely accepted, internalized, and individualized. Identities must because they bring structure to meaning, not to functions. Identities impose a reading of temporal continuity (not constancy) over the years and a spatial delimitation, as they're limited by what I identify as my body.

Castells categorizes identities in terms of power, citing – among other sources – Foucault and Marcuse (sometimes, I get the feeling that we're traversing the curved threads of a spiderweb anchored to old walls with a few window sills that we go back to time and time again). The three categories he identifies are:

Legitimizing identities: These reflect the internalization of what I've called hegemonic normativity. They embrace common sense, the values imposed by institutions through authority, and shape civil society. They do not include, either in individual sensibility or collective awareness, a significant perception of being the object of domination; they therefore do not harbor rebellious purposes or desires for deep, radical transformations at the root of things.

Resistance identities: These disclose the discernment of being dominated by the hegemonic power and show assimilation of dissent. They entail the construction of bunkers and entrenchments in their individual and collective manifestations to avoid marginalization, elimination, or forced reconversion. They're the first step in raising awareness when it comes to articulating a movement that can lead to visibility, normalization, and the transformation of society and its institutions.

Project identities: These go one step beyond resistance: the construct of identity goes from the trenches to deployment on the vanguard. They lead to action because their logic and vision include social transformation, and their aim is to redefine their position in this new order to free themselves from vectors of domination and challenge the privileges that other positions hold at their expense. They turn oppressed subjects into political subjects.

Obviously, my intention is to explore the articulations of resistance and project identities that are more closely related to building bonds. Any sense of self-assignment or social belonging is somehow connected to how we relate to one another, but I will try to focus on the aspects that most directly link these feelings to the world of personal bonds, their influence, and their scope.

Political identities

The daily struggles, politics, and practices related to identity are in a fragile, continuous balance with the ever-present intersectionality of the vectors of power and domination: there exist multiple axes of oppression that give rise to highly complex interactions between them. Recognition and awareness of identity are an essential ingredient in voicing demands and activism against a specific form of oppression, but they can become factors that create division and conflict between oppressed groups.

Charles Taylor, one of the key voices in contemporary political philosophy, suggests:[142]

> "(...) "sharing the space of identity as an alternative to democratic exclusion" means negotiating an identity that's acceptable, or even politically committed, among the different personal or group identities that are desired or must be lived out." Here, the word "negotiate" has a particular meaning: it is not merely a pro-

---

[142] R. Cristi and J.R. Tranjan, "Charles Taylor y la democracia republicana," *Revista de ciencia política*, Santiago, 2010.

cedural negotiation whereby people reach an impartial compromise. Negotiating refers to the merging of horizons, a process of expansion and a broadening of the understandings of participants who are willing to open up to a full relationship with the other."

This, of course, is not a criticism of radical processes aimed at confronting sexism, homoantagonism, racism, capitalism, or any other oppression, nor should it lead to the deactivation of the political subjects that embody them. Rather, it is about problematizing identity along the same lines as queer theory's warning about the dangers of essentialisms, the gender binary, and so on. In her proposal on radical democracy, Chantal Mouffe is even clearer and more explicit:[143]

"If the task of radical democracy is indeed to deepen the democratic revolution and to link diverse democratic struggles, such a task requires the creation of new subject positions that would allow the common articulation, for example, of antiracism, antisexism and anticapitalism. (...) In order that the defence of workers' interests is not pursued at the cost of the rights of women, immigrants or consumers, it is necessary to establish an equivalence between these different struggles. It is only under these circumstances that struggles against power become truly democratic."

But in this recent round of analysis in the field of political philosophy, at no time has the idea that anarchism is one of the political identities with the least inherent links with categories such as class, race, gender, or country of origin been included. In this case, as Laura Portwood-Stacer says,[144] it shows that it isn't necessary to take on one of these identities as a mobilizing factor. Anarchism would be a de-essentialized identity since it has to do with the interpretation and meaning that is given to reality and with desires to change it, rather than with a shared identification, origin, or personal experience. The assessments are what coincide when seen

---

143 Chantal Mouffe, *The Return of the Political (Radical Thinkers)* Verso, New York, 2006.
144 L. Portwood-Stacer, *Lifestyle Politics and Radical Activism,* op. cit.

through a common lens, and they give rise to a purely political position. That's one of the reasons why a movement like relationship anarchy, which involves elevating daily practices to a form of political expression, particularly arises in spaces related to anarchism and gives rise to the formation of such particular identities and political subjects. These practices and this identity offer a unique sense of political action at times when the possibilities for change seem quite slim. According to Stacer, theorists of performativity like Judith Butler have argued that all types of identity are based on the performative, but the anarchist political identity is a particularly conspicuous example.

Relationship Anarchy: from identity to sensibility

Beyond the analysis of identarian trends[145] that a proposal like relationship anarchy sparks in its political dimension, it is interesting to examine how that identity works in the sphere of relationships at a level that's closer to everyday life. On one hand is the question of what it means to identify oneself as a relationship anarchist openly, and the extent to which this entails an opposition to other identities like "normal person" (in the sense of "normative"), "someone in a couple" (or engaged, married, or in a relationship), a "single person" (whether on purpose or while looking for a partner, or even in that peculiar state that I've heard described so many times with infinite perplexity as "a partner isn't sought but found"), etc.

The first question that we could ask, which happens to be along the lines of the previous section, is that most identities in our societies have a lot to do with power. Expressing my national identity places me in a position of power over foreigners (especially those who are poor because, in a capitalist world, the distinctive identity that wealth – or the appearance of wealth – provides prevails over absolutely everything else). Showing my racial, gender, family (my

---

[145] Given that this book is not primarily academic in its aim, I use the concept of identity in a broad sense, mainly focusing on the characterization that appears in this section's approach, but leaving enough room to be able to partially integrate ideas, behaviors, practices, and roles that complement identarian sense.

last name), professional, or religious identity can put me in the place that's always in my best interest, when it is an expression of power.

In this sense, the identarian totem of relationship anarchy (or of non-normativity, non-monogamy, and more) is used starting from very different, almost opposite, positions. The traditional masculine identity can sometimes be a flag flown as a crude warning, meaning, "Girl, with me, you know what you're dealing with." A constant specific alert, information, the task of deconstruction, and deploying every method for preventing this circumstance are all necessary. On the other hand, from an identity of a feminist and a woman, for instance, it may be useful (in this case, through emancipation behaviors that must be valued and supported from all fields) to establish limits, build networks, and propose true liberation that is broad and non-specific in political, supportive, and collective terms in processes of empowerment.

Generally, though, my proposal would be to steer any identarian temptation in the context of relationship anarchy away from identity and toward sensitivity. In other words, rather than identifying with a category, I prefer for the approaches of relationship anarchy to lead me to practices where the highest level of sensibility around their basic aspects is constantly, consistently demonstrated. These practices should be sensitive to any form of authority, domination, or oppression; they must be careful to avoid normative privileges and express the utmost consideration for the needs, desires, and limits of each person to build spaces or networks of collective self-management. This delicacy should allow us to escape submission to the dominant norms and the power structures that these entail without anxiety or pressure.

Contesting normative identities

Relationship anarchy is a response to normative identities. It is in regard to this characteristic that I've mentioned the lines of reasoning that lead to questioning prescriptive labels, couple/friendship dichotomies, allosexism, etc., based on the principles of non-authority, non-normativity, and self-management in previous chapters. In that sense, the same approach could be useful: moving from identity to sensibility. The predefined categories inherit cumbersome baggage that's loaded with rules, structure, rights, obligations, and expectations, but they shouldn't be fought or attacked at the expense of the weakest or those most in need. Giving up those identities should be, yes, but without brushing anyone aside. We should replace them with sensibilities that put consideration before deconstruction; this is because the latter is a task that has to be done collectively and at the pace of those who are slower.

Normative categories could be understood as territories demarcated by limits: borders. These borders defend certainties, frameworks of perceived security that relationship anarchy intends to eliminate. But as an analogy, it wouldn't be fair for us to set aside all the problems and drama related to those borders when we embark on the internationalist and humanist project of bringing them to an end. The aim and the conviction that humanity is all one, with no barriers or boundaries between nations, cannot lead us to deny how they condition poor migrants or refugees, nor to forget the struggle to visibilize their tragedy and recognize their rights as human beings. We will surely abolish borders tomorrow or next week, but in the meantime, let's not abandon those who are their victims today. We will see regulatory labels shed their restrictive, authoritarian character, but in the meantime, it's important to recognize, be recognized, and empathize with those who are most vulnerable or who are going through rough times. When someone is in that situation, they surely need confirmation, reinforcement, and a little bit of symbolic structure that serves as an anchor or buoy to maintain some stability.

Adopting sensibility as a criterion makes it possible to cast the struggle and collective work in a positive light. It offers the ability to turn demands into mutual understanding. As a first step, I can change the words. That will help me think differently. Using new categories can also cause discomfort and thus visibilize and end up contributing to normalization when the listener gets used to that language. It can also spark curiosity and questions. Answering them in an informative, respectful way will make it even more apparent that I relate to others in a different sort of way.

Personal identity isn't only a descriptive notion that serves to bring meaning to my actions and express traits or characteristics that represent me. It is a set of dynamics, self-perceptions, building a model of the world, meaning for my environment and my individuality as part of that universe, as an entity that can transform and be transformed. In Galeano's words:[146]

> "At the end of the day, we are what we do to change who we are. Identity is not a motionless museum piece in a display case, but the ever-amazing synthesis of our daily contradictions. It is in that fleeting faith I believe. I find it the only trustworthy faith, because of how much it resembles the human creature, which is screwed up but sacred, and the crazy adventure of living in the world."

Socially, normatively, personal identity serves to provide me with a fiction of essentiality. That fiction makes me believe that I behave this way because I am this way, that I feel this way because I am this way, that I think this way because I am this way, and ultimately, that I am this way because I am this way. However, I probably actually behave this way because I was taught to behave this way; I feel this way because I learned to feel this way; and I think this way because I was trained to think this way. And I am this way because this is how culture has built me, or because this is how my body, my mind, my conscious and subconscious being have adapted to the environment I grew up in.

So, is this my "natural" way of behaving, feeling, and thinking? This could be said to be true; after all, as I've mentioned before, the natural development of any living organism is based on adapting to the environment it finds itself in at birth. But what would I be like

---

146   Eduardo Galeano, *El libro de los abrazos*, Siglo XXI, Madrid, 1993.

if I had had to adapt to a different environment? I would undoubtedly be different, quite different if those surroundings had been very different.

Therefore, the statements "this is how I am" and "I am what I am," are fictions if I consider being to be something essential that's independent of culture, circumstances, stimuli, and chance. Unfortunately, reality can only confirm one hypothesis; that means that we cannot know what we would be like in another staging of life. No one thrives in an indifferent environment. There is no "normal" environment that can serve as a neutral reference point. There's no such thing.

I do have to admit that, ever since I was born, I've been adapting my character to a script and that I've been so focused on my role that I've forgotten that I'm acting. Assuming that, the first thing that interests me is examining the text with a critical eye, deciding if I agree with my character, and if not, determining what things I want to change. By altering my part of the script, I'm building a new identity – it's probably just as fictitious as the last one, but it's more conscious and less automated. It may be a resistance identity that channels a radical collective feeling.

For instance, the gender binary works to differentiate roles into two groups: actors and actresses, each group having its own traits. The basic features that structure the script of female characters are the need for love to be happy, the obligation to capitalize on their beauty and guard their virtue, self-denial, and restraint; there's a price to be paid for overacting or getting out of character. The male characters' traits constitute active protagonism: they represent the universal, everything outside the feminine; they define humankind as a whole and provide all the necessary richness to the text because, for them, innovation has a reward. The characters also have different roles depending on their age: they must grow up, settle down, work, have offspring, and – in due course – retire behind the curtains for the most risque scenes. Supporting characters, no matter how enthusiastic they are, rarely end up being the most applauded. Generally speaking, those that don't adapt to the play, the scene, or the majority sensibility of the audience will only receive attention if they're put in important scenes from the very beginning.

Going back to the initial idea that I am what I do to change what I am, that I can change my role, especially if I realize that it's the script for a character and not a necessary, inevitable essence, how can we characterize the possible paths to that resistance or project identity? Perhaps I would have to critically change my vision of the character and then assess the option of making that change visible so that it is also perceived from without. For the first part, it's helpful for me to be clear about the objections to my current role and the aims for the transformation I'm suggesting. For instance, I want to challenge my gender identity, how I relate to others, and my way of consuming. I have reasons for all this and the conviction to want to make an effort to do so. If I'm interested in visibility, I will have to find the strength and encouragement to express and externalize it, making it visible to at least part, if not all, of my surroundings.

There is also a more comfortable alternative, of course, and that attitude may be one of acceptance, submission: taking on the role that has been assigned to me. On the one hand, it's the simplest option since I won't have to fight against my own forms of inertia and those from my social context. On the other hand, though, if I really don't feel represented by my character, resignation isn't a very pleasant long-term path, either.

As for the degree of defining the nuances, non-hegemonic identities tend to seek a precision that's not required of traditional roles. Sometimes, they require a lot of introspection, examining the sensations that arise – and which may change – from every angle. This sometimes surprises those who live in the comfort of the hegemonic realm, and this strangeness sometimes leads to skepticism and even ridicule (another form of abuse that could be understood as meta-violence in some cases). Legitimizing identities don't call for confronting consolidated power structures, privileged groups, and structural violence. Neoliberal thinking is based on the assumption that all of us start out from the same basic point. In other words, it denies differences in opportunities; in the level of access to resources and means of personal or cultural development, consumption or production; in subjection to structures of control and submission, etc. This sort of thought is blind to the inequality that finds a perfect complement in the idea that love is just as blind: blind to position, origin, and identity, blind and indifferent to forms of oppression.

Below, I've listed structures of domination and identities of resistance related to non-normative relationships, making the notion of identity more flexible to expand it to tendencies, orientations, and expressions that are framed in subalternity and dissidence, along with details on the circumstances and configurations that determine them. Identities that can lead to insurrectionary, revolutionary, transformative sensibilities. This framing helps to understand and visualize the large number of dimensions in which the cultural context divides and facilitates oppression between people, pitting them against each other. It's worth pausing to go over this list and internalize how many of these axes cross through us and where we are along each of them, whether that position falls in the realm of privilege or submission.[147]

A. POWER STRUCTURE
B. Hegemonic identity
C. Project/resistance identities
D. Structural violence

A. PATRIARCHY
B. Man
C. Woman, feminist
D. Misogyny and sexism (sexist violence)

---

[147] I've used the suffix "-antagonist" instead of "-phobia" in accordance with the recent denominational trends in activist spaces. This is because "phobia" refers to a pathological aversion, not to a moral or political prejudice as is the case here; this also prevents blaming those who suffer from any true phobias.

A. HETEROSEXISM
B. Heterosexual
C. Homosexual, bisexual, pansexual, asexual, etc.
D. Homoantagonism, lesboantagonism, LGBTIQ+ antagonism

A. MONOSEXISM
B. Monosexual (heterosexual or homosexual)
C. Plurisexual (bisexual or pansexual)
D. Biantagonism and panantagonism

A. CISNORMATIVITY
B. Cisgender
C. Transgender
D. Cissexism, transantagonism, transmisogyny, and sissyantagonism

A. GENDER BINARY
B. Masculine and feminine
C. Non-binary, queer
D. Enby antagonism

A. SEXONORMATIVITY
B. Allosexual
C. Asexual, gray-sexual, demisexual
D. Allosexism

A. SEXUAL PURITANISM
B. Normosexual
C. Promiscuous, BDSM practicer, sex-positive activist, sex worker
D. Religious morals, sexual shame, patriarchal biases against promiscuity among women, stigmatizing sex work, the threat of abolitionism, slut-shaming, porn antagonism, BDSM antagonism, sexual negativity

A. AMATONORMATIVITY
B. Alloromantic
C. Aromantic, gray-romantic, demiromantic
D. Aroantagonism

A. MONOGAMY
B. Monogamous, serial monogamous, secret cheater
C. Non-monogamous (open relationships, swingers, polyamory, networked love, polygamy, etc.)

D. Polyantagonism
A. CORPORAL NORMATIVITY AND NEURONORMATIVITY
B. Bodily normative individuals and neurotypical individuals
C. People with diverse bodies and neurodivergent individuals
D. Fat antagonism, dysmorphoantagonism, aversion to neurodivergent individuals

A. STATE
B. Exemplary national citizenship
C. Migrant, anti-system, victim of forms marginalization (racism, xenoantagonism, cultural and economic elitism, etc.), freethinker, anarchist
D. Immigration laws, non-compliance with the Universal Declaration of Human Rights or constitutional and legal mandates of a social nature, state monopoly on authority and violence, repression, laws against civil rights and freedoms, patriotic indoctrination

A. RELIGIOUS INSTITUTIONS
B. Believer
C. Atheist, agnostic
D. Monopoly of spirituality; repressive, dogmatic morality; religious indoctrination; anti-laicism

A. LINGUISTIC AND CULTURAL COLONIALISM
B. Person brought up in the dominant culture and language
C. Speakers of minority languages and those who come from subjugated cultures
D. Undervaluing local culture and language, eradicating a people's cultural traits, cultural standardization, stigmatizing anything not in accordance with the morality of the dominant culture, marginalizing those socialized in contexts of colonial subjugation

A. Neoliberal capitalism
B. *Capitalist, someone who owns capital or means of production*
C. Worker, proletarian, poor/subaltern person
D. Exploitation, ableism, socio-economic neglect

Any combination of these proposals associated with resistance or project identities and practices gives rise to a configuration that is compatible with the non-normative thinking that relationship anarchy outlines. The features that define identarian sense vary widely: some give shape to communities of resistance and activism, and for some people, relationship anarchy can function as a feeling in itself or connect with a combination of identities structured by a critique of hegemonic normativity, of power structures and the violence they engender. Another perpetual feature is the calling to create self-managed networks of affection and care without coercive mechanisms, networks where there is a balance between the imperative for mutual aid and the principle of personal sovereignty, without renouncing either.

As Stevphen Shukaitis says in *Anarchism and Sexuality*:[148]

> "Surely the path to creating a better, joyous, freer, more loving world is not one that is premised upon a constant struggle that leaves one tired and rundown. The question is one of creating communities of resistance that provide support and strength, a density of relations and affections, through all aspects of our lives, so that we can carry on and support each other in our work rather than having to withdraw from that which we love to do in order to sustain the capacity to do those very things. This is to create a sustainable culture of resistance, a flowering of what I am calling affective resistance – that is, a sustainable basis for ongoing and continuing political organizing, a plateau of vibrating intensities, premised upon refusing to separate questions of the effectiveness of any tactic, idea or campaign, from its affectiveness."

---

[148] S. Shukaitis, *Nobody knows what an insurgent body can do*, in Jamie Heckert and Richard Cleminson, *Anarchism and Sexuality*, op. cit.

4.3 Freedom, rights, entitlement, and agreements

Like all widely accepted moral concepts, the abstract ideas of freedom and individual rights seem to be so natural that we wouldn't be surprised to find them written in the clouds one morning. Of course, they aren't notions directly based on experience and empathy, as is concern for preventing someone else's pain or the grief of losing someone who's near and dear. These are more complex concepts that are difficult to conceive intuitively or reflect on quickly. They require a conceptual framework that contextualizes them.

Taylor's atomistic framework[149] serves as the ontological support for the neoliberal conception of rights as something above and beyond the social context. In that framework, belonging to a society, mutual aid, and solidarity are all secondary elements. Rights (which often supplant what are actually privileges) belong to the individual as such, and considering them to be subject to the common good is posed as a danger to freedom.

From a contrary perspective, Herbert Marcuse analyzed technological and consumer societies in the 1960s. In that analysis, he studied, among other things, the needs created at the heart of those societies to manufacture the individual identity of power and to establish a social position — not to satisfy actual needs or aspirations. He also examined the difficulty of effecting profound changes within the system or through a classical revolution, proposing that the only way to do so would be through an awakening of solidarity as a "biological necessity." His influential work[150] contains a broad, powerful critique of the mechanisms of control, domination, and exploitation in contemporary societies. In this regard, he argues that authentic freedoms and rights can only occur in a system that ensures that

---

149 C. Taylor, "Atomism," *in Philosophical Papers*, v.2, Cambridge University Press, Cambridge, 1985.
150 H. Marcuse (1955), *Eros and Civilization: A Philosophical Inquiry into Freud*, Beacon Press, Boston, 1974 and, especially in this case, *One-Dimensional Man*, Routledge, London, 1964.

the actual needs of all members of society are met. It is on this basis that the rights of individuals and individual freedom should be understood.

Obviously, the social anarchist view, as the source of relationship anarchy's principles, adopts this second understanding; therefore, it waves the flag not of individual freedom but of collective self-management in a context of personal sovereignty. This is combined with the commitment to mutual aid and free association and the rejection of coercion and authority (order and personal responsibility are not contested). Ultimately, it's about valuing the idea of individual self-determination that is subject to collective freedom. This conclusively requires there to be no gradients of domination within a network of bonds, regardless of its size: one in monogamous configurations or more than one in general, and always with support, care, and responsible commitment.

Of course, commitments and responsibility aren't the fun part of relationships, just like in other areas of life. Therefore, individualistic freedom is an attractive element. The word "freedom" sounds good; it's a seductive concept to identify with and a perfect excuse to not have to bother with an uncomfortable, tedious task – though not everyone sees it that way – of communicating my desires, my needs, my limits. And above all, a way out of listening to everything others have to say and the search for self-assigned, self-administered regulation by all those who — in that network — have relational activity, interest, presence, who enjoy and suffer its consequences, etc. In short, it's a perfect excuse to justify selfishness and pettiness in many of its manifestations.

My impression is that, both in non-specific social contexts as well as in those where alternative relationship models are tried out – especially when the interactions are mostly heterosexual – there is generally a strong gender bias in this phenomenon. The aversion to communication, to commitments, to solidarity and emotional work are more evident among those who identify as men. In fact, men are taught to negotiate successfully, seek favorable agreements, and trade to win. Women, however, are instructed from all social and cultural spheres to please, to give in, to seek harmony and agreement. The construction of the meaning of masculine and feminine identities — and their most common roles — gives rise to these behavioral orientations that clearly generally represent a baseline disadvantage for the latter in any dynamic that involves negotiation and transaction.

Commitments versus transactions and contracts

I've suggested the idea of voluntary, conscious, responsible commitment as a regulating element of the amplifying effect that the abstract notions of rights and freedom, understood from liberal individualism, produce in situations of power and inequality. However, compromise is, in turn, a concept that only fits in anarchist thought if it is strictly voluntary and not coercive. In practice, within each bond or network of bonds, different power relations may develop; therefore, the game of finding commitments and mechanisms for mutual or collective consideration is not easy to specify and describe. Intuitively, it would have to be presided over by camaraderie, equity, and renouncing positions of authority, blackmail, and victimization.

The situations that arise are so varied that clearly establishing which articulations of the commitments would fit into a relationship anarchist vision and which wouldn't is not possible. But at least we can outline them with helpful points of comparison. One of these examples constantly appears in the everyday activities of people and companies in negotiating agreements, stipulating conditions, and signing contracts. An agreement or a contract is a tool that determines the possible future actions of those who sign it. By resorting to the laws that regulate contracts, the obligations and sanctions or counterparts that would be associated with a hypothetical breach or violation of the agreement must be established either explicitly or implicitly. It is the use of force, which is monopolized by the State, that ensures that these punishments are an effective threat through legal coercion.

The laws outline that, for contracts to be valid, they must be signed freely and without pressure, but no one is so naive as to think that, strictly speaking, the positions are always balanced when negotiating a contract. Whoever needs to sell, for whatever reason, is subject to pressure that weakens their negotiating capacity and gives the other party an advantage. Those who have less knowledge, experience, contacts, financial backing, time, access to information, or other competitive benefits will have a harder time striking a good deal.

Of course, this scenario doesn't evoke the image of a network of mutual aid, solidarity, or the common good in the least. That's why I understand responsible commitment, which makes sense in the framework of relationship anarchy, to be something that presents several key differences from an agreement, pact, consensus, or contract, as we may tend to call it.

The first difference is that, in a contractual agreement, each party contributes or surrenders something that they have ownership or entitlement over. I can sign a residential rental agreement because I hope to have ownership of the money that I'll pay each month and the power to use it for that purpose. The lessor has the ownership or usufruct of a home and the ability or power to assign it to me so that I can live there. A responsible commitment, however, is not an exchange: it is the recognition, expression, and celebration (because I think this should be experienced with at least some enthusiasm) of a purpose that is voluntary and adaptable as well as reliable and firm. Again, it would be naive to say that nothing is desired in return. There are always expectations of reciprocity, which is surely understandable, but there are no demands. Above all, no one grants their own personal sovereignty in exchange for the personal sovereignty of another or others.

A second difference that's quite significant is, as I've said, the fact that contracts carry penalties for non-compliance. Sanctions that are included in the same document or that come from applicable legislation. In the sphere of relationships, there are misunderstandings, breaking commitments or expectations, feelings of injustice or abuse, or mistrust; it doesn't make sense to address these with sanctions or punishments (though these are frequent practices in normative relationships). Again, the only reasonable path is formed by communication and seeking an interactive consensus, the latter of which evolves according to the wishes and limits of everyone involved.

The model based on agreement, exchange, and transaction often leads to feelings of guilt and displays of victimhood. Blame and retaliation only entrench the lack of solidarity, defending what one considers their own, blackmail, and confrontation. These positions of authority are sometimes disguised as conditional tolerance in a passive-aggressive style: "you can do whatever you want, but you won't see me again" (that is, if you do what you want, you'll be given the greatest punishment); they sometimes cloak themselves with dignity: "if you do that, it's because you don't value me" (because we're exchanging submission for something that has a value); or they may be a direct threat: "you'll see what happens" (I'm not going to tell you what the punishment will be, but there will be one)...

Commitments in the field of relationship anarchy, however, must be voluntary in nature and based on communication – communicating wishes, needs, and above all, personal limits. The limits I'm proposing differ from contractual stipulations or clauses in that they refer to oneself. I can set limits on what can affect my body or what I consider my space, my privacy, my belongings, or the rights that correspond to me as a human being. Under these conditions, limits put things in their place, show where each person is at all times, and when they are reflected in the commitments of others, they can establish a context of understanding and orderly coexistence that is not coercive. Such a context can and should be adaptable. If, after 15 years, I breach a clause in my rental agreement that said I couldn't have pets, I run the risk of being accused of breach of contract, even though that issue wasn't addressed at any time in communicating with the landlord after so long (maybe they would have been bothersome at first, but now the whole neighborhood has pets).

That would make no sense in a non-normative relationship, where there aren't any rules set in advance but responsible commitments. Imagine that we established a set of agreements years ago that allowed me to do such and such but which hasn't been mentioned since, and now I maintain that prerogative without even discussing it. That claim would obviously be a sign of bad faith in the relationship, even if it might be lawful from the point of view of contract law. As for crossing boundaries, this would also be a clear manifestation of contempt for a key element: explicit consent. The fact that a boundary was established in the past doesn't mean that in the present – when there may be even the slightest doubt – you don't have to ask if those delimitations are still the same.

On the other hand, one important characteristic of responsible commitment in the context of relationship anarchy is that it is established with a person as such: just a person, not with their identity, label, or role as a "partner," "friend," "lover," or "spouse." In other words, this commitment doesn't automatically change if the structure of the bonds is ever modified. In the hegemonic model, normative relationship labels define the characteristics, scope, and intensity of commitments. If someone goes from being a "friend" to a "partner," the commitments are instantly updated, naturalized, and clear; they're suddenly greater in intensity, significance, impact, and breadth. When you stop "being in a relationship," the opposite effect takes place just as suddenly. If we look only at the spectrum of friendship, the picture seems to be more stable in that sense; if we look at biological family, some changes don't make sense, and others are more complex over the longer term.

Following the logic of relationship anarchy, the structure has no real value, except if someone in the affective network needs it — symbolically or exceptionally — due to a history of vulnerability or denial of identity, as I've mentioned before. Therefore, the commitments cannot be associated with the position of each person in that structure; they are the product of personal communication or communication through the network. As a result, they are geared towards the people I share things with, not their positions in my configuration of bonds – or the configuration that is legible to the rest of society.

If we take on a way of understanding long-term, sustainable coexistence without authority, abuse, or tyrannical behavior, commitments will generally be oriented towards respect, consideration, help, affection, solidarity, dedication, etc., and they will stay active, be centered around people, and have a deep sense of loyalty, sincerity, and trust through communication.

Finally, any idea or desire that I want to bring into a commitment or a boundary (or an agreement or pact, if, despite it all, that is the path I choose) would have to be subjected to analysis and dialogue. It's important to scrutinize what I perceive as a need in order to explain why it's important to me, looking for the ultimate reasons and not just staying on the surface. This is because commitments and limits (and, when appropriate, agreements) can't revolve around mere whims. Transactional dynamics, these "trading cards," are already problematic in themselves, as they respond to a logic of property rights. However, if these exchanges also involve whims or arbitrary, capricious desires, they simply become a frivolous, childish game. True, it sometimes isn't bad faith but has to do with concerns that simply reflect a cultural mandate. That's why dialogue and detailed analysis of each of these desires and exactly what they're in response to can help the process become a more careful, reflective, genuine, restorative experience.

Freedom doesn't exist (without equity at the starting point)

The central idea of relationship anarchy is that relationships aren't established in coercive or normative terms. This means that no one is forced to do what they don't want to do and that the rules that regulate how relationships are managed do not come from an external normativity. They are the conclusions of a collective process of communication (between two or more people). The characteristics of this process are important: it must be freely accessed on equal footings. To ensure this starting point, the power gradients that exist must be detected and addressed in advance, and they must constantly be attended to in this regard. It is crucial that the freedom I claim for myself is also accessible to others, not only in theory but in practice. Even if this is not the case from the start, at least there must be a collective will to head in the direction of achieving that goal.

The processes of self-regulation (creating the context of commitments and guidelines for behavior) and self-management (enjoying the course of relationships and resolving possible conflicts) can keep the network of relationships running smoothly as a criterion, or they may end up generating dynamics of competition. We've grown up in a monogamous, patriarchal system that encourages these dynamics. The search for a mate involves a contest where only one will win. On top of that, there are specific competitions for each gender with their own peculiarities that guarantee combativeness and the exaltation of the rivalry. Therefore, if we let ourselves ("going with the flow" or "being real"), we'll end up entering those mechanics of struggle and competition.

By ensuring these two requirements – freedom being accessible to everyone and management being directed to the common good and not to competition – can lead us to demanding that relationships are endowed with a more prescriptive regulatory structure than we'd like or than what we might expect in an anarchist-inspired format. On the one hand, these are not rules imposed by the social mandate, and on the other, the objective is to ensure truly accessible freedom in the form of personal sovereignty and to make it compatible with the principle of mutual aid so that the network of relationships is supportive and fair. A regulatory structure that takes the form of freely acquired commitments is usually needed, and this is the tool that will allow the most vulnerable among us to be treated according to anarchist principles in a real, balanced way at a particular time and in a particular scenario (in the end, probably all members of a network of bonds will be in that situation at some point).

In other words, it's about being equitable in considering relationships, not people. The same demands apply to every relationship, but not every person can be asked for the same degree of autonomy, spirit, strength, will, and consistency at all times and contexts.

4.4 Family of origin, chosen family, and raising children

The term "chosen family" was coined by Kath Weston[151] at the end of the last century in a pioneering study on the day-to-day lives, relationships, and family in the LGBTIQ + community in the United States. The uniqueness in how the people belonging to this community formed relationships led to them having as much or more bonds in terms of help, assistance, and protection with friends, lovers, or ex-lovers than with their biological families or families of origin. The reasons varied and included prejudice and rejection by the latter.

Fortunately, things have changed over the decades, but that trend is still partly present today. To a certain extent, it also applies to the community of people who identify with non-normative relationship styles. On the one hand, dealing with one's family of origin often has little content that's truly relational in terms of connection with depth and meaning. There is little communication when it comes to intimate aspects, and tastes, socio-cultural settings, and moral assumptions are quite different.

Depending on the geographical and cultural environment, family get-togethers are limited to celebrations, meals, and mourning (which follow strict protocols and stereotypes and where the tastes,

---

[151] K. Weston, *Families We Choose: Lesbians, Gays, Kinship*. Columbia University Press. New York, 1997

limits, etc. of family members who are less involved in these traditional practices are considered "extravagances").

Family normativity

Normativity is also demonstrated to be as powerful and invasive as in other areas of relationships. Numerous obligations are taken for granted and attempted to be imposed under threat of exclusion, accusations of ingratitude, blackmail based on disappointment, lost hope, frustration. There's a debt to be paid, a respect that is beyond reasonable – not respect for people, who obviously always deserve it in its highest expression, but respect for the system of thought and the moral doctrines that a cautionary family agreement intends to spread to all its members.

In other cases, the family institution is configured not as a single-minded society but as a battlefield where the same conflict is repeated over and over again. Though there's an inexplicably fraternal truce between every event, each meeting brings a new contest. Opinions, judgments, evaluations, and heated words are traded without anyone listening to anyone else.

In short, the family of origin is generally not a source of genuine bonds in the sense of communication, sincerity, accessibility, and listening without judgment. It is frequently so, though, in terms of support with logistical aspects, illnesses, financial assistance, and other situations related to vulnerability, all according to a normative precept. We should also note that this trait has a markedly patriarchal bias: it is women who are mobilized for caretaking. This is a problematic process from many angles, but in practice, in this society where care is not guaranteed, nor are housing, functional independence, or economic sustainability effective rights, this is a highly valuable lifeline. In this regard, then, there is a functional complementarity with other networks of bonds.

As for the possibility of reconstructing the family of origin's network of relationships in accordance with the principles of relationship anarchy, the most significant difficulties arise from the very structure of kinship configurations. These aren't created by a process of communication and commitment to self-management, but by a predetermined circumstance (either biological or legal). Of course, nothing stops these changes from developing over time, but it takes more to overcome inertias that are so ingrained. Furthermore, the cultural mandates and sanctions mentioned earlier support this maintenance of automatic inertias, expectations, and coercion.

Raising kids outside a bubble

The opposite perspective is also an interesting one, focusing on who will constitute the families of origin for a new generation in the future. Raising children in non-normative structures of bonds is an issue that has been dealt with over the last decades based on the evolution of forms of marriage and cohabitation: first, among separated couples and single-parent families, then homosexual couples, and most recently, the still incipient wave of open relationships and unions or networks of more than two people.

Pregnancy and the first years of child-raising drastically alter the mother's personal life and the lives of those who are part of the environment that she relates to most intensely. The normative order is for the future mother to make the conscious decision to get pregnant in agreement with a man (her partner), and that he is the one who provides fertilization of the ovum, usually through sexual activity with reproductive purposes or – if that's not possible or not effective — through medical procedures. Another mechanism for normatively accessing parenthood is through adoption. Though it depends on the specific country, generally only heterosexual families, homosexual couples, or individuals are legally declared adoptive parents. The non-normative configurations are especially complex in this case: they clash with legal systems, which advance at very slow, careful paces, since protecting minors is logically considered to be a greater good in most laws.[152]

---

[152] I'm referring to "modern" states and their laws. In traditional cultures, the casuistry is much richer. For example, a popular African proverb says, "It takes a village

In Western countries, social services generally doesn't tend to take proactive measures against non-normative family configurations unless there are obvious situations of neglect, mistreatment, or abuse. However, if there is a legal battle for custody or a similar issue, a structure of cohabitation that's outside of what is defined can be problematic. Turning to new relationship models after the separation of a couple with offspring can be used as a legal weapon against one of the parents on the grounds that this alleged "unstructured" lifestyle poses a risk to the children. This is yet another example of normativity that crosses social and cultural barriers reaching the administrative and legal spheres.

In any case, going back to child-raising itself, whether done as a single parent, as a couple, or in a network, parenting requires time, effort, energy, and commitment. Above all, it initially involves relating to dependent individuals, children who require constant attention. Right alongside the stories of happiness, pleasure, and joy of pregnancy, childbirth, breastfeeding, etc., we often hear the most unromantic narratives of sacrifice, fatigue, and the difficulties and insecurities of that stage in life from those who have lived through it. Like other transitions we all go through – big projects, illnesses, challenges in school and at work, or adversities of any kind – the demands of parenting create personal instability and also generate imbalances in the network of relationships. Commitments have to be tailored to the new realities of vulnerability and the need for support from those who are facing these situations.

---

to raise a child." This an aphorism is specifically from the Igbo and Yoruba cultures of Nigeria (www.afriprov.org), but it demonstrates an idea that's widespread on the continent. In Tanzania's Sukuma culture, a beautiful example of ancestral poetic expression says that "One knee does not bring up a child;" in the Swahili culture of Central and East Africa, this becomes "One hand does not nurse a child" (source: African Proverbs, Sayings and Stories Webpage, afriprov.org). The responsibility of supporting and raising a new member of the community belongs to the entire community. The concept of extended family also still exists and even thrives in societies in southern Europe, South America, and others, given the strong presence of grandparents, aunts, uncles, and even close yet unrelated individuals in upbringing.

On the other hand, there are clear advantages offered by collective responsibility, understood as the possibility for more than one or two people to be involved in upbringing to different degrees and modalities. In addition to the issue of number itself, which has obvious logistical benefits, there is a clear shift in perspective when the formats for bonds are flexible and based on commitments (which may explicitly include child support and education) rather than on a cultural prescription and implicit expectations that create obligations to perform this task. These commitments are based on freely accepted responsibility, not on elements like romantic passion or sexual activity enduring. (The instability of these factors in the normative model often leads to ruptures in cohabitation, which affects the children's lives.)

It is about the predisposition, the calling to care for and raise or accompany the children, the focus on precisely that and not as a secondary effect of the bond with the mother or anyone else involved in upbringing. The affective network may include those who are interested in raising children and those who don't feel the slightest inclination towards this task, those who offer support in this area and those who contribute in other matters. The work of a parent (or a nurturing person in a broad sense) is a choice in life, and making this decision and carrying it out are matters that deserve their own space. It isn't a reality that should be experienced as a result of other options.

Finally, there is still little information regarding the question of how children are affected by how they perceive their family's format or network of protection, their support, education, responsibility, and caregivers and key figures. In addition to studies on monogamous non-heterosexual families, which are somewhat more abundant, there are only a few pioneering longitudinal follow-up studies on other non-normative families, specifically polyamorous ones.[153]

---

[153] M. Goldfeder, E Sheff, "Children of polyamorous families: a first empirical look," *LSD Journal*, 2013. Y C. Klesse, "Polyamorous Families: Parenting Practice, Stigma and Social Regulation," *Sociological Research Online*, 2018.

As I've said before, in some ways, the situation goes back to the time when we began to study the impact of separated couples on offspring and their development and integration. The hypotheses of the time suggested that the spread of divorce would result in an increase in crime, the abuse of minors, addiction to alcohol and drugs, weakening of the parent-child relationship, an increase in promiscuity, earlier loss of virginity, harm to mental health, higher suicide rates, deterioration of the educational level and thus lower probability of pursuing higher education, the risk of marginalization and impoverishment, and much more. Today, there is no need to comment on the extent to which these suggestions were misguided.

Observations from recent studies on parenting in non-normative structures already cited show that children's perceptions of the key figures in their lives are similar to that found in traditional models of extended family or of father-and-mother couples with previous histories of separation or widowhood. There is consideration for the different caregivers, or for the other kids one lives with, that is similar to the regard reported by those who have grown up with grandparents, aunts, uncles, cousins, or with their adoptive siblings, father, mother, etc.

The members of the network who have more frequent interaction and cohabitation are framed in roles closer to motherhood and fatherhood; those who demonstrate less intensity in relating to them are seen as very close but don't have that regard. The varying degrees of the affective sexual bonds between the adult members of the network generally have no bearing on the children's relationships with those adults, so any changes in those relationships (as long as there is no violence and abuse) are innocuous for them. After all, from their point of view, there are always more people available to take care of them, help them with their homework, read to them, tell them stories, or take them for a walk.

As a whole, in these studies, researchers have concluded that children seemed well-integrated in the structure; they're intelligent and have self-confidence, and they have typical "problems" for their age, such as frustration at having to share toys or not being able to make decisions about what to do, what to eat, and when to do so. The feeling was consistently one of relative abundance of resources in terms of people to play, share, and interact with.

As for adolescents, like most in their age group, their primary concerns were on identifying and differentiating themselves, both within their family network and in society at large. On some occasions, they negatively judged their family formats, considering the management of relationships to be too complex (at that age, they were already aware of it). In other cases, they were proud of it, compared to what they interpreted as scarcity and lack of care in the families of their fellow classmates and friends.

4.5 Models of life, cohabitation, and care

In relationship anarchy's approach, there are logically no aspects as specific as housing preferences, the choice of living together or not, what form that cohabitation, if chosen, takes, etc. But there is always the possibility of sharing time, resources, spaces, and moving toward a shared life to a greater or lesser extent with one or more people in a network of affections, which may be broader or narrower. The only thing that does stem directly from the approach is that the possibilities of cohabitation are not limited to those established by cultural normativity; they go much further. In this section, I discuss various possibilities in this regard and the aspects that may impact its development.

Intentional communities

French anarchist Emile Armand[154] compiled dozens of experiences of living together in communities that constituted true social experiments, especially between the end of the 19th century and the beginning of the 20th, in an extensive volume published in 1934.

---

154 Émile Armand, *Formas de vida en común sin Estado ni autoridad: las experiencias económicas y sexuales a través de la historia*, Innisfree, London, 2014.

Among them was the Colonia Cecilia in Brazil and its "loving camaraderie," the Oneida Community and its "sexual communism," the Home Colony in California, and the Vaux Libertarian Center in France. The latter's 1903 founding manifesto, for instance, reads:

> "In the Colony, no attempt will be made to apply any system, above all on love; monogamy will not be applied any more than polygamy, polyandry, or absolute community; we will strive to reach harmony as completely as possible, and each individual will determine their life accordingly. Each individual understands woman to have the same titles as man, since there will be complete abstraction of the sexes: only free individuals will be recognized. Consequently, whether or not [male] comrades have gone before the law to join their [female] companions, they will never be able to assert any proprietary right over women, nor will women be able to use any such rights in relation to men."

We've noted that the countercultural revolution analyzed in a previous chapter took place in the 1960s and early '70s. It is estimated that, in the U.S. alone, some tens of thousands of communities of cohabitation emerged,[155] hundreds of which still exist. They vary as much in character as those from six decades before, or more, and they constitute another large-scale attempt from which much can be learned.

Today, under the influence of networks as a new substrate for communication, the movement of so-called intentional communities is growing; they are the heirs of utopian communities, cooperative communities, and others. The meaning of the term "intentional" in this case quite appropriately connects with the notions of normativity and self-management. An intentional community is distinguished from a circumstantial community (any building, town, city, nation) because, in the former case, members have chosen to live in that community because of its goals and ways of operating; individ-

---

[155] Timothy Miller, *The 60's communes: Hippies and Beyond*, Syracuse University Press, New York, 2015.

uals join the latter by chance (birth, for example, or finding an attractive, affordable home there) or circumstances (work, school...) rather than the will or intention to live with and like the other members of that specific community.

To determine whether this attribute is applicable to a community, it must have at least two features: the intentional one, which I've already mentioned, and that of community – the common principles, values, and objectives that have to do with its way of life, on the one hand, and, on the other, a minimum level of solidarity, functional agreements, and processes for collective decision-making so that the community can run harmoniously. If there are no common objectives and agreements, we're looking at a circumstantial community. When asking members of these intentional communities how they describe their projects and experiences,[156] concepts such as commitment, mutual help, and cooperation surface.

In fact, one branch of this movement is communal anarchism, which includes these issues as primary axes while also adding the primary concepts of the community's conscious, responsible autonomy. They're based on the ideas that each member's activity is in line with their abilities, and that the resources and care each person receives are also in accordance with their needs. The absence of hierarchies and impositions is also a key element. The different groups would, in turn, relate to each other on the basis of those same principles, and so on.

The Fellowship for Intentional Communities website, www.ic.org, lists more than 1,000 communities around the world. The types of projects outlined are: communes (where virtually everything is shared), eco-villages (organized around ecology and sustainability), cohousing (individual houses on a community property), shared housing, student housing, spiritual or religious com-

---

156 According to the Fellowship for Intentional Communities's website: ic.org.

munities, eco-neighborhoods or transitional communities (which favor agroecology, permaculture, and degrowth), and finally, traditional or indigenous communities.

The communities' sizes vary greatly depending on the type of project and the particular issues at play in each case. Some descriptions list a maximum size that doesn't exceed the Dunbar number. This number was proposed by anthropologist Robin Dunbar[157] and roughly gives the number of individuals that can fully and effectively relate to one another in a group. Basing it on diverse experiments and assumptions involving groups of primates and humans, the size of the cerebral neocortex and its processing capacity, and several other factors, Dunbar determined this value to be 150.

The descriptions that appear are extraordinarily diverse and interesting to read. I've included two of these listings below: one rural European community (in Spain) and another urban North American location (in North Carolina, U.S.). The first is described as follows:

> "[People] ...between 42 to 63 years: With a clear decision to live in the country in contact with nature and the elements. With a serious inner work, aware of his/her ego and his/her personage, both of its light and darkness, for the sake of a healthy communication and living. Lovers of simple life, austerity and asceticism in a contemporary sense. With polyvalent ability to work in the different subsistence tasks: domestic (order, hygiene, kitchen, administration, etc.), gardening, maintenance, firewood, etc. With community and cooperative spirit, valuing likewise the need and respect to individuality. With financial solvency or a minimum savings made.
>
> The process of participation: 1) Introduce yourself as you consider. 2) Let's talk, first phone conversations. 3) Come for a trial period of 1 month. 4) If farovable on both sides, the stay extends

---

157 R. Dunbar, "Coevolution of neocortical size, group size and language in humans," *Behavioral and Brain Sciences*, 1993.

to 1 year. 5) After the first year, if still favorable and it is so desired one can be member of the project and built his/her individual space."

And the second:

"(...) is a diverse urban cohousing community guided by kindness, respect, and mutual support. Together we are creating an oasis of individual and community well-being. Our 5-story cohousing condominium (...) is within walking distance of a vital cafe and shopping district, a university campus and hospital, and public transit. Our indoor spaces are designed to be open and airy, blending with our woods-and-gardens environment, with indoor and outdoor spaces that support privacy, group activities, and neighborhood interaction. (...) [here] we can truly be ourselves in this diverse and welcoming mid-sized city full of history, culture, and charming neighborhoods

Membership is largely self-selecting. After filling out a membership questionnaire, potential members are invited to an information session and a plenary circle meeting. The meetings will give them a feel for what is involved in belonging to our community. If they choose to become members, they meet with one of our financial advisers to verify eligibility to purchase a condo. We require 20% equity as a down payment toward your condo unit purchase. There is no developer in this process, so every dollar invested goes toward purchase of the member's residence. Membership is capped at 23 households; if filled or if there is no available condominium that meets an interested party's needs, we welcome additions to our wait list through a defined process."

Cohabitation

Previously, when discussing the relationship escalator, we saw that two of the clearly distinguishable steps were "establishment," where habits are adjusted to those of the other person and making an effort to spend time together is both done and required; and "union," where they live in the same house, sharing expenses and basic assets. In a non-normative relationship style, these steps are not prescriptive, but they are an option. They're not limited to a specific number of people, nor do they require labels for the types of bonds – such as a couple, romantic, affective sexual, or friendship – nor do they presuppose a level of intimacy or specific practices; simply the willingness to share time, space, and essential parts of everyday life is, of course, a significant possibility.

It is clear that homes, their set-up, furniture, architecture, services, schedules, jobs, vehicles... almost everything in society is designed for a specific way of life: the traditional family. Some of these aspects are easy to adjust to alternative relationship models; others, not so much. But what are these models in more detail?

From least to most cohabitational involvement, the list would start with a configuration that does not involve sharing a home or physical assets. Time, affection, care, support, and dedication don't necessarily depend on where you live or what you have in common. Sometimes, some of the people you have relationships with may not live in the same city or country. In that case, you have to work out travel, which will depend on the geographical configuration of the network. On other occasions, there is seasonal cohabitation, which may be more or less symmetrical or balanced. Residence may be shared by each of the members in turn, or by several permanent members and others that come and go. Sometimes, they may enjoy seasonal residence, such as in the summer.

When there is permanent cohabitation, its members may organize themselves in a community with apartments in the same building, a cohousing model, or the same house with separate wings, rooms for each member, or sharing all rooms. Separate apartments have individual services; in co-housing, equipment and some basic services are shared; and in shared housing, cohabitation is more intimate.

In the next chapter, I will discuss some of these possibilities in the context of relationship anarchy from a more practical point of view.

Legal recognition of bonds

Analyzing the forms of relationship recognized in various State laws around the world is interesting because it characterizes what societies understand important and significant relationships to be, as opposed to those that do not have any legal significance, in a very precise way, although with some inertia or delay. This normative relevance goes hand in hand, except for the delay I've mentioned, with perceptions and customs, moving from traditional models to new common forms of relationships, such as couples that don't live together, people sharing a home after ceasing to be couple, the union of divorced people with children, homosexual partnerships, etc.

The canonical object of regulation in this regard is what various legal codes identify as "the family." The restrictiveness or scope given to this social element is not homogeneous. The preamble of the Universal Declaration of Human Rights, promulgated in 1948, offers a paradigmatic example that begins by identifying all of humanity as one great family. In its considerations, it establishes that "... the inherent dignity and of the equal and inalienable rights of all members of the human family is the foundation of freedom, justice and peace in the world." However, on delving into the details, it adheres to the principles of Western monotheistic societies, leaving no room for ambiguity or social development beyond the traditional institution of marriage. In article 16, section 1, it says, "Men and women of full age, without any limitation due to race, nationality or religion, have the right to marry and to found a family. They are entitled to equal rights as to marriage, during marriage and at its dissolution" Section 2 goes on to say: "Marriage shall be entered into only with the free and full consent of the intending spouses." Section 3 reads: "The family is the natural and fundamental group unit of society and is entitled to protection by society and the State." Article 25, section 2, though, rightly uncouples the protection of children from their preferential family model, saying: "All children, whether born in or out of wedlock, shall enjoy the same social protection."

The same protection, seen from a more modern approach that is more respectful of diversity, was mandated in an international legal treaty adopted forty years later in 1989: the Convention on the Rights of the Child. Its preamble says: "... Convinced that the family, as the fundamental group of society and the natural environment for the growth and well-being of all its members and particularly children, should be afforded the necessary protection and assistance so that it can fully assume its responsibilities within the community, recognizing that the child, for the full and harmonious development of his or her personality, should grow up in a family environment, in an atmosphere of happiness, love and understanding," and in article 5, it refers to the family not in terms of matrimony, as in the previous case, by as follows: "States Parties shall respect the responsibilities, rights and duties of parents or, where applicable, the members of the extended family or community as provided for by local custom, legal guardians or other persons legally responsible for the child." And the rest of the document talks about "family" or the "family environment" without specifying any special formats or restrictions.

The breadth of the definition of the family group and the reference to extended family or community surely has more to do with respect for the different cultures around the world (many of which were still considered backward and primitive by the "advanced" West in the 1940s) than with any predictions of what could be new forms of relationship.

In a recent work,[158] Alejandro Martínez Torío analyzed how the new relationship models fit (though he focuses on polyamory, maintaining the hegemonic anchor to amatonormativity and, therefore, moving away from the work's introduction on the approaches of relationship anarchy) in various legal systems, including the civil code of Catalonia. The first distinction that Martínez Torío makes targets

---

158 A. Martínez Torío, "El Poliamor a debate," *Revista Catalana de Dret Privat [Societat Catalana d'Estudis Jurídics]*, 2017.

precisely one of the key conceptual differences between polyamory and relational anarchy, ensuring that:

> "Nor should polyamory be confused with the cohabitational situations of mutual aid that the second book of the Civil Code of Catalonia (CCCat) regulates, which consist of the cohabitation of two or more people in the same habitual residence who share, without compensation and with a desire to live together over time and help each other, common expenses, domestic work, or both. Thus, they constitute a cohabitational relationship that is governed by the agreements that have been stipulated or, failing that, by what is established in title IV of said regulation.
>
> (...) Article 240-2 of the second book of the Catalan Civil Code establishes that persons of legal age united by kinship ties on a collateral line, without any limit of degree, and those who have relationships of simple friendship or companionship may constitute a cohabitational relationship of mutual aid, as long as they are not united by a marital bond or form a stable couple with another person with whom they live. Here, then, we find another difference with respect to polyamory, which does require a stable affective bond between their members; on the other hand, forming polyamorous relationships does not require cohabitation in the same habitual residence."

To me, it is striking that a civil code (this is only one example – there are many other cases of legal entities that could be cited[159]) establishes a specific distinction around bonds of "simple" friendship and companionship. To begin with, qualifying these concepts as simple (in addition to being horrible nonsense in ethical and aesthetic terms) very clearly outlines the hegemonic moral substrate and, above all, implies that a difference can be legally established be-

---

159 There are also exceptions, such as the advanced Portuguese Law no. 6/2001, dated May 11, on Shared Economy, which has been in effect since 2001. This law does not put any conditions on recognizing the union of several people who share housing and economy, and it equates this situation to that of a marital union in many significant respects.

tween some types of relationships and others. This recognition explicitly allows the State authority to inquire about the nature of people's relationships down to the most intimate level. In legislative areas like immigration, the recognition of a migrant's nationality by association with someone who is a national of the receiving country (which must necessarily take the form of marriage) becomes an extreme case of this interference, with investigations, questionnaires, confrontations, entrapment... all to find out whether the relationship is "real" or "one of convenience." This is not only an abominable coercive practice, a violation of privacy, and an attack on an individual's most fundamental dignity: it doesn't make any rational sense. It's intended to distinguish an agreement that seeks to "satisfy certain needs for support between the parties" from an agreement that seeks to "satisfy certain needs for support between the parties" – that is, to differentiate between two things that are the same. The distinction is that there are some needs that are morally accepted and others that aren't.

In line with trying to widen the legal loopholes so that the rights of those who have decided to relate to others in different ways begin to be recognized, proposals have been made based on different sensibilities[160] that propose a path through strategic essentialism (using essentialist arguments for legal and political purposes, even if you don't agree with them). It's about making the argument that new relationship styles must consider sexual orientations (or traits alongside these) to take advantage of the ground gained by the LGBTIQ+ community, which has achieved visibility and recognition of rights like those associated with egalitarian marriage in many countries.

Of course, relationship anarchy can hardly be understood as an alternative to marriage. Thinking that the fight for recognizing plu-

---

160 Some of these are collected in C. Klesse, "Marriage, Law and Polyamory: Rebutting Mononormativity with Sexual Orientation Discourse?," *Oñati Socio-legal Series*, 2016.

ral forms of marriage could be one of its aims doesn't seem reasonable. In any case, it would be presented as a fight against the binaries, amatonormativity, and allosexism contained in the legal codes of different States, as illustrated by the examples I've already mentioned in this regard. The "enemies" to be defeated: gender as a limiting and defining factor; the differentiation between a view of love as help, support, companionship, care, respect, consideration, passion, and dedication (not necessarily all at once) and its substitute, printed and initialed on paper with the State seal; and finally, sex as the center of the moral/legal system of relationships.

Chapter 5. A way of sharing based on commitments and boundaries: relational keys

> "Simplicity and sincerity generally go hand in hand, as both proceed from a love of truth."
>
> — Mary Wollstonecraft

Up to this point, I have tried to bring together, interpret, and contextualize all the information possible on relationship anarchy. This proposal emerged in the anarchist environments of Northern Europe; at little more than a decade old, it has been the subject of a variety of analyses and has come to be understood in different ways from a wide range of perspectives. My interpretation has focused on a collective, feminist, queer, and openly political perspective, lifestyle politics as the source of a revolution from the ground up. The time has come to touch down. All the theoretical constructs, the references to trends of thought, criticisms of ideologies and structures that set up gradients of power, authority, and domination, and the narratives of struggles and rebellions have to become tangible.

5.1 Touching down

Anyone who agrees with the key aspects and the direction of the last four chapters will be interested in the practical results I build toward based on these in this chapter. They are inferences and conclusions that stem directly from those essential foundations, steering clear of magic formulas, expert prescriptions, and well-intentioned recommendations and advice. If the hypothesis intrigued you, this part is how it translates to the everyday reality of relationships.

If you've not been interested in the theoretical framework developed so far, what comes next will probably not be inspiring. But you never know. Sometimes, the rhythm is more seductive than the melody, or the melody is more so than the lyrics... and petrichor, that scent of rain on dry lands, can more than make up for a summer outing interrupted by stormy weather.

Individual respect and cultural criticism

I wouldn't be proposing anything new by saying that all people are worthy of respect and consideration simply by being people, unlike opinions, ideas, or actions, which do not always deserve that recognition. I understand that many behaviors (whether aggressive, cruel, or criminal) are not respectable or tolerable, nor are many ideologies (those which are violent, authoritarian, or irrational). However, those who carry out such behaviors or defend those ideologies are still people and are therefore at least deserving of the guarantees and privileges of the Universal Declaration of Human Rights, an inalienable ethical basis.

By way of analogy, there would be similar applications in the field of relationships when we empty them of normativity, as proposed throughout the previous chapters. Relationships are established among people who, as such, deserve a certain minimum of consideration, respect, and deference. Relationships themselves can take a thousand forms and may be the object of much more critical, provocative analyses that are not as constrained by any minimal requirements. In other words, there are specific relationship styles and behaviors that, based on ethical principles, may be deemed inappropriate, harmful, or unacceptable, and others that may seem healthy and proper. These are discretionary assessments – moral judgments – yet they're ethically grounded and legitimate and may be useful in practice.

Therefore, the key aspects that I will inquire about in this chapter are of two different types: those that apply to people and those that apply to relationships. As a fundamental belief, I must reiterate that the former category goes beyond moralities, worldviews, ideologies, beliefs, and utopias. They are anchored in the rights of the individual that have been established throughout history. Relationships, however, can be set up according to principles that are compatible with the fundamentals of relationship anarchy to varying degrees; I will consider these configurations to be subject to analysis and opinions. Based on the conclusions developed so far, there are relationship traits that surface as toxic, authoritarian, coercive, individualistic, selfish, patriarchal... As I said at the beginning of the book, I'm not seeking equidistance but radicalism in its most committed sense. This is where this assault on domesticated civility is especially fitting: respect for people does not extend to ideologies, thoughts, or practices and behaviors.

However, in a sphere as significant and complex as that of relationships, the radical commitment to ideals requires thoroughly positioning the perspective from which it is formulated. This book is written from the awareness of a specific position, the result of ideas and evaluations developed in the first part of the book and complemented with a long history of active listening to the experiences and contributions of many; still, the distillation, composition, and above all, the positioning from which they are illustrated are personal and, therefore, partial. I think that must stay at the forefront during these pages, an active awareness that the point of view presented is cisgender male, heterosexual, white, European, intellectual, and urban. This defines a perspective that is inevitably Western, rationalist, and ableist, one far from other interpretations that are needed. Combining different points of view, not just staying with this one, is essential; it goes beyond complementary – it is the foundation needed for understanding.

Relationship cartography

Perhaps the analytical and relatively dispassionate prism offered by this perspective is useful, but it only offers a cartography. In this case, the general map of the most common relationship approaches is illustrated in the following figure. It is an archipelago with two main islands. In the largest area, amatonormativity reigns, and three cultures coexist. The central and northeast regions are based on affective and affective-sexual exclusivity, respectively. The southwestern corner does not uphold this normative trait, nor do the cultural fragments in the coastal areas influenced by the small island. The different regions of the big island, in this case delimited by borders and not by shades of gray, represent specific styles of relationships. Of course, the continent, society as a whole, cannot be seen: it would be to the northeast of the archipelago, enormous compared to the islands and completely filled with a uniform dark gray.

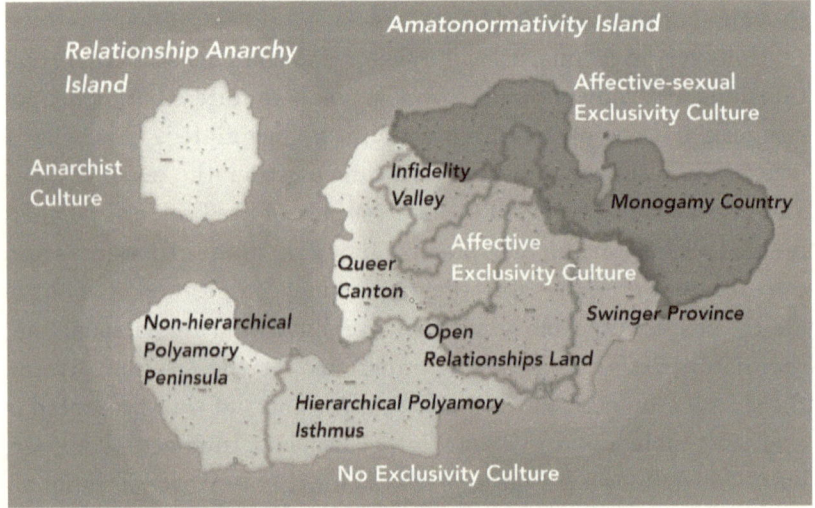

Map of the most common relationship approaches.

The approach I'm proposing to describe and tour these territories will start from the critique of normative thought, but not of its specific content in the context and time where each individual lives; I will consider any one of those contexts to be as legitimate as any other. The critique will instead focus on its structural dimension and its adoption as psychological and emotional automatism. In other words, the goal of this chapter is to bring as many questions, attitudes, and automatic behaviors as can be identified to the surface, always in the field of relationships, and to offer arguments and tools for reflection and analysis so that they become self-managed critical opinions (individually or, better yet, collectively, in networks) following and relying on the results and conclusions of the long journey of searching and inquiry that I've illustrated in the previous four chapters. Each of the reflections I'm going to raise, some in the form of a proposal, others as questions, warnings, or indications to tug at a subjective thread, will always have the specific purpose of highlighting something that can be taken for granted; I'm proposing for it not to be assumed, but to be assessed. The examination may be more or less expeditious, more cautious or more challenging, more reflective or more emotional, but the awareness that at least one moment of critical observation has been devoted to it will mark the difference between normative submission and relationship self-management. I don't know if that effort will have positive results. Under no circumstances should it be understood as a solution to anything. It's something I can do if I feel the need or desire to do so. It is just a possibility.

5.2 Critical deconstruction of the ideology of the couple

Imagine being in a conversation or at a meeting and asking to talk about desire and commitment without using the term "couple." You will soon realize that it's not easy. This idea is so prevalent and rooted in conscious and unconscious thought that even those who have defied many social mandates and live in a free, alternative, independent way end up talking about it even if it is in the plural. As a legitimated vessel of affection, sexuality, and coexistence, the couple constitutes a true ideology, with most of the features historically and sociologically attributed to this concept. In his influential work *The Sublime Object of Ideology*, Žižek writes:[161]

> "The most elementary definition of ideology is probably the well-known phrase from Marx's *Capital:* 'sie wissen das nicht, aber sie tun es' – 'they do not know it, but they are doing it.' The very concept of ideology implies a kind of basic, constitutive naivete: the misrecognition of its own presuppositions, of its own effective conditions, a distance, a divergence between so-called social reality and our distorted representation, our false consciousness of it. That is why such a 'naive consciousness' can be submitted to a critical-ideological procedure. The aim of this procedure is to lead the naive ideological consciousness to a point at which it can recognize its own effective conditions, the social reality that it is distorting, and through this very act dissolve itself. In the more sophisticated versions of the critics of ideology – that developed by the Frankfurt School, for example – it is not just a question of seeing things (that is, social reality) as they 'really are,' of throwing away the distorting spectacles of ideology; the main point is to see how the reality itself cannot reproduce itself without this so-called ideological mystification. The mask is not simply hiding the real state of things; the ideological distortion is written into its very essence."[162]

But following a pragmatic critical approach, what are the keys that can help me deconstruct this thought (which is neither reconstructing nor reformulating or articulating it in another way), a thought that all my mental and emotional routines recur to repeatedly and

---

161 S. Žižek, *The Sublime Object of Ideology*, Verso, New York, 1989.

162 Along these lines, ultra-conservative sectors are attempting to instill the notion of *gender ideology* as a tool to discredit feminist movements and the struggle for LGBTIQ+ rights. It originates from the Vatican State's opposition to the United Nations international conferences in 1994 and 1995 on population and development and on women, where *sexual and reproductive rights* were recognized using the term *gender*. Their strategy is established and disseminated each year at the World Congress of Families, and it is taken up by far-right forces around the world, especially in countries where they enjoy significant power.

constantly? I will review the axes and arguments found in the third and fourth chapters, bearing in mind that I will not seek to provide the ingredients or recipes to cook some alternative order, but the tools first to visibilize and then challenge the meal that has been universally presented to me as the sole obligatory option.

Couple privilege

The first challenge I come up against at the start of a relationship (even within the framework of the shared will to follow the principles of relationship anarchy or other similar principles) is that of the tendency to visibly label it with the "partner brand" and to demand, or at least to hope and wish for the privileges that this badge entails. I automatically tend to demand special attention from the other person or people and more dedication than what they give to those whom I don't identify as their partners. If I can renounce those categories, internalizing that resignation as much as possible, I will have then managed to avoid many problems: all the ones that stem from the automatic configuration of permanent structural demand. I'll then develop the idea that demand is an important factor in wearing away at appetites and passions, so a continued source of demand is potentially a persistent mechanism in destroying desire (in its broadest sense, not just the erotic one).

On the other hand, you might think I have the "right to establish" some minimal boundaries on the level of dedication I require to be comfortable, or to consider a bond to be significant. From my point of view, it is an understandable temptation, but as a supposed right, this requires assuming that I have power over the other person's time and reality; that doesn't make sense as a boundary since it doesn't refer to my own body or time, nor does it imply that there is some question of consent.

What does make sense is for my reaction to a level of interaction or dedication that is insufficient for me to include distancing myself, changing my priorities, or reducing the attention I give to communication or contacts. I understand that, as long as these possibilities are not used as a warning, threat, or blackmail, they are totally legitimate expressions of my conscious and responsible autonomy.

In short, I believe that exercising couple privilege, in addition to being questionable from an ethical point of view, supposes an erosion of bonds. The response to a perceived lack of interest from other people should not be handled through the invocation of a supposed right, but by fitting one's attitude to the circumstance. Though this is actually considered a right according to the ideology of the couple, this presumed right does not exist as such under the hypotheses of relationship anarchy but as a privilege, where it exists at all. The two most significant difficulties are, perhaps, how to just walk away from a level of attention that is attractive to me and that I want – and that I come to think that I need at all costs to be happy – and how to communicate what I feel without that becoming a demand or a pressure.

The first question of moving away from demanding a supposed right, from insistence, and from reiteration depends, on the one hand, on my motivation: if I have unwavering conviction in how I want to relate to others or in not wanting to contribute to a situation where some flaunt the privilege of being able to make decisions that affect others and, by extension, third parties, by following the most basic sense of solidarity and justice, I will have the necessary motivation to make the effort to avoid these scenarios. On the other hand, it also depends on not living in a situation of lack. The continual privation of affective stimuli, vital sensations, or pleasant breaks from monotony creates a state of need that doesn't leave any room for moral imperatives.

For instance, ecclesiastical celibacy, normative monogamy, and other structures of potential prolonged repression of desire often generate behaviors that range from anxiety to abuse and violence. Even with strong motivation, states of anxiety and lack make it more difficult to maintain behaviors that respect other's autonomy. It is therefore important to take this possibility into account as well to avoid reactive attitudes that may generate even more anxiety and pain. Normally, things are only relatively easy – and not even that – when everyone is in a good place individually and possesses certain material conditions, psychological capacities and tools, self-knowledge, self-control...

The second issue – communication without demand – depends on aspects similar to the first one: motivation and ability. First of all, I must be clear that I don't want to express my wishes (which I can often subjectively perceive as my needs) in such a way that they become obligations imposed on other people, beyond responsible, voluntary commitment on their part. I also have to be able to renounce that communication without feeling as though I am repressing or curtailing my freedom of expression. It's a complex balance, and my impression is that it should be weighed as a cost-benefit calculation: if I express all my impulses and desires, even going so far as reproaching when they're not fulfilled, I am being transparent and exercising my assertiveness; at the same time, I may be applying pressure and giving rise to more or less subtle emotional coercion and blackmail.

These coercions and blackmail will alter the character of the relationship and have negative consequences (at least from the perspective of relationship anarchy). There's no simple formula, but somehow the burden of conflict management must be shared between those who want more and those who want less. Another consideration is that boundaries must always be respected, and there is thus a very clear final ethical basis in establishing minimums, boundaries, and consent.

Expectations

Predefined expectations (due to hegemonic normativity) are another of the key ingredients for the ideology of the couple. Those that emerge automatically as personal aspirations of the members of the relationships would be internal expectations; external expectations would be the ones that represent the expected progress towards which the family and social environment trusts that any bond will be directed.

External expectations are mechanically aligned with hegemonic normativity or, in other words, with the relationship escalator model and the myths around romantic love. To some extent, they can be adapted to what the environment perceives as peculiarities of the people in the relationship (always two in monogamous normativity; more than two in non-monogamous models of minority normativities), but there are strong limits on such adaptations. Those limits will be more or less expansive depending on the sociocultural environment where the process takes place.

Nowadays, at least in some environments within urban Western societies, the necessary measures of rebellion, tenacity, and character that make it possible to counterbalance external expectations are relatively attainable. Some act under the weight of these influences, but many others can relativize them in such a way that they don't bear a fundamental weight on our decisions.

It is also important to consider the relationship that exists between the judgments and prejudices that my social environment conveys to me and the image I project to that environment. These are opinions I may be able to manage, but they can be annoying or even harmful in the long run. It's yet another reason to avoid labels, stereotypes, and reproducing the hegemonic models. If I behave like a normative partner with someone, even if I am not, the environment will read "normative partner" and apply the corresponding expectations. There are two options: avoiding the use of labels and incorporating the normative ways of acting and expressing yourself into your own life, or else accepting the applicable consequences of the expectations and prejudices associated with them. However, internal expectations are not so easy to overcome. First of all, identifying them is not so simple. It's not about external forces wanting to impose a way of acting on me that I don't share. It's my thinking that comes up with a set of perspectives and projects future scenarios that I logically perceive as my own and would swear are the sole product of my personal determination. But when I examine them, they coincide with what is expected of me and my relationships in many respects.

Of course, this is not about automatically rejecting anything that might raise suspicions of being "too normal." "Normal" actually has many advantages. It just seems interesting to take my expectations apart and critically examine them, applying a certain amount of intellectual and personal honesty to that critical analysis, without going beyond a relatively healthy level of demand, without going into an obsessive pursuit of unattainable, absolute objectivity and coherence.

Affective sexual scarcity

If we're playing at analyzing it from an algebraic point of view, the hegemonic structure of bonds establishes a binary relationship of an unreflective, symmetrical, intransitive sort in the set of all people. Furthermore, if we restrict ourselves to heteronormative morality, this binary relationship defines a one-to-one correspondence between the set of men and that of women. In economic terms, this would mean that each individual need to pair off would, when satisfied, capture a resource exclusively, removing it from the set of goods for the long-term, thus unleashing a crisis of scarcity in a stationary regime. This entertaining game of analogies leads to outcomes that are often not so fun; despite affecting many people, we don't perceive these directly because they occur in a context of cultural immersion. They have been and are in effect all the time; they constitute what's normal, natural. This is a scenario where not being assigned to a partner is a situation that can only be considered satisfactory if it is temporary. In the long term, not addressing that circumstance means failure. When such an assignment occurs, the goal is to make it last over time. This isn't always possible, and a rupture is yet again considered defeat.

But if the "normal" situation is being in a couple, while the opposite is only tolerable for a certain period, say 10% of the time for simplicity's sake, the ratio of people who are "available" at any given time will be only 10 % of the population. This will then generate an even greater sense of the scarcity of opportunities and fear of being in that situation. This fear may prolong the periods that individuals stay with a partner, beyond when it is "truly comfortable." This will lead to a feedback loop, a vicious circle where the fear of loneliness lengthens the time as a couple. This reduces the percent of people available for a new pairing, which in turn accentuates the fear of loneliness, and so on... In addition, anxiety will lead to the minimum conditions we demand of the other person to relax, and the probability of spending more time "really at ease" decreases even more and the extra "bonus" time is longer and more painful every time.

There is a note of dystopian parody in this hypothesis and in the caricatured description of that scenario, but there is also a backdrop of sad reality. In fact, the economic analogy serves us even more if we compare this situation with the economies of scarcity.

In economic regimes where a population or group is suffering from a state of scarcity, the mechanisms of production and consumption are close to a subsistence economy and are characterized by a very low level of creativity and openness. Goods, ideas, and opportunities are not easily shared, and although there may be specific movements of solidarity and unity, people become possessive and selfish in an extreme situation.[163]

In our societies, scarcity is used as a sales pitch. We tend to perceive something as more valuable when it is offered to us with the

---

[163] Recently, there has been growing interest in what has been called post-scarcity economics, proposed by anarchist author Murray Bookchin (M. Bookchin, *Post-Scarcity Anarchism*, Black Rose Books, Montreal, 1986). This concept is linked to another growing movement, the transhumanist movement (H+): this cultural hypothesis studies how using technology to overcome the limits that the environment and biology have historically imposed will affect human beings. In this case, what will happen when there is no shortage of consumer goods (when they are not subject to supply and demand and they don't have a set price or limit) is analyzed. It's the utopia of a world where the meaning of ownership would gradually disappear, and where people would only maintain their attachment to goods of sentimental value; for all other goods, there would be no limits on access or replacement.

label of exclusivity and declared to be not available to everyone. Advertising messages try to create a feeling of competition among the potential audience by saying that something is available in limited quantities, for a certain time only, or is simply so expensive that few people can afford it, and if I can buy it, it means that I belong to an exclusive and privileged elite.

Recent experiments, like the one by Lee and Seidle[164] featuring watch ads described as "limited edition," "exclusive," or "limited supply," versus those like "latest model," "available," or "large assortment in stock," showed that on average customers would pay up to 50% more for the first ones. The feeling of scarcity, urgency, is also used to cloud and disturb the judgment of those who receive these messages. The ability to compare, calculate, and establish measures and contrasts rationally decreases dramatically when there is a certain level of anxiety and nervousness in the sale or negotiation procedure.

Considering the pros and cons of a decision requires a relatively calm state of mind. When my brain assumes that it is operating in a context of scarcity, rapid, visceral reaction mechanisms are set in motion that exaggeratedly value highly conspicuous short-term factors and ignore significant longer-term aspects. In psychology, terms like "tunnel vision" or "goal inhibition" are used because I not only act more in the short term, but I also overvalue one goal and forget the importance and impact of others that my unconscious will begin to consider secondary. Under these conditions, a balanced evaluation of costs and benefits becomes difficult. Decisions are made impulsively because they are mediated by constraints on the supply. Not only do the decision-making processes suffer; my perception of successes and let-downs, of hopes and losses, is also impacted. The significance and impact of each spell is magnified compared to how you would react in other circumstances. The impulses

---

164 S.Y. Lee, R. Seidle, "Narcissists as consumers: The effects of perceived scarcity on processing of product information," *Social Behavior and Personality*, 2012.

for possession and control are triggered by the insecurity caused by the sensation of falling into the void when abandoned and not having a support network to catch you. The perception of a world of affective scarcity leads to emotional dependence and anxiety.

One of the myths of romantic love, the myth of our better half, reinforces this cognitive distortion in an extraordinary way. We've been taught that there is only one person in the world for us. We soon learn that this is perhaps an exaggeration, but if it's not just one, there are only a few. After all, we're special and selective because exclusivity gives things value, and there's nothing more plain and ordinary than saying, "I'm open to everything." When it comes to choosing our romantic partner, we bring up issues that we would never consider, for example, with offspring. This is because there is no myth that there's just one special, perfect little being free from defects that fate has in store for us, who will fulfill all our longings – and that having more babies as that first one grows up is a betrayal. In addition to constituting an economic scenario, the threat of scarcity has historically been exploited by reactionary ideologies as a political strategy: the strata most heavily punished by the system, by its injustices, inequalities, and crises (or what we're made to believe are crises, though they are actually the consequence of unilateral ruptures by the elites of the already precarious social balances) take refuge in a struggle over the crumbs against those who are even more vulnerable: migrants, refugees, those who are racialized, the poorest, those who are stigmatized because of their culture, language, or origin. The liberal populist modus operandi of turning the next-to-last against those who are behind them has worked for centuries, and it continues to be a political success at many times and in many places.

The paradigm of consumption, supply and demand, continuous growth, and the created needs for aspirational goods (which don't respond to real needs but to the search for status) as bases of the socioeconomic system also lead to an artificial construct that could be described as the feeling of an "induced shortage." This construct is fed by elements of personal lifestyle such as the relationship escalator, and at the same time, it feeds them, always rushing onward with growing needs, obligations, and financial and personal burdens that seem to have no end in sight. Or it surfaces as the objectification of people: the tendency to establish consumer relationships where I seek to satisfy a desire without considering the other's wishes. I don't see them as another human being but as part of what's available (and not in metaphorical terms as an exercise of analysis and parallelism like this one, but unfortunately, in a literal internalized sense).

In a society that's thoroughly riddled with consumption, it's difficult to get around a sense of ownership over the people around us, especially when certain rights of belonging are socially recognized, as in the case of couples, or that of sons and daughters (for those who are legal minors, however, the circumstances are different and specific as there is an ongoing process of personality formation and moral, legal, and material responsibilities). In privileged situations, such as that which men hold in patriarchal societies or in new normativities such as polyamory or other forms of non-monogamy, the idea of possession is extended to frequently give rise to a tendency toward accumulation. Coming from where we come from and living where we live, in capitalist societies based on unlimited growth and consumption, facing the possibility of owning more than one good often leads to the tendency to accumulate more – the more, the merrier.

Desire and desires

An unsustainable escalation in the search for satisfying needs – whether basic or aspirational – and for their specific instances in the form of desires constitutes precisely the key element of the capitalist model of consumption. Though people's desires are many throughout life, there is a specific modality that aims to break away from the pack, to stand alone, to be "The Desire" in capital letters. It is the allosexist dogma framed in the ideology of the reproductive couple that gives special significance to desires of a sexual nature, singling them out and turning them into a noun that is articulated by its own grammatical number to distinguish itself from the rest of humankind's appetites and desires.

But what particular thing does desire act on in its hegemonic conception? What is it heading toward, and what do its intensity and focus depend on? The answer can be summed up in a very illustrative concept: erotic or sexual capital. This is about symbolic capital, again a parallel borrowed from the economic world. It falls along the lines of Pierre Bourdieu's "cultural capitals"[165] that Catherine Hakim compiles[166] in a controversial interpretation that claims to be feminist, yet which contains significant, dark aspects that refer to a neoliberal, fundamentally patriarchal conception of social interactions. This is an example of neofeminism or post-feminism that actually cloaks the anti-feminist notion that we've already reached a playing field where men and women are on equal footing. Women, then, just have to take advantage of the opportunities within their reach yet which they still can't see (they have to open their eyes), opportunities including their sexual capital.

But I think that the concept itself is useful precisely to understand why that image is toxic under a radical feminist gaze and a relationship anarchist philosophy. Erotic capital, even if we strip it of the gender perspective and treat it as an undifferentiated personal trait, embodies the quintessential power gradient in relationships.[167] It isn't the only factor that tends to unbalance the scales –

---

165 P. Bourdieu, "The Forms of Capital." Pp. 241-258 in *Handbook of Theory and Research for the Sociology of Education,* edited by J. G. Richardson. Greenwood Press, New York, 1986.

166 C. Hakim, *Erotic Capital: The Power of Attraction in the Boardroom and the Bedroom.* Basic Books, New York, 2011.

167 In fact, I think that in this case, the gender perspective would work just the opposite of how Hakim suggests it would: in relationships, significant erotic capital in a person read as a woman hypersexualizes, impedes, conditions, and creates as many long-term problems as it does short-term benefits. It is by no means the first

I've already spoken of many factors – but it is one of the most visible and surely the least structural, the most individualized. And it is perhaps also one of the most difficult to manage and deconstruct.

I don't have any recipes for this management (or almost anything else not prepared on a stove or in an oven), but again, I'll dare to outline the role the principles and theoretical conclusions I've arrived at in previous chapters could play. If it's a question of approaching desire from a perspective removed from amatonormativity and allosexism, overcoming the hegemonic idea that "The Desire," the one that's important, valuable above all else, is sexual (as I said, we refer to all other desires with the same word but in the plural, as if we dissolved them through multiplicity) and even more valuable if it is associated with the affective, perhaps a first step we could take would be making it into a cross-cutting issue. Cross-cutting "The Desire" to discover "the desires."

Deconstructing desire is an aspiration that is often discussed in writings and environments for reflecting on ethical non-monogamies. The objective is to analyze whether gender, sexual characteristics, body aesthetics, ways of dressing, moving, or seducing that stimulate me, and so on coincide with those promoted by heteronormative culture and, if so, to question it. After all, the non-monogamous community has made an effort to deconstruct the cultural mandate of sexual and affective exclusivity and, in many cases, some of the elements of the patriarchy that are supported by those exclusivities leading to behaviors of objectification, possession, and control. Ultimately, it's about trying to redirect desire to other bodies, aesthetics, ages, games, etc.

But cross-cutting instead of deconstructing could be, as I've said, a goal that's more in line with relationship anarchy: breaking the boundaries of what I like and am attracted to, not only thinking about physical intimacy but other practices, as well. It can be easier,

---

time that a vector of oppression has turned positive qualities into obstacles and inconveniences, or even into factors that directly breed violence.

less self-repressive, self-blaming, and self-coercive to think about what I like to do with someone and what I enjoy with them (in the singular or plural) rather than to determine the particulars of attraction a priori in the physical, in the sexual arousal, and try to focus specifically on what stimulates me in that particular moment. A cross-cutting reconstruction of desire that pluralizes it, that manages to encompass more perspectives and more joyful behaviors without privileging or prioritizing pleasures, just as I try to do with affections.

Lack and precariousness as starting points

The ideology of the couple starts from the idea that a lone individual is incomplete; only by forming a dyadic union do they become a full member of society and life. Therefore, the search for relationships is approached out of lack. I'm missing half of my whole, and if I can capture it, I will have achieved success in terms of relationships. But if I lose it, if it gets away from me, if it rejects me, I'm back to a situation of loneliness and failure.

Lack as a starting point generates unhealthy behaviors that are highly recognizable, and the fear of returning to that state causes even more harmful consequences. It's the ideal companion for scarcity: it isn't easy to find someone who complements me, and being unsuccessful in the search means that I continue to be a truncated, imperfect being. Structural lack leads to structural fear and the need for attention as normalized behavior, the constant demand for normative inspiration – normative meaning it is enshrined in law and is where obligation arises from. Duty quenches desire, or at least they're two points that are galaxies away from each other in the emotional universe. This also creates positive feedback: more demand creates more disinterest, more withdrawal. It then fuels insecurity and produces an attitude of even greater demand.

Breaking the loop isn't easy, but it's very important to do so as soon as possible. To that end, that loop's operation must be recognized, and one must act from both ends, drawing heavily on will and solidarity, bearing in mind that the answer cannot be docility or submission, nor can it be rejection or imposition.

From the point of view of relationship anarchy, bonding is important, valuable, perhaps even vital, but all bonds are worthwhile. There is no mandate to concentrate the entire set of values, duties, and attributions that the myths of romantic love impose into just one person. I start out from the wealth of a network that supports me, cares for me, and will be there for me. I have room for more stimuli, more magnetism, more passion, more understanding, all of that – or just a part of it. I can care for others more, and they can take care of me more, learn more, and enjoy more. And my latest interest may fit my life sustainably, but if it doesn't, it won't be so dramatic or a terrible failure.

Voluntary, intentional, responsible commitments

The norm dictates that each type of relationship entails different commitments, no more nor less. I expect and offer the commitments associated with the label I apply to my bond. And I'm reassured by the promise that precisely the same commitments are expected and offered. I may find it more difficult to take them on, I may just break them, I may not have even considered whether I need them to be provided. All the same, I still hope they do, and it hurts me if I find out or suspect that those commitments are being violated. Because, even if I have never brought them up, breaking them means I've been cheated on. It's cheating because "it's understood" that those norms have to be respected.

Researcher Elizabeth Brake introduced the term amatonormativity[168] to refer to the collectively accepted axiom that a relationship must be romantic, a couple, exclusive, sexually satisfying, if possi-

---

168 E. Brake *Minimizing Marriage: Marriage, Morality, and the Law*, Oxford University Press, Oxford, 2012. E. Brake, "Do Subversive Weddings Challenge Amatonormativity? Polyamorous Weddings and Romantic Love Ideals," *Analize – Journal of Gender and Feminist Studies*, 2018.

ble, socially recognized, and better when heterosexual and reproductive so that, in that relationship, the most culturally significant commitments are credible and reliable. In fact, as I've mentioned, these commitments – basically perpetuity, care, shared goods, and fidelity – appear automatically, without further ado.

Relationship anarchy proposes a rebellion against this amatonormative pattern and positive, active insubordination that brings us together, that makes us committed, that allows us to weave alliances of care, feelings, complicity, affection, passion. Everything at once or not, always headed south or traveling in unpredictable paths, in intimacy or a larger ring, in a loose net or a tight warp, in a network of constant communication or a wide space of respectful intimacy, thoughtfully or carelessly, with your feet on the ground or flying high with hopes and dreams... It's also about making sure that commitments are no less responsible or less valuable in some cases than in others, no less free, voluntary, or sincere. But this isn't so easy: if nothing is planned, predefined, pre-cooked, then everything has to be built from scratch and decided on without standard itineraries. Among the many difficulties I can find in putting this into practice, the most basic ones are: how to distinguish a free and voluntary commitment from a concession stemming from an implicit agreement associated with imbalances of power and lack of assertiveness? Or if I assume that everything is balanced and sincere, how can I make sure that my commitments today are not the basis of a coercive structure for myself or others tomorrow?

In the first place, the most important thing is for the commitments not to be arbitrary; they must have a meaning, and they must respond to reasons that are shared and analyzed. In many cases, only with this exercise of communication and reflection will we be able to avoid the most common pitfalls where we bear expectations that don't really exist, or take needs for granted that aren't actually so important. Secondly, when analyzing commitments, we should remember that other people, other situations, and all sorts of changes may arise in the future... and build them together, taking these eventualities into account as much as possible, as far as we can predict. Third and lastly, if we remember that commitments are not clauses of a contract or an agreement, nor immutable dogmas, nor State laws or social norms imposed beyond our control, we will keep changes from causing ruptures, deceit, or betrayal. My fidelity is towards other people, not to the commitments themselves, and certainly not to the relationship labels that automatically invoke them.

The exercise of loyalty consists of discussing any factor that affects my relationship with the commitments taken on: if it is hard for me to fulfill them, if I find them to be uncomfortable, if they are becoming obsolete, or if I'm noticing any of these things in someone else. This is a fundamental difference from a normative relationship model, where the norm is determined by my type of bond; if I want to modify it, I have to change the relationship's category – in practice, that means destroying the relationship to replace it with another. In a relationship anarchy model, which is non-normative, commitments are made without looking at "pre-printed forms," and they're self-managed without the need or obligation to change titles, categories, or labels.

Affective individualism

Over about 10 years, I personally experienced the process of trying to build a way of life that didn't elicit the strong dissonances I'd experienced until then without any references, in a self-taught manner. I didn't want to recreate a model that I knew wasn't right for me, but I didn't know of any alternatives. In fact, I thought that relating to others in another way was a particular concern that I couldn't really share, an adventure that had to be undertaken alone, a paradigm that had to be developed individually and couldn't be exported or imported from other people or places.

I explained "my model" as best I could, and without much conviction, because I didn't believe that anyone would really be interested and because I myself found my speech unconvincing. It was a model

I was refining little by little. It didn't include cheating but also didn't include particularly high amounts of communication. There were forbidden words like "love" and "relationship" since I wanted to get as far as possible from commitments, as if those words were responsible for what I had perceived as a misguided, repressive, suffocating model — the hegemonic one — even though I had experienced it with a wonderful person who I know was not to blame for those feelings.

Later on, I started to find references, readings, people I could talk to, grow with, and get excited with again without fear. Now, I call what I built without help "affective individualism." Now, I believe that you have to grow by relying on the work of others and on interactions in life. Now, I know that before starting this collective journey, I did what I could, and perhaps I couldn't ask for more, but that I got to a place that I don't like today.

Affective individualism consists of surrounding oneself with impassable barriers and borders, confining feelings, words, fantasies, desires, emotion, union. It's containing rather than exploring. Because the contours of what's possible always exist and are defined by our material and social circumstances, our reality, the axes of power that overwhelm us, the very accidental nature of life as a fortuitous biophysical episode. But they are to be challenged as much as humanly possible. As Leonard Cohen sings,

> "Ring the bells that still can ring
> Forget your perfect offering
> There is a crack, a crack in everything
> That's how the light gets in."

Caretaking

The way the moral imperative of mutual aid, a classic element of social anarchism, cross-cuts the sphere of bonds constitutes one of the ethical bases of relationship anarchy. Replacing the cultural mandate that creates disconnected bubbles of affection, care, and protection, the family or clan self-centeredness discussed in previous chapters – replacing all that with a way of caring for each other that doesn't make solidarity, care, or consideration depend on the hierarchical category of the bond.

If I provide caretaking and feel cared for by a network of people whom I may be tied to by passions and attachments that may be different, with different ingredients: more or less intimacy, attention, shared life, and so on, then I will not experience interest in a new affection from a place of lack, I won't cling to a sinking ship, I will savor and appreciate the good in people without feeling the anxiety that it could end at any moment. In that ideal situation, I will give away my engagement and my help, and I won't put conditions on them because I know I won't need compensation; perhaps returns won't come from the same place where I put energy in, but from others. But that will end up supporting us collectively because we will be a network.[169]

Here, the gender perspective must once again function to keep people who are socially and culturally raised as women from shouldering most of the burden of caretaking and providing attention for others. It is essential to be highly aware of how we specify our practices so that the multiplicity of vectors of protection and support does not give rise to a multiplication of the components of inequality and oppression in terms of gender or other axes such as social position, functional diversity, or the origin of those who make up the network.

These inequalities can also create feedback loops of exclusion. If someone is in a situation or moment of vulnerability, they can come to be perceived as a burden. In the absence of the normative mandate of the couple or blood relations, they may face a process of progressive forgetfulness. This will create needs and demands from the

---

169 According to the valuable concept of "indirect reciprocity" mentioned in section 5.3 and in the glossary entry, "mutual aid."

person who has been distanced; their complaints and demands contribute to even more distancing. To prevent these dynamics from taking root, the first step is to be aware that they may occur; the second is to be ready and use willpower based in the conviction that they are unfair.

In a recent work, Mari Luz Esteban[170] analyzes caretaking, as proposed by forms of feminism, providing an anthropological perspective and focusing on the over-dimensioning of the term, its historical and cultural decontextualization, and the risk of sentimentalizing the concept, hypertrophying its emotional dimension. Her analysis establishes a strong resonance with relationship anarchy's proposals as she establishes a dialogue between feminism and anthropology that can suggest alternatives or complements to the concept of care and compensate for this hypertrophy. She specifically proposes incorporating the notions of mutual aid, self-care, and reciprocity. In her own words:

> "(...) the fact that current research focuses above all on representations and the social organization of procreation and upbringing is making other types of relationships of solidarity and reciprocity that are fundamental for people invisible, leaving them aside. Besides, studies like those on communities of mutual aid allow us to relocate and simultaneously use the concept of caretaking with others, such as that of mutual aid, which is the one I favor. This concept of mutual aid was first used by Russian anarchist Pyotr Kropotkin in the book entitled *Mutual Support: A Factor of Evolution*, which he published in 1902 while in exile in England. (...) When I say that mutual aid allows us to reconsider the centrality of caretaking, I mean that, at least in the networks I've focused on, doing and sharing together aren't just caretaking, not in the usual sense of this term; everything is shared, as we've seen, from economic protection and moral and ideological support,

---

170 M.L. Esteban, "Los cuidados, un concepto central en la teoría feminista: aportaciones, riesgos y diálogos con la antropología," *Quaderns-e de l'Institut Catalá d'Antropologia*, 2017.

to free time, political activity, etc., including caretaking at times when the network's participants cannot fend for themselves.

(...) we can affirm that feminist work's revision around the concept of caretaking lets us see the contributions of a radical critique of the current hegemonic economic vision centered on the market. But, in my opinion, a contextualization and redefinition of this concept is essential, in addition to exploring other possible concepts such as mutual aid that allow us to cross the borders of current family relationships and ideologies and move in spaces "between." In other words, the debate on caretaking is not only a debate linked to social and economic inequalities between men and women or between groups with different social positions (immigrants/indigenous people), which it is. It is also a debate that forces us to return to family, friendship, kinship, parenthood, sustaining life, and the interdependence between human beings."

Recognition

Mathematician, philosopher, and linguist Ludwig Wittgenstein (curiously, an aeronautical engineer by training and a disciple of Bertrand Russell) said, "The limits of my language mean the limits of my world." The idea of renouncing the labels that categorize the ways we relate to each other and delimit our ways of feeling, living, and helping each other can also mean dispensing with the lexical, semantic, and pragmatic framework that supports our needs for recognition. When I spend time, energy, passion, and dedication on one person, or several, and I have them in my thoughts often, their presence in my reality is so important that I may feel the need to give them an important place in my symbolic universe. I may aspire for that person or those people to name me as well, granting me recognition in the form of a singular, distinctive signifier: my girlfriend, my boyfriend, my boy, my girl, my partner...

As with expectations, when it comes to recognition, there are two slightly different elements: internal recognition and external recognition. The first is feeling that the people I interact with intensely "owe me." I don't want to be treated like everyone else. I need, or rather, I want to be considered and named in a special way.

The second type, external recognition, has to do with how the rest of the world sees us. I may also wish for us to be identified as members of a named relationship. We can aspire to have a presence in the referential space of others who also matter to us.

Both forms of demand for recognition are sometimes associated with insecurity, instability, or the search for an identity that goes beyond the individual. Internally, my fears of abandonment or irrelevance may be influencing factors. Externally, those may be the need to feel a minimum level of integration in the shared environment and not having to explain certain things over and over again. After all, recognizing that categories are cultural constructs does not mean that these categories don't exist around us and affect us.

Every person or group of people answers these questions differently, from the commitment to adopt the categories in a descriptive way and to be highly aware that they don't become coercive instruments, to the most resistant and insurrectionary attitude of maintaining non-normativity at all costs in all regards, including in language. What is clear is that the need for recognition and the feeling of "being special" from another person or other people is to give them a significant amount of power over me.

I consider it necessary to have enough tools and security to feel that I am special without validation from anyone else. I have to be able to provide my own recognition. Interdependence with the rest of my network of relationships gives me pleasure, growth, happiness, but it isn't other people who have to recognize my uniqueness or prove my validity in any way.

In short, labels, as I've discussed at various points, are not coercive per se, but automatic expressions and subconscious performative effects can be hard to handle. Of course, supposing that the categories don't exist would be oblivious, and suggesting the obligation to dispense with labels would be simply proposing another normativity. The conclusion therefore can't go beyond assessing these risks and insisting that having all this information is important to be able to use it, share it, and turn it into another tool in our common toolbox for collective self-management.

Delimitation in time

In most cultures, from the most ancient to today's and from great civilizations to human groups of a geographically smaller scope, rites of passage, manifestations of collective confirmation, and demonstrating support and recognition in the most meaningful episodes of life have been developed. The ritual that accompanies death, for instance, helps loved ones accept and cope with the loss and share their pain. Rituals of welcoming new births, reaching adulthood, and different biological and social processes, marriage, emancipation, greeting, farewell, and so on, are observed.

It's not surprising that we uphold a strong tendency to mark and share the important milestones that have to do with bonds. The normative model requires delimiting the changes in the type of relationship and making them visible. From the moment that each relationship label has duties, rights, and expectations (internal and external) indelibly associated with it, there is an obvious need to make it clear as to what situation we're in. Otherwise, we won't know what we can and should do, and we risk being criticized and censured by our environment (although the latter is no longer so important in many social contexts today). As developed in previous chapters, the challenge to normativity as a relationship model leads to the fact that this delimitation is no longer necessary.

From a practical point of view, I would actually say that this is one of the most important differences between what relationship anarchy proposes and the other ways of understanding bonds. Both monogamous and non-monogamous models, such as polyamory, preserve and share the practice of delimiting and identifying bonds. In particular, they maintain the logic of rupture as the end of one form of relationship (amorous, a couple, intimate, etc.) and the transition to a new one (friendship, companionship, distancing, etc.).

What does this mean in practice? That there can't be any more changes? That, by the mere fact of not being labeled, relationships are indestructible? Obviously not. It doesn't mean that circumstances won't lead to bonds deteriorating, to people no longer sharing things, that passion won't gradually lose its initial impetus or that conflicts, incompatibilities, and differences will no longer arise. The point is that if we aren't forced to decide "whether we are or we aren't," these modifications will have consequences that are limited to the change itself. That is, what has to change will change without dragging the entire structure of the relationship with it.

In some way, it is about rebelling so that the signifiers stop imposing their authority by defining the stages and practices, and that what matters is what is signified. The rupture should not be the center of countless hours of conversation, anguish, suffering, and doubt. Instead, we should talk about what we want or don't want to do, and if need be, what we can no longer share should be the only thing that causes pain.

Feeling rejection, pain, and frustration are inevitable when another person stops wanting to be with me in moments and experiences that brought me happiness, or wants to do so less often or in some other way. Still, it's likely that you still have many other things to share with that person, above all love, affection, and the desire to care for each other. There may be more or fewer limitations, but everything won't disappear just because we've moved to another relationship category. Common examples of these practices, which can vary in intensity or disappear, include cohabitation, physical intimacy, attentive communication, or participation in family, social, and recreational events.

It's possible that my reaction to this proposal is disbelief, skepticism, "I couldn't do that," "I need to know where I stand." Denying these feelings doesn't make any sense, but perhaps a parallel can be useful to explain the extent to which the cultural construct may be determining this perception. In a workshop, exercise, or therapy oriented around "couple relationships," it wouldn't be unusual for us to find a section where the goal is to facilitate clean break-up processes without any negative consequences. However, in a similar context oriented at how to relate to your family of origin, it would be odd to find an item dealing with how to "break up with your mother or father properly, definitively, and without any consequences," for one example.

The idea of serial monogamy suggests that you have to make clean breaks with one person in order to devote all your attention to another, to rebuild a subsequent union in its entirety after demolishing every important link with the previous one. Somehow, a "couple identity" must be destroyed to forge a new one. The process of building a new identity is often a journey of empowerment, but in this case, it is more like an exodus. Everything must be abandoned in search of a new promised land.

Negotiation

The most cited reference in the study and practice of consensus is known as the Harvard Program on Negotiation, collected in the work of Fisher, Ury, and Patton in the 1980s.[171] It is undoubtedly a well-intentioned paradigm that seeks mutual benefit, objectivity, and justice, while trying to minimize possible grievances to the other party to avoid resentments that may deteriorate the agreements' sustainability.

But while this vision is surely useful in certain areas, it very conspicuously overlooks the problem of power relations. As Clara Coria says,[172]

> "Negotiation takes on positive or negative signs depending on the ethical context within which it is put into practice. Thus, for instance, in a context of corruption, negotiations are corrupt. In a

---

[171] R. Fisher, W. Ury, B. Patton, *Getting to Yes: Negotiating Agreement Without Giving In*, Houghton Mifflin Harcourt, Boston, 1991.

[172] C. Coria, *Las negociaciones nuestras de cada día*, Paidós, Barcelona, 1997.

context of extreme competition, they're tough. In a context of solidarity, they are alternatives to finding solutions that consider the parties' needs. It is the ethical context in which each negotiation is inserted that gives it its attributes."

And it is not at all about substituting negotiation with submission:[173]

"Yielding out of appeasement is very different from strategical yielding, which involves accepting to renounce some of one's own interests to make an agreement that finally resolves the disputes possible. Yielding out of appeasement opens the door to condescension, which ends up turning into submission. It is the result of multiple invisible instances of violence. Violence that, given how everyday it is, ends up being naturalized and goes unnoticed. Everyone knows – though we may not always remember – that violence not only resides in the unmasked attitude of hostility, frightening gestures, or scathing words. Violence occupies spaces that aren't always evident. And its most covert form is not the least harmful.

There are countless types of violence that are "invisible" to our eyes simply because we aren't used to considering them as such. Many hide behind and shield themselves with unexamined habits, social prescriptions, and personal inertia. Some of the most common forms are self-imposed silence, self-contempt, and the sanctification of women's roles."

The consequences of applying an anti-authoritarian and anti-oppressive paradigm to the dynamics of self-management at the relational and affective levels go through recognizing the great difficulty that normally involves detecting and neutralizing these invisible forms of violence and, thus, looking at the idea of negotiation with suspicion – assuming that there are asymmetries and imbalances, power gradients that induce us to accept concessions regarding our agency and our boundaries. But without demands and cessions and

---

[173] Ibíd.

a process of negotiation and agreement, how can I come to an understanding in my relationships that lets me be at ease? It's not easy to answer this question. The principles of self-managed social anarchism that relationship anarchy has inherited include the concepts of freely accepted and revisable commitments, responsible autonomy, and personal sovereignty – an ethical tripod. This foundation can be built on with dialogue, a relational reference based on commitments and boundaries.

Commitments bind me based on my will, and boundaries only make sense when applied to my body, my time, my space... True, we can come up with endless sophisms that adulterate commitments and define fraudulent, deceitful boundaries. Any logical structure can be stretched, manipulated, and distorted until it is conformed to an oppressive, tyrannical claim. But if we are able to cling closely to the ideas of strictly voluntary commitments and specifically individual limits, it will be more difficult for the result to incorporate authoritarian practices.

Surely, only through experience and effort can I arrive at that precise alignment. Or maybe it's too complicated in practice. The truth is, those of us who have tried for years with interest and motivation aren't always sure that we're doing it well, but to some extent, it does work and serves as a guide or a horizon we can move toward if we agree with the basic principles of the proposal.

In this case, I think examples may be useful. My understanding of the ethical principles of relationship anarchy as it relates to agreements (there are, of course, many other interpretations) could be illustrated by practical guidelines such as these:

- Communicating using expressions such as "I'm affected by..." or "I'm not comfortable..." instead of "you can or can't..." or "you should or shouldn't..." Expressing what you'd like to say in the first person singular.
- Defending my own values and principles, not attacking or criticizing those of others.

- Striving to ensure that other people don't decide what I do or should do, what I participate in and what I don't... but using just as much effort or more to make sure that they have that same capacity.
- Establishing limits on my space, on what is explicitly directed towards me, my things, my time, my dignity, and my rights, without trying to disguise the desire to impose obligations, constraints, or demands on other people as limits.
- Adapting based on clearly specified commitments in terms of upholding respect, providing support, care, understanding, listening, and tenderness, but not adapting in the sense of giving in to requests in exchange for something else (or in exchange for nothing, which in practice translates into a postponed "collection," because what I perceive as a concession is tallied up as a debt).
- Maintaining the level of privacy that I feel comfortable with and respecting that required by others.
- Similarly, moving forward (or not) with physical intimacy at the pace that makes me feel comfortable and respecting others' paces, following the rule of minimums, that is, the pace of the slowest or most vulnerable individual.
- Applying the same criteria of respect to the speed with which aspects such as understanding, generosity, sharing time, relationships, etc., can grow. Even when, for whatever reason, there are setbacks instead of advances.

I repeat, these are only ways of approaching interaction that won't necessarily change the outcome, core, or functioning of relationships, but they can serve as a starting point. Finally, understanding commitments to be serious and solid yet flexible can help them become broader and less cautious. If I have to think out everything, down to the last detail of anything that might come up in the reality of any person or circumstance that will interact with my relationships in the future, I'll need very conservative commitments to avoid affecting others and bringing restrictions and coercion onto them.

I believe that if we approach commitments as instruments that orchestrate a score of affections and fraternity – not as transactional terms, clauses of a commercial contract, or articles of a bilateral treaty – the rhythm will be freer and the melody more human.

Communication

In spaces of relationship activism, we often share a sort of joke that in a normative bond, the relationship is only discussed at times of conflict and problematic situations, yet in a non-normative one, it's in the most lively and interesting times of the relationship when communication and dialogue occur the most.

In reality, there is also a practical and emotional limit that makes an excess of dialogue and management exhausting. The general objective of relationships is not to talk about them but to enjoy company, affection, laughter, adventures, humor, and intellectual and physical excitement. But it's true that communication — especially about what is important and may condition the relationship — is crucial in a non-normative bond: there is no standard or reference point that can be accepted "by omission." Limits and commitments aren't stereotyped, so they must therefore be addressed. They aren't fixed and immutable, and they aren't dogmatic; it's necessary to analyze motives and reasons at play and to understand that they can evolve. In practical terms, it's about communicating as fluently as possible without the dialogue itself becoming a mandate. Beyond personal work that the shyest, most introverted people may need to do, it's not a particularly complex issue. We simply have to deal with all the topics because, in a non-normative model, no issue can be taken for granted if it hasn't been discussed.

The most difficult aspect that requires careful analysis is distinguishing between sincerity and transparency. As I mentioned in the previous chapter, there is little doubt that honesty is a commitment that should be part of any ethical relationship. But this commitment's exact structure doesn't have to be automatic. In fact, how it is managed is a highly relevant aspect. Starting from a basic foundation that ensures that the people I interact with are always informed of the essential elements that affect our boundaries, commitments, and the relationship structure, any approach regarding what, when, and how to communicate all other matters would fit into conceptions of relationship anarchy. In other words, the principles of relationship anarchy leave no room for a normativity that requires a certain level of transparency, much less the total renunciation of privacy. The levels of visibility can be adapted to needs, provided that this transparency is genuinely voluntary and not required or imposed.

In practice, again, the way we normally manage communication in friendship relationships is a useful reference to understand how a dynamic consistent with the fundamentals I've explained can be established. We share certain things with some friends and perhaps less with others. Usually, this depends on the interest they convey, the degree of understanding they exhibit, and how their reaction relieves or supports us. Little by little, depending on these parameters, we sort out our communication style and the scope of what we share with each person. Normally, in friendships, we don't feel obliged to say anything that we don't want to reveal (except something that directly affects another person) or demand more transparency than what arises voluntarily. In the case of relationships where there are strong levels of codependency or very marked expectations, it is common for some communicative acts to have a tactical component, whether consciously or unconsciously, and to be more selfish than generous. We often use communication to relieve ourselves of responsibilities, to vent. In this sense, we should remember that sincerity must be accompanied by an equal amount of empathy. Non-empathic sincerity can be crude and harsh.

An example of tactical communication is when it is used to create crises or changes in relationships by confessing to breaches of boundaries, deception, or cheating. Other examples are "emotional sincericide," the atonement of guilt through recognizing sin, provocation to trigger a conflict, the threat of disappointment when others don't react according to certain expectations, blackmail...

Trust

I believe that building trust has a lot in common with building communication styles and commitments. In fact, this is even more impervious to normativity. We don't always have the most trust in who we should, according to cultural expectations and mandates. We have more trust in those we feel closer to, who we share more empathy with, who react to our confidences with support and help, and not doubt, suspicion, or judgment.

A very direct reference already mentioned in the second chapter is that which originally came from feminist movements (fundamentally, difference feminism from the 1980s) in the form of *sorority* (sisterhood) and *affidamento* (reliance). From that current, we can learn and take away practical ideas. These terms have gained momentum through the work of the Women's Bookshop Collective of Milan, being disseminated in the writings of Marcela Lagarde, and beyond. This conception is related to fraternity and trust, mutual recognition, solidarity, and support. Danila Suárez Tomé captures its essence and practice in the following way:[174]

> "Sisterhood is not a call to love each other, to be forced to get along, not to criticize ideas and actions, or to disagree with other women. No. That's a misunderstanding that ultimately leads us to weigh ourselves down with rules that are impossible to comply with and to avoid debates and discussions, which power all change. Sisterhood speaks to us about creating opportune pacts where we can find more and more women; generating new bonds between us and in relation to other groups and other struggles; including new subjectivities, too, because not all of us who experi-

---

174 D. Suárez Tomé, "Sororidad y praxis política feminista," *Economía Feminista*, 2017.

ence patriarchal oppression recognize ourselves as women; gradually accomplishing objectives that have been agreed on in foundational understandings; strengthening differences so as not to violate plurality with the ideal of homogeneity. In short, sisterhood is a political pact between peers, where those who agree are precisely those who had never been able to agree before and who were, as a result, left out of the public sphere and the political arena.

Once, in another panel where I was talking about sisterhood, I was asked if this ideal was perhaps too impossible to achieve and would ultimately end up bringing us a lot of frustration, insofar as the problems, arguments, and differences cutting through feminism seem to be irreparable. And it's true, sometimes we get overwhelmed and believe that it's impossible to move forward. But we can think about it from a different perspective: a single way of thinking and the absence of conflict is a situation reserved for those who support the status quo and who benefit from it. When what we want is to change the world, when everything has to be done and built, when we choose non-violent paths and value diversity, it's natural for things not to be so simple and comfortable. I propose taking these difficulties that we experience on our journey through feminism as a symptom of health, movement, and the power to change, and sisterhood as a regulative ideal that we must keep in mind in every feminist action, even if it seems (and may even be) unattainable."

On the other hand, a balance must be maintained between trust and respect. More specifically, I believe that it is necessary to ensure that the former is not built at the expense of the latter, that trust isn't developed at the cost of respect. It's easy to fall into this trap; the line between trust and over-familiarity can be a thin one. I'll say more about this in the section on respect in relationships.

5.3 Difficulties, obstacles, and collective ways of overcoming

In this stroll through the ground floor of the landscape of alternative ways of relating to others, we find ourselves laden with the burden of a hegemonic model that is patriarchal, normative, and dogmatic and that tends to minimize the space for rebellion by constituting not merely a model but a means of complete immersion. Around me, I only see normative bonds that make it difficult for me to imagine how far other relationship models can go. After all, plurality only grows when fueled by diversity, and I can only barely intuit some distant oasis in a desert of uniformity on rare occasions.

So, with hardly any references to go on, with few anchoring points on which to build and go further, it isn't easy to overcome all the difficulties that relationships entail, plus those derived from putting together a new, uncertain structure. Proposing a way of life based on a free, supportive network is almost an impossible mission in an environment where monogamous bubbles, the scarcity of affections outside of those bubbles, the feeling of lack, the need to possess, and the expectations are so overwhelmingly dominant.

Now, I want to go over some ideas and experiences on how to overcome these conditions, and how to deal with feelings of scarcity, lack, dependence, expectations, idealizations, guilt, and oppression. Of course, I want to continue to leave any miracle recipes aside, but I would like to provide starting points for each person to elaborate thoughts and model their own tools that, when applied to daily practices, bring the utopia of lives traversed and sustained by affections and collective solidarity a little closer to reality.

Jealousy and compersion

As Marcel Proust described in *Swann's Way* from his wonderful work *In Search of Lost Time*, "His jealousy, like an octopus which throws out a first, then a second, and finally a third tentacle, fastened itself irremovably first to that moment, five o 'clock in the afternoon, then to another, then to another again. But Swann was incapable of inventing his sufferings. They were only the memory, the perpetuation of a suffering that had come to him from without."

Curiously – another of those poetic turns of chance that reality takes – one of the most popular parallels in many relationship activism communities for describing and illustrating the complexity of the feeling of jealousy is the "8-Armed Octopus"[175] that North American educator Reid Mihalko used at the end of the last decade in his articles and workshops.[176] The octopus's arms correspond to 8 emotions that, like tentacles, can grasp and trigger the feeling of anguish, pain, and suffering that we identify as jealousy. These emotions are:

1. The need for possession and control that goes along with the myth that I'm special and irreplaceable.
2. Insecurity and the feeling of vulnerability in the relationship.
3. The fear of loss and abandonment.
4. The fear of rejection and frustration, often associated with low self-esteem.
5. The panic of loneliness that is related to dependency and the absence of a support network, an active social life, etc.
6. The feeling of injustice and inequity that occurs when the other person has an easier time finding relationships and plans for socializing and having fun.
7. Low self-esteem and self-image in terms of inferiority.

---

175 "Battling The 8-Armed Octopus of Jealousy," on reidaboutsex.
176 By the way, that author was recently accused of violating others' consent (including some who attended his workshops), and after accepting the seriousness of the damage he had caused, he is now in a process of restorative and transformative justice. The way to approach such a serious matter using unconventional assumptions based on responsibility and accountability in a collective environment is interesting, to say the least. More information at "Information about Reid Mihalko's Accountability Process," on reidaboutsex.com.

8. The feeling of emotional scarcity and that it isn't easy to escape a situation of lack.

The problem of jealousy that arises in a monogamous relationship is different from that which occurs in a non-normative relationship. In the former, of all the issues listed, the clandestine breaking of a commitment – cheating – hovers over all the rest. In the latter, affective sexual exclusivity is often not one of the commitments taken on; therefore, jealousy has more to do with the difficulty of overcoming those emotions, despite understanding that it would be better to manage and overcome them.

This is one of the most studied and discussed issues in readings, workshops, and conversations in non-monogamous spheres. Strategies, mechanisms, experiences, and practices are shared time and time again, and they're continually refined and evaluated. It is undoubtedly a useful exercise to acquire skills, tools, and empowerment, but the idea that jealousy creates suffering and conflict always stays the same. It's important to realize that there is no point in adding more distress on top of the situation and feeling guilty for not being able to control those feelings. That work must be done by everyone in the network, not just those experiencing them. Like almost everything in relationship anarchy, solutions are collective.

Another concept that's often been used for years in the literature on ethical non-monogamies is that of "compersion" – and no, that's not a typo. This is a positive feeling defined as empathic satisfaction stemming from our happiness for another person we have an affective or affective sexual bond with when they are enjoying another similar relationship. In some ways, it could be an antonym or counterpoint to jealousy. It's based on stories of experiences where new relationships in the lives of those closest to us can enrich and feed our own relationship indirectly at different times and degrees. It isn't easy to say to what extent this is a common feeling, or if it is only reached through work of deconstruction or solidarity and altruism.

What is clear is that possessiveness, lack of solidity in the relationship, insecurities, feelings of inferiority, fear of abandonment, and ultimately, everything that characterizes what we call jealousy makes it absolutely difficult to feel compersion.

It's striking that the set of emotions that make up the feeling of jealousy is culturally managed in our societies in a particular way. It isn't like other feelings that are considered controllable; it's accepted as something intolerable, something invincible that can dominate me and has no remedy. Until a few years ago, many countries recognized extenuating circumstances or even had a differentiated definition for "crimes of passion." These were judged less seriously because no one could supposedly overcome something as insurmountable as murderous jealousy.

This is surely an example of a self-fulfilling prophecy. If no one around me has ever considered the possibility that jealousy is just another feeling that's as manageable as any other, I'll find it as unbearable as I've always been told and supposedly understood it to be. Babies and young children, for instance, have a tendency to want to appropriate everything they see and that catches their attention. This feeling of attraction to things that belong to others is routinely managed by adults by calmly, peacefully repeating that they cannot take it, it's not theirs, they can't touch it, etc. When we get to be 10, 20, or 40, we don't have any difficulties or dramatic episodes walking through a market or a shopping center just because we can't take everything we see and like with us. Sometimes, we might really wish we could, but we suppress that urge without getting too upset or considering it a grave misfortune. We've simply learned to live with it.

Jealousy, on the other hand, has been presented to us as a drama beyond all management – even as proof of love. There is no love without jealousy, or so we've been told. How awful is that? Having reached adulthood and with bonds that have been created and are in progress, doing the work that culture itself could have done isn't so simple, but it isn't so difficult, either. It involves the same type of learning, just preceded by "unlearning."

As for the aspects that set relationship anarchy apart from other forms of non-normativity in this regard, consider labeling relationships in such a way that some have a special character that's defined and delimited and others do not. That can mean that the arrival of new people to this privileged network of bonds carries a greater potential threat. If that dividing line doesn't exist, nobody can cross it, not in any direction. That threat then fades away; it stops operating in the same terms. On the other hand, the lack of structure could feed feelings of insecurity, low self-esteem, vulnerability, etc., ultimately reaching an end result that might be similar to that of other models and approaches.

The need for symmetry and "feeling special"

The community of people who proposed relationship anarchy as an evolution of what was initially called radical relationships often explained their proposal by pointing out a parallel between what we understand as friendship and the relationship we call the couple. Among the examples they cited is the fact that friendship doesn't need to be fed with continual, confirming contact, or at least requires to a much lesser extent. The same is true of other relationships, such as those with our family of origin. This is largely because the nature of these bonds does not contain at its core the question of establishment, survival, and rupture. Of course, any bond is susceptible to getting complicated and breaking apart, but there is no internal line of questioning: "Do I still love you? Do you still love me?" "Do you make me happy? Do I make you happy?" Drawing on that parallel, transferring those phrases to a socially normalized adult friendship seems almost childish; after knowing each other and spending time together for a few months, would you ask, "Are you still my friend?" "Am I/are you a good friend?" "Is the friendship over yet?" Or in the case of a typical family relationship, "Do you still consider me a good sibling or parent?" (In the last case, confirmation doesn't refer to the bond itself, which is immutable, but to its quality).

All these phrases may make sense in any relationship in times of severe crisis or special circumstances, but they are only recognizable as statements of continual or periodic confirmation for relationships we call sentimental or relate to love or the couple, which are usually of an affective sexual nature. This is understandable: in an amatonormative relationship, that status corresponds to a position that must be defended. There is always the threat that we'll be kicked off the pedestal where, in monogamous normativity, only one person fits; in other structures, such as polyamory, more than one person fits, which requires significant work for everyone to fit comfortably on a platform that may be wider and more flexible but is also more complex to manage. On top of that, my position on another person's pedestal, or other people's pedestals, requires a place for them on my own pedestal as just compensation. Therefore, there are two closely related needs: the need for it to be confirmed that I'm still "special," and the demand for fairness or symmetry in this regard. These two conditions generate very specific dynamics. While things are going well, they manifest as the constant exchange of pampering and messages of affection that act as verification, gratifying vital signs of the bond. I don't mean to say that they're not generally sincere expressions, but they often have a more phatic function than an emotional one. It's about actively maintaining supervision over the affective connection.

But when wear occurs, when some conflict arises or simple irregularities and personal ups and downs for an individual or the relationship, the expectation around the level of continuity in certifying the bond suffers; there seems to be a break in what the habit and inertias had been. That break leads to doubt, to the need for more confirmation, to demand, mistrust. Small changes that may have gone unnoticed before become glaringly obvious, seemingly enormous; their scope unhelpfully amplified. Therefore, the proposal that could stem from the relationship anarchist conception is to once again bring the mechanics of confirming all bonds as close as possible to what usually happens with friendly relations. By changing the dynamics, the particularly vulnerable, threatened condition that amatonormativity instills in the most important bonds can be modified as much as possible.

In short, it's about trusting people and relationships more because – though some may be more significant, active, present, intense, passionate, or established than others. Which would you choose: a plateau surrounded by frightening abysses where you have to move carefully so as to not fall off the cliff, or a smoother terrain that might have its ups and downs, but no precipices and unfathomable chasms – no peaks and valleys that breaking up with one person and replacing them the next in line brings?

When the couple is no longer the measure of everything

I have a very vivid, specific memory of the moment my last normative relationship ended, almost 20 years ago. It's not the evocation of some vague idea of liberation, a mixture of fear and curiosity to see how this new stage would go, along with grief, longing, and excitement. That happened, of course, and I remember it, too. But for some reason, what really stuck in my memory was the feeling that I was suddenly free to look after and listen to anyone at any time. I certainly wasn't getting out of an oppressive or suffocating relationship, not at all. I wasn't surrounded by prohibitions, and there was no reason for that feeling to be so dominant.

It is true that cohabitation brings routine: every night, you have dinner, and after talking a while, it's the sofa, reading, and so on, until you have to go to bed at a reasonable time to get up the next morning. So, on a day-to-day basis, settled into that inertia, getting a phone call or a visitor in the middle of the night, for instance, is only acceptable when something serious, an emergency comes up. However, I felt that I was different then, that I was free to assure anyone that they could call or come by to see me at any time, for any reason. I've spoken about the dangers of certain notions of freedom and the practices they lead to, but now I realize that this was a beautiful freedom because it was directed outward, a feeling of availability to listen, to receive, ultimately to provide attention and care. Fortunately, it's not something that has been necessary often, but I still get the same feeling and emotion every time someone comes by for me to lend them my ear and my shoulder. Seeing things the other way around, these years have shown that, when people go into the bubble dynamics of the couple, they generally stop caring, paying attention, and deepening the rest of their relationships, or at least they do so to a much lesser extent. When that happens, the story may have several outcomes that are all quite predictable, and the words and expressions used are meaningful. Most commonly, there is "I'm getting to know someone," then "there's a special someone," "I'm starting a relationship," "I'm with someone," and the like.

The first impression received when these situations occur is that there is an immediate risk of withdrawal. In fact, when the new relationship is monogamous and normative, the risk becomes a near certainty. When it's not, there is a high probability that, in order to maintain it, we will have to subordinate logistics to what the "primary partner" imposes; this is not only the logistics of things but also often the affective dynamics themselves, communication (we almost become a little secret, or we are at least asked for more discretion than before), and meta-relationships, the network we've gained access to through the other person that often also experiences distancing.

As I mentioned earlier, the normative structure built based on these scenarios is called "couple privilege." It's given this name because the implications often go beyond the free decision to undertake "something special." This is because it affects more people than those involved in making decisions and because it is a cultural model that grants automatic benefits and prerogatives (both in the hegemonic monogamous world and in most non-monogamous communities).

As with other issues, it's difficult to propose functional guidelines that are applicable to daily life. We can only try to be aware of the existence of this normative order, which is easy to overlook because it permeates everything and arises from standardized practices. We must also attempt to understand that it results in upholding that exact same order with its isolated bubbles and the tendency to make networks of affection, solidarity, support, and collective conscience impossible.[177]

Obsessions, addictions, dependencies, and interdependence

Let's go back to the proposals around which relationship anarchy revolves: mutual care, free and voluntary commitment, and responsible autonomy. Now, I'm going to focus on how any changes affecting that last leg can throw the entire structure off-balance. When aspects pertaining to other people (such as their possessiveness, their instinctive territoriality, their desire for security, having all their needs covered at all times, for control) – when those go beyond my intention of maintaining a conscious, careful autonomy, a situation of dependency is established. Since relationship dynamics often tend to seek out symmetries and reciprocities, it's common for this dependence to be a two-way street — or more, in an affective network — and in the end, a process of codependency arises.[178]

---

[177] In a 2016 study, Natalia Sarkisian and Naomi Gerstel concluded that being in a relationship reduces the number and quality of social connections for both men and women, even if we take structural explanations into account. The bonds of those who aren't in a relationship are more integrative and involve more cooperation and social involvement. In N. Sarkisian, N. Gerstel, "Does singlehood isolate or integrate? Examining the link between marital status and ties to kin, friends, and neighbors," *Journal of Social and Personal Relationships*, 2016.

[178] Of course, everyone is interdependent on others, especially with our networks of support and affection. Here, I'm referring to a harmful emotional dependence precisely because it affects these networks by putting stress on them and in many cases breaking them to create new islands or affective bubbles.

Interestingly, the recent craze to identify dependencies or "addictions" in almost any continual, repeated behavior (sometimes there are just things we like to do, that's all) hasn't reached relationships, nor will it, to the extent that they operate as a culturally accepted behavior. Similarly, we'll find that the practice of reading before bedtime is not popularly identified as an addiction (in terms of the "pop psychology" we'll see in the checkout line at the grocery store). It's precisely because it constitutes a valued, cherished pastime in cultured spheres – meaning it is a hegemonic trait. Still, according to the responses to a standard test, it could meet certain criteria associated with addictions:
"Do you do it every day?"
"Yes, every day."
"Does it affect your daily life?"
"Yes, I have a harder time falling asleep if I don't."
"Could you quit easily?"
"No... it would be difficult for me, and it would make me unhappy."

In other words, faced with evidence of a similar nature, the perception and judgment that the community has about a behavior depend on how and how much it aligns with cultural mandates and values: when applied to psychoactive substances, video games, or social media, it's an addiction; when referring to reading or spending time on any activity that fits in and is valued, it's a habit or a respected practice. This is what happens with affective dependencies and codependencies (if the sexual component takes precedence, we're once again going beyond what is decorous and respectable, and the word "addiction" resurfaces everywhere): a behavior that would be classified as obsessive if it were any other activity – such as always having the same thing for breakfast, lunch, and dinner, or eating at the same restaurant every day – yet it seems perfectly normal to us when that object of insistent attention is a person we're tied to by a normative affective bond (the couple).

It's important to clarify that I am not defending a dubious ideal of egocentric individualism. Relationship anarchy looks toward the collective, interdependence, the network. I, on the other hand, am taking a critical look at another ideal, the romantic myth, which consecrates one person as the source of all love, trust, well-being, passion, intellectual and emotional stimuli... It's inevitable that we'll develop exclusive dependencies on anyone we assign all that responsibility to. In fact, that dependence leads us to yearn for stability as the supreme good, and the value of the relationship no longer comes from the things that we do and enjoy together, from tenderness, attention, affection... In the end, the important thing is the strength of the bond and security, not the pleasure, affection, and happiness it provides.

One interesting idea that could alleviate the problem of codependency (though it is certainly difficult to put into practice until it is widely accepted and shared, at least in a community) would be based on the notion of indirect reciprocity. If I take on life with a clear dedication to building networked relationships, I don't have to expect that what I do for someone, according to my potential and their needs, will be returned to me by that same person. It may be that my needs tomorrow will be better suited to the potential and availability someone else in the network has to offer. The important thing is not who solves the problems, but that they are solved. Some people support and sustain others with emotional, physical, logistical, and material help, but the vectors of assistance don't have to run in both directions. Everyone has abilities and availabilities. This network or indirect reciprocity doesn't generate personal dependence or codependency between two individuals. Instead, it reflects the collective phenomenon of interdependence among the network's members. It's more akin to the idea of group solidarity than rights of ownership and feelings of fear around loss.

Blackmail

Blackmail and manipulation are two very common forms of coercion in any type of relationship. In those where there is a normative substratum imposing predetermined rights and obligations, they are often used to enforce these prerogatives against impulses, resistance, or conflicts. Relationships governed by explicit agreements and negotiations, on the other hand, are not free of this form of conditioning; suggesting negotiation about what another person or other people can do implies claiming that you have some implicit right or power about them. This starting point favors the imposition of coercion in the form of a concession subject to arbitrary ends. In other words, it's along the same lines as saying, "I won't forbid you from doing this, but if you do, this is the consequence..." or "You're free to do it, but then...."

Foucault said that, in the context of social and criminal reprimands for crime and the way it was addressed by the penal system throughout history,[179] "the punishment often exceeded the severity of the crime, thereby reaffirming the supremacy and absolute power of the authority." In this case, the punishment is usually the threat of abandonment, prolonged silence, expressing disproportionate sadness, or suffering that feeds on itself. They are passive-aggressive behaviors based on mechanisms that are set in motion almost automatically and that contribute to making relationships and life a little more miserable.

Again, a reading based on relationship anarchy would first involve avoiding normativity — because it functions as an adhesion contract that doesn't allow examining or changing clauses and commitments — and secondly, avoiding a sort of liberal management that follows the mercantile contractual paradigm of exchanging concessions. On the other hand, the proposal is to adhere as much as

---

[179] M. Foucault, interview with Jerry Bauer, in Playmen 12 (1978), 21-30; also in M. Foucault, Dits et Ecrits (Paris: Gallimard, 1994), III, 671

possible to a model of establishing clear limits that are centered exclusively on myself; on what I won't accept for my body, my time, and my personal dignity; on demanding explicit consent about it; and on being in dialogue and taking on free, intentional, responsible commitments of care, support, sweetness, attention, and affection.

In short, and again insisting on the fundamentals, it's very important for boundaries not to affect others and for commitments not to be demanded of others. Those limits should be personal and individual, and commitments would be free and voluntary. The idea is to keep noble feelings like love and tenderness from becoming alibis for possession (and, therefore, objectification). It's to highlight its positive essence and reject its coercive version.

Dangers of identarian feeling

A proposal as radical, far-reaching as relationship anarchy will inevitably arouse a predisposition to identarianism. If I understand, share, and clearly recognize myself in a revolutionary formulation about something as palpable in life as relationships, it isn't strange for an identification to develop. Then, there is the rising temptation to designate myself as a relationship anarchist, as well as the practice of tailoring my opinions, expressions, and behaviors around my membership in that "new club." On the one hand, identarian feeling is interesting and useful. It allows me to show my way of seeing things from a broader perspective, one that is less singular and pathologized in the eyes of some; it's easier to express (though not always easier to understand) and more predisposed to socialization, to meeting people like me. But on the other hand, there is a danger that the collective roots of an identity will, over time, give rise to a new normativity. The fact that the very essence of relationship anarchy is self-management renders this meaningless, but in the absence of vigilance, it can't be ruled out.

As with labels (those that apply to relationships), identities (which affect people) can also tend to be descriptive or prescriptive.

A fundamentally descriptive use of identity is useful, as I've mentioned, but a genuine — prescriptive — identarian interpretation constitutes a risk of renormativization, a new opportunity for prejudices, exclusions, and violence in general. It may also entail self-censorship and self-imposed punishment which, instead of alleviating the difficulties that arise from trying to live differently or challenges the dominant cultural norm, aggravates these, adding to them and further complicating the management and resolution of day-to-day relationship problems.

After all, we're starting out from a cultural construct that doesn't include the network (it includes it less and less) as an emotional structure for support. In this regard, our general references are isolation, alienation, competition, suspicion, surveillance... Most of the collective feelings traditionally promoted in our societies are those that aim to confront other human groups: against other nations, there's patriotism; against physically different people, racism; against those who love in a different way, homophobia; against who are not of our social stratum, classism; and so on. Therefore, establishing a new normativity, demarcating the community that will take it on, isolating it in some way, competing to see who is more of a relationship anarchist, and not trusting anyone suspected of not "really" being one is the least revolutionary, radical, subversive, and transformative thing that can be done. It is precisely the most mainstream – and the most reactionary. It's what we've been taught to do: monitor ourselves.

The solution – in case relationship anarchy seems like a good idea to me – is simply to try and apply it, to try to surround myself with people who also want to try it out, to take it for granted that we will make a thousand mistakes, that it won't be easy, that we will have to communicate about what's important, respect time and space, be flexible, and not throw in the towel at the first sign of difficulty or frustration. Let's not forget that the hegemonic relationship model generates many frustrations every day. Let's not demand what we don't ask of the dominant system from an experiment in learning and insubordination. Let's not expect that swimming upstream will be more comfortable than going with the flow (following the modern, illustrious "flow" that is so popular in the world of pop culture and sugarcoated ideas).

The natural, the cultural, and the political

One of the most-used arguments on the naturalistic fallacy (introduced by English philosopher George E. Moore at the beginning of the 20th century) is that which assimilates the good with the natural. If something is natural, it is desirable or morally acceptable, and if it isn't, it is unacceptable. This theoretical device has lost strength in the intellectual realm over the last century, but it is still easy to use in a narrative that appeals to less-reflective intuition.

It continues to be used in homoantagonistic discourses that warn that heterosexuality is natural and that the species would have disappeared if homosexual relationships were the norm. It is used in sexist arguments that ensure that it is natural for females to stay "safe with the young" and for males to "go hunting," or that the latter tend to "spread their seed" while the former try to "keep their attention exclusively on the long term." In addition to the fallacy of this naturalistic reasoning, most interpretations about what is natural – and what isn't – are so conditioned by the culture and expectations of society, academia, religions, morals, and so on, that they can end up being far from offering any verifiable intersubjective evidence. Therefore, the perspective I propose as most compatible with relationship anarchy challenges the authority of any interpretation and accusation that refers to what's natural as a source of moral judgments, as a goal, or as a utopia. I neither know nor care what's natural (as knowledge, I do, but not as an ethical foundation). It is important to me that my conduct and my relationships with other people meet the criteria that I consider most acceptable, effective, fair, and equitable. In other words, I care about the political in the broadest sense of the word.

However, we must also understand that the idea of origin, of where we're from and how we got here, holds an important power of fascination and persuasion. I've already spoken of the interesting book by Christopher Ryan and Cacilda Jethá, which analyzes the evolution of human sexuality since the Paleolithic.[180] "I am a 63-year-old widow, and I consider this to be one of the most important books I have ever read. I wish I could live my life over with this information."

Therefore, it can sometimes be a good idea to reclaim and propose that what moves and fascinates us simply serves us, no more. In this case, it may be useful to keep a path clear from what we think we are (even though it is actually a simple interpretation) to what we want to be, not putting even more stepping stones along our complicated route.

Continual management: relationship bureaucracy

One of the essential needs of any non-normative relationship —or one that aspires to reach some level of self-management— is communication. Having the shelter of an adhesion contract that's premade by culture and social customs requires much less effort in communication than developing a specific relationship framework that is suitable for a bond or a self-managed network of bonds. We must reflect on what our boundaries are, what commitments we can sustain, what level of contact and intimacy we want, under what conditions, and so on.

It's easy to agree that communication is a good ally and that it's a positive characteristic of self-managed relationships. Sometimes, though, the network is overloaded by dialogue dedicated exclusively to managing the network itself, which collapses and minimizes messages of affection, contact, intimacy, or fun. It's a kind of "paralysis by analysis." We could call it relationship bureaucracy.

---

180 C. Ryan and C. Jethá, *Sex at Dawn: The Prehistoric Origins of Modern Sexuality*, op. cit.

On occasion, I've heard quite an illustrative comparison: it's like buying a car with one or more people to be able to travel, get around easily, go on trips to the beach or the mountains... and after a year, we realize that the car has been in the shop for more time than it got us to the places we wanted to go when we bought it.

It's not easy to come up with a solution when this happens. In fact, the very design of the remedy can lead to even more management and further breakdown. Of course, there has to be a simple strategy for lightening the load; the first step is precisely recognizing that something is happening. From there, I don't know if there are general rules, but the evolution may be positive, or it may end up being the case that the people who are trying to form these relationships are too far away from a minimum level of finding common ground, of moving away from normativity, of dependency or the capacity to offer care or take care of themselves.

Lightening the bonds is always an option to keep in mind. The reference points we've grown up with are characterized by a tendency to cling, to persevere, to save the relationship at all costs, because we conceive it as something that is or isn't. Flipping the kill switch may be reversible, but it is always quite a serious move. In this case, the proposal may be to relieve the pressure, reduce the seriousness of the interaction. It isn't easy to overcome inertia, but when this can be achieved, surprisingly happy and lively new ways of relating may emerge without abandoning the essential commitments, which must still include being supportive and showing up when something truly important happens. In some ways, it could be seen as loosening the ballast of everyday life to increase the flight altitude and to see and better care for what really matters.

Who's with me?

Right. I'm convinced. I already am or want to be a relationship anarchist. Ah, but there's not anyone else around who shares this conviction. What do I do?

Clearly, a proposal like relationship anarchy that's based on a personal vocation yet is collective in scope doesn't make sense in a context where there isn't anyone else willing to investigate and experiment. It's also a radical approach that requires deconstructing many attitudes, ideas, and behaviors that are firmly ingrained in our lives. It isn't a quiet stroll; it's a journey that's full of difficulties and that only makes sense to undertake based on a personal need and a decision that's been carefully considered.

This is why it's highly likely that there isn't anyone else around who knows and shares a formulation that, besides all else, hasn't been widespread so far, outside some limited circles (it is this book's modest attempt to start to change that). Thus, the possibilities are limited. Depending on where we are, there may be non-normative activism or groups related to non-monogamy that aren't far away. Many people try to go to these group meetings to meet other people, though it is generally heavily stressed that these activities are not places to "hook up."[181] They're places for exchanging ideas, readings, experiences, etc. Still, it is true that the mere fact of sharing such major concerns often leads to relationships of varying depth. They are also environments where the need to have done personal work on consent, gender, and inclusiveness is strongly emphasized.

Another possibility, of course, is interacting with people who don't know about or have never had a particular interest in renouncing the hegemonic model. In fact, these are the sort of people we'll meet most often. When some interest is perceived, the topic of relationships usually comes up, and we share our views on the matter. Reactions to the statement, "I relate to others in a different way,"

---

181 In fact, a considerable part of the problem in managing these activities lies in providing a space that's as free as possible of individuals, especially cishet men, who are looking for "easy sex." In some areas, the term *polyfakes* has become a popular way to refer to them. In this sense, even though it isn't possible for those who facilitate these meetings to guarantee a safe environment, we always try to include notes, warnings, and workshops specifically on the concept of consent, and those attending are encouraged to react immediately if a scrupulous respect for boundaries and spaces is not upheld.

and a more or less detailed explanation of what relationship anarchy is, vary widely. Many fall into one of the following categories:

Rejection: fundamentally out of fear of the unknown, or because what's proposed is understood to mean something else. Depending on gender and context, this may vary. If the contact is heterosexual, the proposal is commonly read by a person socialized as a woman as being quite similar to a relationship without commitment or one of exclusively sexual interest.

Unthinking acceptance: because there is a "crush" at play, or because only part of the description (the novel and rebellious part) is understood. Again, depending on gender, a person socialized as a man and educated in patriarchal terms may often read this as an opportunity to form a relationship without any commitments.

Sincere interest: when the approach catches their attention and is of intellectual and emotional interest. Of course, this is the most pleasant and exciting situation, especially if the questions are accurate, aimed at the key aspects and the hardest difficulties to combine with practice and reality. It's also an extraordinary learning opportunity because the understanding that emerges from each dialogue represents a new ingredient added to that formula. A composition that may end up being one of the most fascinating of all those that can be experienced on this journey of life.

In the first two cases, as I've pointed out, there are highly accentuated and harmful gender constructs at play. In the second, there may also be a highly negative evolution in the relationships' dynamics (though not always): as the bond develops, there is a realization of what everything they told me initially actually means. The result is usually a serious conflict, one that is more painful the longer care and affection have been developing.

Even in the third instance, the most favorable one, one's ability to adapt may be overestimated; there may be significant differences in timing; and the connection may not be possible or work very well.

Understanding and sharing the principles of a new way of relating to others does not guarantee that all the difficulties that come with such a major change can be overcome. Of course, no form of relationship will necessarily work out with everyone we try it with.

As time passes, other relationships may also appear, potentially monogamous, normative, or hierarchical ones, and that will bring distancing. The question of whether or not an amatonormative relationship is compatible with a network built on relationship anarchy is debatable and complex. In practice, though, there is a tendency to stop attending to and caring for relationships that aren't the primary one (or the only one recognized as a couple, in the case of monogamy).

A particular problem arises when you don't live in a big city. The difficulty of finding people interested in what lies beyond the conventional, the lack of a sense of anonymity, external judgments, and economic and social dependence on the regard and esteem of small areas that are relatively isolated from towns – and the lifelines they may offer – make relating to others in a different way more difficult in rural areas. An interesting reference in this regard is "You Need Help: Seeking Poly People and (Relationship) Anarchy in Small Town, U.S.A" by Christina Tesoro in Autostraddle.com. There are also groups that address these exact problems, like the *Xarxa d'Amors Rurals* in Catalonia.[182]

Closets

Just as how communication with those I have more intense interactions with can be considered in very different ways with varying intensities and nuances – all valid as they depend on the preferences, needs, commitments, and boundaries of the people involved – com-

---

[182] https://www.facebook.com/AmorsRurals. See also https://www.autostraddle.com/you-need-help-seeking-poly-people-and-relationship-anarchy-in-small-town-u-s-a/

munication to *the outside world,* all the people around me, also depends on many factors, and it can take many different forms that are compatible with relationship anarchy.

Applying a straightforward interpretation, you might think that — given that I'm approaching relationship anarchy as a political and personal approach at the same time — only an attitude of openness and actively spreading the word makes sense. I can't convince anyone about what I practice and what I believe in if I don't talk about it, if I don't put my reality on display and defend it. Though activism is important and laudable, it isn't essential, and it would be ridiculous to suggest that it is forcibly required, a mandate, when what we're talking about is precisely overcoming those normativities.

I've posited a view of relationship anarchy as lifestyle politics or prefigurative politics. Of course, it's not a common political movement — conceived of as a party or a union — but a proposal that builds reality by walking the walk, not talking the talk. In daily life, not by participating in campaigns and elections. It's clear that, without some kind of sharing, there would be no way to change anything at the social level, but sharing and building majorities is not the objective here. It isn't even the fundamental mechanism as in other political spheres – though it is also true that the more visibility and standardization there is around these issues, the easier it will be to compose and expand networks of affection, mutual aid, and deep bonds that are at once free and have commitment.

Therefore, coming out of the relationship anarchist closet is a possibility that contributes to those important processes of visibility and normalization that other circles like the LGBTIQ+ community have previously done. But it's essential to recognize that, as always, various factors heavily condition that possibility: gender; social class; geographical origin; administrative, financial, work, and family situations; the socio-cultural environment, and many more. For instance, if I am socially read as a woman, it will be hard for me to explain my relationship choice without my environment automatically interpreting it as me attributing traits such as promiscuity, sexual availability, moral glibness, and other generally negative characteristics to myself. If I'm also not heterosexual, a migrant, poor, racialized, undocumented, hold precarious jobs, am providing for children, find myself in a sexist, traditional family environment, etc., then it is probably not the wisest choice to express my unconventional views and my relationship practices publicly.

And if I decide to make my vision and my experience public, to whom, how, when, and why express how I relate to others? Of course, it's not necessary and perhaps not even a good idea to shout it from the rooftops. At least to start with, it's helpful to choose people you trust, regulate the tone and how much detail to provide, try to perceive the impressions caused, and analyze the feedback received. Then, determine if that communication has positive or negative outcomes in terms of greater understanding or rejection.

It should also be kept in mind that, by coming out of the closet, I'm exposing others who have a known relationship with me in my surroundings. There is thus also a collective component to this personal decision. In any case, it's understandable for these issues to be the subject of conversations in the network of affections, not only to make a collective decision but also because these are potentially upsetting aspects, of course, and it's natural to share them with those who are closest to us.

And... what if I'm a woman?

Patriarchy's degree of prevalence and generalization as an organizational system that oppresses people who are socially read as women (regardless of their biological characteristics, which, as mentioned in previous chapters, can be distributed across a broad, multidimensional space of physical, biochemical, and functional traits) is such that it permeates every aspect of culture, social interaction, and all of reality.

This oppression is unlike any other, as Simone de Beauvoir described it, due to the strong structure of bonds that unites oppressors and oppressed. When we challenge that structure, as proposed here, if we don't do so from a perspective that considers and weighs gender in a singular way, giving it priority, the previous model's characteristics of domination and submission will probably be repeated or amplified. In other words, it is not enough to ensure that the theoretical framework is egalitarian and equitable.

In an ecosystem of bonds impregnated with the imposition of inferiority, objectification, control, and patriarchal power, it is necessary to apply a force in the opposite direction to compensate for the imbalance we're starting out from. Specifically, all the elements I've addressed so far as formative ingredients for the forms of hegemonic relationship – the myths of romantic love, the ideology of the couple, dependencies, guilt, essentialisms – all of these harm the oppressed community more than the dominant one. This is because the social construct eliminates affinity with women in men. A boy's identification with the feminine is censored and ridiculed from childhood on.

The message is that women aren't comparable to me: they're something else entirely, and I have to remember that. It's the same way that a soldier is convinced that the enemy is not like him, so the tendency and even the ability to empathize is greatly reduced and he can kill. This reason alone can explain the deep misunderstanding that such a high percentage of men have, and their unwillingness to put themselves in a woman's shoes. It cannot be ignorance, cruelty, or apathy. Men who are moved by much less obvious injustices respond defensively (the familiar "not all men"), in paternalistic ways (mansplaining), or with exaggeration or sarcasm when faced with unequivocal situations of sexist violence. It's just as the feminist adage says: "They're not crazy, they're not monsters, they're not sick. They're healthy sons of the patriarchy."

I think it will be interesting to look at an illustrative example, given its cross-cutting nature and distance from ideological and intellectual conditioning factors. Serena Williams is an American tennis player who has won four Olympic gold medals and 23 Grand Slam titles, and she is also incidentally a feminist activist. She was recently the subject of a poll published by YouGov[183] that had an unusual outcome, one that I find chilling because of the clarity with which it evidences the arguments made in the previous paragraph. The survey showed that one in eight men in the United Kingdom – some 12% – is convinced that they could score against Serena Williams in a tennis match! No need to say more.

Finally, when getting into the world of relationships – and, above all, when it comes to potentially intimate bonds – sexism's most difficult specter appears with implacable force. Ideas like women giving away their virtue (transactional phrases like "giving it up" are often used in reference to a woman's body in awful, hyperbolic metaphors) when they experience sex and intimate affection freely with different people or without offering the obligatory resistance (in their virtuous role as fortresses to be conquered, another form of objectification). These same behaviors in men are seen as qualities of a successful male. It is such an obviously pathetic, unfair, dangerous attitude that it is incomprehensible how it is still so prevalent in society.

So, what guidelines could be derived from the foundations of relationship anarchy in this regard? I think the first step is keeping oppressions and privileges visible and monitored at all times, making sure they aren't silenced. The only possibility for those who hold privileges to be able to give up space is to listen, listen, and listen. I also think that it's necessary to problematize the roles of caregiver imposed on women as who's responsible for providing support, the ant hard at work for daily and affective chores; so do the roles of demanding care and being a victim, providing themselves with

---

183   https://yougov.co.uk/opi/share/surveys/results/survey/344ce84b-a48d-11e9-8e40-79d1f09423a3

power and taking responsibility for their own agency, grouping together and supporting themselves as an oppressed community in non-mixed groups that develop and disseminate the corresponding critical view from that essential perspective. Feminist writer Audre Lorde has said, "For the master's tools will never dismantle the master's house."

Obviously, all this information, opinions, and positioning on my part (which doesn't free me from still having automatic behaviors and adopting patriarchal attitudes on a daily basis) comes directly from paying attention to, listening to, and reading women and female authors, thinkers, and experiencers – those who really get out there and live life.

And... what if I'm a cishet man?

As I'm basically a straight, cisgender man, I'm in a privileged place in many respects. My cultural construct has been the one reserved for masculinity, with all the nuances that may arise, even though my family may have been very progressive and egalitarian, or if I was raised among women or feminist militants, anywhere... Unless I come from another planet, my references at school, around town, in mass media, books, comics, games, and in social groups when it comes to going out, flirting, loving and being loved... all these variables still fall under hegemonic masculinity.

As stated before, as a child, I learned either directly or indirectly that any attitude, behavior, or gesture reminiscent of a girl may be ridiculed and censured; that girls dress differently, play other games, and have other interests. We've been conditioned to internalize that girls aren't like us; they're human, but a different kind of human. We no longer think that they're inferior, as in different times. We've now swallowed the lie that they're better at many tasks (especially the ones we're least interested in sharing), that they can do several things at the same time (whereas, if we can get away with it, we don't do any of them), and other stereotypes that are just as convenient.

They're not inferior, but they are something else; they're in a different place entirely. And the empathy I'm capable of feeling (really feeling, not just intellectualizing based on my notion of justice and equity) quickly dwindles with that distance. In addition, the very expression of empathy is something that's more typical of women's socialization. Feelings generally convey vulnerability, and that fragility and delicateness is the farthest thing from what a man looks like, as we've learned. We must appear to be strong and powerful like John Wayne or rebellious and elusive like James Dean, but never overly sensitive like... like who? Like a girl. For all these and many more differential cultural constructs, the general exercise of relating to others should require a man to undertake a weighty deconstruction of the most awful, harmful aspects of masculinity. But if, on top of that, the relationships won't have the structure imposed by society, the bar is set even higher.

The monogamous heteronormative structure that is centered around the reproductive couple is obviously organized in a way that favors men, but it at least establishes minimum boundaries and obligations. They are authoritarian guidelines, obsessive with regard to possession and cohabitation, in many cases objectifying, demotivating, rigid, and suffocating. But still, they establish a framework within which there is some choice to move around and where getting out can be considered to be rather orderly, except in the most dramatic cases (which, unfortunately, are not uncommon).

However, a form of relationship where there is no such framework, rigid but at least known, can be exploited by the dominant party to obtain even more advantages. Under the guise of flexibility and complicity, peddling ideals of liberation, emancipation, and openness to modernity, we might end up building a new paradise for men and a new hell for women, as we learned from the forays of the '60s and '70s.

So, what proposals should we be crystal clear on, looking at things from this point of view? I think that it is first necessary to admit and include in my discourse, both inwardly and outwardly, the reality that no relationship with me can be considered emotionally safe. Conveying trust is offering something that cannot be given. No matter how informed, conscientious, hardworking, aware, and well-read I am, my original socialization and education have built a personality framed in privilege, in territoriality, in non-empathic firmness, in paternalism, in the objectification of the female body, in control, and in automated, vigorous replies (to put it in neutral terms and not delve further into the quagmire). Of course, we have the ability to change our behavior and to think before we act, but let's not overestimate self-control. Deep down, there are inclinations, a predisposition, and a basic identity that will surface quite often.

Because we are not afraid, or at least not of the same fears. Canadian writer and activist Margaret Atwood has said, "Men are afraid that women will laugh at them. Women are afraid that men will kill them." If we aren't able to understand this vast difference, to find the necessary psychological tools to empathize, perceive, grasp those feelings, to imagine that we had been the subject of the gaze of others who judged us as objects for years, without our desires or feelings coming up in that gaze at any time or in any way. Able to imagine that, at the same time, a contradictory, ridiculous virtue was expected of us in order for our basic dignity to be recognized, that we also weren't believed or listened to when we raised our voices...

The number of examples of all this and the number of possible suggestions and warnings is astronomical. I highly recommend reading *Playing Fair*[184] by Pepper Mint and putting those ideas into practice. The range of relationships that this book addresses is beyond what I understand as relationship anarchy, but most of the contributions are quite timely and tremendously necessary. Another

---

184 Pepper Mint, *Playing Fair: A Guide to Nonmonogamy for Men into Women*, Thorntree Press, 2017.

essential reading that goes deeper into the issues and reasons underlying all this reflection is We Should All Be Feminists by Chimamanda Ngozi Adichie.[185]

In short, when the culture has put you in a place where your behaviors are evaluated more in your favor than those of other people, your word receives more attention and respect; you have the tools at your fingertips to avoid many instances of vulnerability and aggression; you experience much less fear and enjoy so many other privileges. All of this together means that it is impossible for you to see who is underneath you. You can't see past your own nose. You neither see nor hear whoever is telling you that they're there and is explaining what's happening to them. The only way is through constant, attentive listening. Just practicing thoughtful cautiousness, paying particular attention, making an effort so that what you see and hear makes it through your wall of prejudice (plainly said, getting you out of your own head), past your tendency to take the hint personally and try to evade it (again, the well-worn "not all men") instead of understanding what privilege is, overcoming that temptation to be on the defensive and at best-seeking equidistance. And dismantling so many other things... only in this way will we be able to get a partial glimpse of that other reality, and at some time perhaps contribute to changing it from a position of listening, not of command or leadership.

Recently, an activist group described a conversation between two women and a cishet man who was explaining to them how great it was to break out of conventional relationships, saying it was actually easier than it seemed, that it was so modern and satisfying, not problematic at all. On hearing this, the conversation continued: "Has breaking the norm been as comfortable for you?" "No." "Well, it's so easy for this gentleman because he isn't breaking any rules."[186]

---

[185] Chimamanda Ngozi Adichie, We Should All Be Feminists, Knopf Doubleday, 2015.
[186] Post by Nuki Feminazgul on *Poliamor Catalunya*, 2020.

5.4 Sustainable relationships

The hegemonic model of relationships is presented as a cyclical repetition of patterns; a mechanics of emotional consumption, objectification, and substituting some people, whose bond has been bled dry, with new ones, a replacement; from one unsustainable experience to the next in a dynamic that continues without any alternatives. The pattern that was valid in our societies until the second half of the 20th century, when marriages were understood to be lifelong, has morphed into the general conviction that most relationships have an expiration date. Little attention has been devoted to assessing whether this lack of sustainability could be due to the format of affective sexual bonds and the implicit assumption that relationships have to be the same as the norm has always imposed: total, absolute, exhaustive. A standard relationship works by filling in all the emotional and vital space available. The general idea is to dedicate as much time as possible to "the couple," except for the time spent at work and on hobbies, friends, one's family of origin, etc. Any model that strays from that basic starting line is subject to criticism and the idea that there's something wrong about it. In fact, popular doctrine holds that it must also be "quality time." The definition of this quality is vague, but as a rule, it is socially unquestionable. It is a construct aimed at creating a social bubble that's isolated from all the other bubbles. If the air inside it runs out after it has existed for a while, the bubble is punctured, and the search begins again to create a new one. This way, the wheel keeps turning.

A possible paradigm shift would aim to ensure that relationships are not necessarily perishable, but not in prescriptive terms, instead seeking formulas for sustainable bonds. This is not a self-justifying end. Maybe I'm not interested in this, maybe it doesn't seem so important to me, or maybe it just doesn't suit me, and I prefer to assume that bonds have a certain life expectancy, just like people and most things. That's a valid option, but, on the other hand, I may be interested in exploring the idea of a change in the format of relationships that makes it possible to sustain some deep, thrilling, passionate bonds, those that are full of solidarity, tenderness, desires to share... So, in that case, what are the keys to fulfilling this longing for lasting, joyous bonds? Is there some magic formula? Of course not. But I suspect that the recipe, if there is one, would include ingredients like adjusting the times, spaces, and frequencies of interaction to reciprocal wishes, thus avoiding saturation; well-being and not resignation or stubbornness as a general disposition of the relationships; choosing the type of contact, interrelation, or coexistence based on the will and desires of those involved, in a way that's not conditioned by the normative patterns; and finally, fulfilling the commitments, consideration, affection, and maximum emphasis on respect for boundaries, rigorously observing the requirement of explicit consent at all times.

Dosage and sustainability

The medical definition of an overdose mentions the fact that it can only be applied to substances or behaviors that have some expected positive or practical effect. In a suicide or murder, it doesn't make any sense to say it was a poison overdose. The amount needed (or more) to poison or kill someone, if that's what you're trying to do, would have to be called an effective dose, not an overdose. So I'm interested in talking about satisfactory bonds in this case, those I want to enjoy and preserve. A relationship that's damaging to start with is toxic at any dose, and there are so many of that sort. But can a wonderful, affectionate, tender, passionate relationship that's full of respect, admiration, and affection lead to an overdose? Can something so wonderful become burdensome, annoying, and boring over time? Inevitably, there will be some sarcasm in the reply that yes, that has been known to happen. We're facing such extensive evidence that, as I said before, it has translated into a conviction for much of society, at least for the most recent generations, that relationships generally have a limited duration and that it's most common for them to end over the years to give way to new ones.

Today, it is normalized and widespread for breakups to happen because "love is over," "the passion's gone," or "it's not like it used to be." And what about applying the hypotheses of non-normative relationships? Can this dynamic be changed? It's possible. In fact, my experience shows that it does, considerably so. I think it's a good idea to start from the hypothesis that sustainable relationships are possible, though we must assume that attempts can fail and that this doesn't mean that the ideal is unfeasible. The very aspiration of sustainability may also cease to interest me at any given moment. But that isn't the case for me; I'm interested in it. It's a very clear, valuable goal in my life.

Specifically, the normative mandates that I aim to confront and rewrite in terms of self-management – in the same way that I'm repeating myself on each topic – are, in this case: that of absolute dedication as an obligation; constant attention as a vital mission; daily regularity as a duty associated with the significance of the bond. Ultimately, the proposal is to adjust the measures to the needs (something which, by the way – here, applied to relationships – is quite typical of classical social anarchism). Taking care of each other, but also taking care of desire — desires — attraction, fascination: not killing each other with an overdose. Rebelling against the norm does not mean suppressing impulses; it means deciding how and how much we see[187] each other to take care of and protect the desire to continue seeing each other over the long term or whatever term we may want, while preventing exhaustion and seeking sustainability.

---

187 By drawing on the pharmacological simile, another interesting nuance is that dosage includes not only the dose, but also how it is administered – that is, not only how much we interact but under what conditions. For instance, hanging out with someone on the sofa or in the kitchen every day when you get home isn't the same as planning specific outings to go to the movies, have dinner out, go to a concert or on a walk, or visit somewhere. At that rate, the former assumes a higher probability of breakdown in desire than the latter.

How to propose it and carry it out, the details and recipes, go beyond the scope of what I can produce here, especially since those suggestions couldn't be universalized. My experience has generally been very positive, but once again, I must repeat that every story comes from a specific place (and is also associated with privilege on various axes); therefore, it isn't easy to extrapolate. One detail that is important and likely can be generalized is that the optimal dosages are not necessarily the same for everyone involved.

The aim of sustainability could only reasonably be achieved if the level of interaction is closer to the minimum, the most restrictive of those sharing the bond – the person who would be the first to suffer from an overdose. But this, in turn, may bring up anxiety among those who have to give up their desired level of interaction, especially if it is a relationship between two people – even one framed in a broader network. Anxiety may lead to a dynamic of dependency, demand, insistence, power gradients... and end up impacting the continuity of the bonds more negatively than positively. I think this phenomenon must be monitored and kept in mind if it comes up, or if it's suspected that it could.

Well-being

One of the many constructs of idealization and mythification that have shaped the idea of love in recent centuries is that of romanticizing suffering. Self-denial as a virtue for women, men's courage in tackling frustrated attempts time and time again, impossible loves in literature, cinema, the social imaginary... all this has contributed to the inconceivable fact that well-being is not a clear objective in relationships. Something as sensible as having to be well, at ease, happy in a relationship of any type – it seems like that notion doesn't quite fit into our canon, and it especially doesn't fit with the social practice that can be seen everywhere, all the time.

In fact, malaise – which is harmful, by definition – is cloaked with a certain chimerical mystique composed of bits and pieces of religious traditions, of romantic thought, and Western assimilation of Eastern traditions over the last half-century, with its tendency to opposition, contradiction, and antagonism as forms of narrative and reflection. Ideas like "happiness doesn't exist, it's a state of mind," "you learn more from failure than success," "worthwhile things aren't easy or comfortable," and other similar notions form a framework that conceals and constitutes a breeding ground for resignation, tenacity in the face of pain, and the unjustified and unjustifiable prolongation of painful, heartbreaking processes, and even for the acceptance of abuse and domination. Therefore, in the face of this normalized cultural disposition, I'm defending the original anarchist perspective, which is utopian and anchored in a concept of happiness not mortgaged off by postmodern constructs that are rugged and convoluted. It offers a vision of life as a personal search for fulfillment, yet it doesn't consider any good to be such if it isn't held in common and achievable by the community. In short, it doesn't leave room for conformism, submission, or compliance. If a relationship isn't satisfactory, I suggest either doing the work to make it so, transforming it, or moving away from it.

Respect

Another trait that is normalized and accepted by a senseless instance of common sense, again shaped by different traditions and historical evolutions, is that of the progressive and accepted loss of respect as bonds move forward in time and grow deeper. In fact, the normative criterion – which declares an affective sexual relationship to be a special bond that's different from any other – amatonormativity, and couple privilege automatically leads to an admitted over-dimensioning of familiarity and trust, to implied agreement, to the assumption of tacit approval, and therefore, to the loss of a significant form of consent (it isn't the only one – I will discuss that essential aspect in more depth later on).

In order to overcome this configuration, which is clearly virulent, the aspiration and difficulty in this case is to separate between trust and familiarity, on the one hand, which are positive features of a bond, and on the other, assuming power and control, which underlies the dynamic of losing respect. A simple key that I've discussed, analyzed, and also used often in practice is thinking that other people would always deserve more respect for being close, loved, connected to me, no less than anyone else. That means not invading the living space, decisions, privacy, and so on of someone I relate to more than I would dare to do to someone else I don't know. If I wouldn't call someone in my neighborhood or at work on the phone at midnight except in case of an emergency or out of serious need, I wouldn't do that to any of my most intimate relationships, either. If I wouldn't drop in unexpected on just anyone, I'd treat my most valued relationships the same way. Asking for and offering help, always; invading or letting others invade my space, never. In short, I'm talking about respect for the conscious autonomy, privacy, and agency of others, their capacity for making decisions and taking action without interference, and always within a framework of consideration and awareness of the community.

Falling in love and limerence ("New Relationship Energy")

Being smitten or falling in love – a concept that's been around forever – has been called NRE (*New Relationship Energy*) in non-monogamous communities in the many books, blogs, and articles on the subject. This, of course, refers to the emotional and partially biochemical high that causes us to stop paying the same attention to those we share bonds with when someone new appears who stimulates us in a powerful way. In the scientific field, the concept of limerence is also used in this sense, especially when it is a heavily accentuated, prolonged, obsessive state. Contrary to what we might think, the most quoted, looked up, and reviewed difficulty in affective networks and non-exclusive relationships in general is not how I manage jealousy or possessiveness, since these problems are alleviated by how their causes are addressed, but how I manage NRE (both mine and that of someone I have a relationship with). Because, just as I noted when dealing with jealousy, falling in love as a sort of fit has also been mythologized and elevated to the category of an emotion that is spiritual, ungovernable, and invincible. And if it is experienced as a gift of life, there is nothing to object to – quite the opposite.

It's wonderful to get carried away by an unruly, heart-pounding wave of passion, no doubt about it. The problem is when that enthusiasm creeps into reality beyond the interaction with the new person and affects others (or my own inner balance). To a certain extent, this is unavoidable, and everything of intensity that happens to me ends up affecting my network of bonds. But it's about trying to prevent those effects from leading me to stop caring for, communicating with, and considering the importance of everyone else I relate to in a meaningful way. An even greater problem surfaces when, in addition to influencing consideration for other people, the NRE acts as an excuse to get carried away and break basic commitments. We fall into the temptation to take advantage of the cultural pattern, which subordinates everything else to falling in love and makes everything forgivable because of its all-encompassing influence, forgetting an important ingredient of relationship dynamics: thinking about others and empathizing with them.

In short, I think it's helpful to recognize the value of the high that a new affective sexual connection, or any other kind, can bring (or even a connection not necessarily with a person but with an exciting project or a professional, academic, or life challenge, etc.) and accept it as a positive thing, along with the fact that those who experience it are happier, more positive, and contribute more. However, on the other hand, it's also necessary to identify the dangers, to avoid compulsory compersion and enthusiasm from the rest of the network – understanding that others aren't going through the same process of consuming enthusiasm that I am – and, from the opposite direction, to give and demand the same respect, avoiding the objectification and trivialization of the new relationship, which is new but still involves people, as all relationships do. Maintaining the existing links in these cases requires the same care as always, or maybe even a little more, along with extra empathetic communication.

Forms of cohabitation

Earlier, I discussed intentional communities. The most visible examples are public groups that are open to participation because they promote relatively large-capacity housing infrastructure. Still, any group of people, even a small one, can have the collective characteristics, values, and motivations related to a way of life that includes solidarity, pacts of cohabitation, and collaborative forms of management based on commitments, mutual aid, and cooperation. All this defines a minimum basis from which we can speak of cohabitation formulas that are compatible with relationship anarchy. Of course, someone living alone or only two people living together can also lead a relationship anarchist lifestyle through a network set up without aspirations of group cohabitation. In fact, this is a common model.

The option of creating living spaces is interesting for many reasons: saving resources; solidarity and more direct, daily, real help with situations like parenting or in scenarios of vulnerability, grief, or illness; and as a response to possible tendencies toward isolation, especially in later stages of life. But it is also true that the experiences that have taken place so far have yielded irregular results and evaluations, ranging from the most positive to reports of serious problems of living together that worsen over time and ruin otherwise interesting, exciting ideas. In reality, as I've noted in the section on dosage and sustainability, there is a certain obsessive, permeating character in daily cohabitation that is routine, forced, and has no alternative. In this regard, one proposal that's along the same lines as those I'm proposing under various headings is "crosscutting" cohabitation, as well – keeping that main common space where you can spend as much time as you want, while each individual or subgroup also has other more private, isolated spaces. Always sharing shouldn't be mandatory.

Take, for instance, a communal infrastructure with two levels of cohabitation: *1)* private rooms, and common areas for spending time together and things like laundry, kitchens, a dining room, a library... everything you need to be able to live long-term, and *2)* apartments or standalone houses in another space where you can go to from time to time, or even most or all the time, without any rules governing those periods. Of course, commitments around coexistence must prevail in the common space to make cohabitation and harmony possible; still, the option to choose solitude or intimacy in a small group would always be available — at all times. It is one model among many other possibilities that brings together the key aspects of relationship anarchy, centering around the calling for collective life, help and cooperation, forming a network, all while combining it with respect for personal autonomy.

In any case, the idea is to challenge the heteronormative structure of the nuclear family, where the only life path is finding a partner of the opposite sex, having offspring, and raising them between two people (either together or at alternating intervals if a breakup occurs, which is already accepted and assimilated by the hegemonic model). That is a possible option – the default, actually – one that's just as legitimate as any other, but the interest here is exploring and valuing less alienating perspectives, ones that don't take us out of the collective framework where we could develop without exacerbating individualism and centering around the family or clan – those axes of industrial and post-industrial capitalist societies.

Consent

In the legal field, consent is an expression of civil law that reflects the public expression of the will to accept rights and obligations, thus defining one of the contours of the theory of autonomy of the will. In recent years, this has been one of the most mentioned concepts in debates about sexist violence as seen from the gender perspective. In the context of this book, the main concern goes beyond the patriarchal and heterocentric "he desires – she consents" and the circumstances in which that sort of consent is valid. Even so, it seems important to go over it through today's feminist lens, which aims to base the expression of will in the sexual, physical, and emotional sphere in women's empowerment.

The idea is for this unequivocal display of will regarding intimate relations to take place in an active, positive, explicit way. For it to be specific, meaning that it is valid only for a specific situation and not automatically extending to any other practice or moment, and that the manifestation of will must be maintained throughout the entire process and can be withdrawn at any moment. So far, everything is in response to a clear right to impose limits on one's own body and one's own emotion.

However, beyond boundaries, other debatable elements have surfaced, such as the need for consent to be enthusiastic and inextricably linked to desire. First, let's recall that desire, as I've mentioned in a previous chapter, stems in part from a complex, normative cultural construct that draws on allosexism and the heteropatriarchal model. It's also easy to sanctify and idealize it in line with the myths of romantic love and therefore separate it from conscious will and responsible autonomy. I insist on the point that desire, just like jealousy and other passions, has been sold to us as an uncontrollable force that we have no choice but to submit to if we are sensitive, emotional people and not "cold, calculating robots." However, we may be willing to engage in sexual activity, or any other interaction that involves bodily or emotional intimacy, for many reasons, not only out of desire.[188]

Thus, in the realm of establishing bonds – and especially their subsequent development from the perspective of relationship anarchy – the analysis could be in line with what we've said about agreements, pacts, and consensuses as the inheritances of a commercial, mercantile device. This type of consent is linked to the concession of

---

[188] Authors Stef Papin, Cristina Gozalo (K. Sagaris), and Loreto Ares explain these matters well, "Más allá del deseo," on pikaramagazine.com. Also Clara Serra in "Deseo y consentimiento no siempre coinciden," on ctxt.es.

something that is asked of me in exchange for something else that I'm asking for (and which is often a cultural stereotype that I've not reflected on or am sure responds to a real need). This consensus, as a whitewashed, sugarcoated version of the commercial contract, could be replaced by a more organic and procedural concept comparable to the calling to offer aid, the commitment to mutual care, awareness f the network, and interrelation.

Beatrice Gusmano describes this idea with great clarity:[189]

> "While the liberal definition of consent is to give permission beforehand, care takes place not only before, but also during and after things have occurred, "acknowledging the human condition as a state of interdependency, rather than acceptance of the liberal illusion of personal autonomy" (Bauer, 2014: 106). Liberal consent operates in a fictional linear dimension, without taking into account unexpected events, new relationship energy, vulnerabilities, desires, and crossroads – that is, precisely the raw material of intimacies, from which arises the art of care: a relational practice shaped in creative ways by affective contingency. Moreover, while liberal consent affects a limited number of people (usually two) who make an agreement, care can radiate all over because it isn't bound to a specific situation: it's a way of being in the world, of caring about, of assuming responsibilities, of admitting vulnerabilities."

Conclusions and proposals for starting to relate in a different way

Ultimately, in emotional and behavioral terms, the general idea is to consider the set of all my relationships of all sorts as a network, and to prevent those with whom I have bonds with romantic, affective, and/or sexual components at a given moment from holding privileges over others. To do so, the most direct option is to avoid using labels that define the bonds, or reduce the weight these carry, because it's hard to keep the title I give to each relationship from

---

[189] B. Gusmano, "The Kintsugi Art of Care: Unraveling Consent in Ethical Non-Monogamies," *Sociological Research Online*, 2018.

letting some of its regulatory burden weigh on those who it is meant to describe.

Freeing myself from relationship labels can also help me exonerate myself from guilt, lighten expectations, express desires and needs more freely, build meaningful commitments, and set clear boundaries, not experiencing relationships out of insecurity or fear of loneliness. This is because the concept of breaking up also loses its gravity, as it ceases to be an abrupt fracture and instead becomes an evolution. The pressure to comply with all that is expected of us, internally and externally, is mitigated, as is demand from within to fulfill all of someone's needs or those of a particular relationship category. In short, it alleviates the obligation to comply with norms I had no part in creating.

Using a criterion similar to the one we use for the bonds we call friendship can be a good starting point. The goal would be to apply that criterion along with an added level of communication, care, consideration, and respect for all my relationships. This is not at all a simple task: there are no models I can follow, and I can't expect outside recognition. External forces will use all means at their disposal to pigeonhole each relationship into a category. It's the socio-relational version of *horror vacui:* what isn't understood is filled in with whatever label is closest at hand.

I also believe that it is important not to be discouraged when I realize that I'm not treating everyone in my network the same; that's not what it's all about. Nor is it about spending the same amount of time (those dosages are different for every interaction), or feeling my pulse race in the same way, or leveling out any other feature of the relationships. Making everything uniform is not the issue. The goal is for there to be no privileges that objectify, that establish hierarchies of rights, that turn some people into an authority and others into underlings. If I laugh more with one person than another, nothing is going to change that. Trying to control it is an undoubtedly problematic aspiration that has nothing to do with relationship anarchy. If I'd rather go to the movies, or fuck, with one person more than another, there is nothing wrong with that. I certainly shouldn't beat myself up about it. It makes sense for me to have different degrees of intimacy, different desires, different ways of enjoying myself with different people. Also, all of that can vary over time without any drama, schisms, fractures, artificial distancing.

Other outcomes of relationship anarchy's general approach that overlap with the previous ones are: I can lower the need to continuously verify my position, as to whether or not we're a couple, friends, or something else; I can gradually empty out clichés like "working on the relationship" to simply enjoy it; I want to stop considering long distance relationships to be a challenge where each encounter has to be wonderful and fill the other person's life until the next meeting; I don't have to account for sexual orientation in an exhaustive, exclusive way because it isn't a factor that will limit the character and type of possible relationships; the explicit, precise definition of sexual identity is also going to become less important to me as a requirement when it comes to bonding; I have to consider and minimize the influence that vectors of power like geographical origin, race, or social position have; I'll have more tools to situate the different dimensions of oppression at the heart of all vigilance so that – specifically in the case of gender – there is no lack of listening by people socially read as men, and there is an awareness of our privileges; and with the help of an entire network of affections, it is possible to reduce the consequences of those privileges and move forward so that they will, at some point, cease to exist.

In short, I understand that building networks is possible because it is already happening. Some of us are lucky enough to experience and share webs of bonds where love and support are as solid as in any normative family relationship, and much more sustainable. My feeling, which is personal and subjective, may respond to an idealization or a fantasy, but I don't think that's the case. I'm convinced that it is real.

Chapter 6. Making what's nameless visible: relationship activism

"You can't give up on something just because it won't happen in the time of your own existence. I couldn't live if I didn't believe that imagination can create new realities."

— Gioconda Belli.

"Only those who are capable of embodying utopia will be able to fight the ultimate combat; that of recuperating the humanity that we have lost."

— Ernesto Sábato.

Throughout the book, I've discussed the concept of *lifestyle politics* and mentioned proposals such as that of Laura Portwood-Stacer. Now going into more detail, she defines the term as follows:[190]

"When individuals who desire social or political change are compelled to shape their own personal behaviors and choices toward the ideals they envision, this is known as lifestyle politics. While the stakes of each specific episode of activism may be low, the moments of confrontation are multiplied for radical lifestyle activists because every minute decision one makes is implicated in a fight for a new society. The way one dresses, the food one eats, even the people one chooses to have sex with, can become overtly political acts. Radical lifestyle politics reconfigures the everyday life of the individual into an ongoing struggle against domination."

---

190 L. Portwood-Stacer, *Lifestyle Politics and Radical Activism*, op. cit.

This definition comes from the anarchist tradition and absolutely fits in with the idea of relationship anarchy. But this type of activism carries a number of specific needs to have any chance of being effective. The most important one is that it cannot be restricted to one person or a few people. It has to become a movement. Political movements often pose an open confrontation, organize based on location, set up demonstrations, protests, occupations of public or private space, and even give rise to political parties. But in the case of *lifestyle politics*, the site of direct confrontation is occupied by cultural work, the search for visibility and recognition, the definition and contribution of content to subcultural identities such as urban tribes, subversive communities, reflection, activism, etc.

This author continues on anarchist activism:[191]

> "(...) anarchism is a "political culture," which entails "a family of shared orientations to doing and talking about politics and to living everyday life." In this, anarchism is typical of contemporary social movements in which a very blurry line separates everyday life and political orientation, if any such line exists at all. Anarchists present a rather extreme case, since, as anarchist writer Cindy Milstein suggests, "Embracing anarchism is a process of reevaulating every assumption, everything one thinks about and does, and indeed who one is, and then basically turning one's life upside-down. "The radical subversiveness of anarchist political philosophy translates to the striking contrast between the ways of life pursued by anarchists and those in the mainstream, hence the idea that one's life is turned "upside-down (...)"

In fact, Portwood-Stacer introduces the concept of "chosen identities" after Kath Weston's concept of "chosen family." In the same way that there is nothing prior given as in the family of origin for one's chosen family, in the case of the anarchist identity – which can be extended to relationship anarchists – there is no primary trait such as social class, race, or place of origin supporting it. There is no physical appearance, religious group, sexual orientation, or social

---

191   Ibid., p. 14.

position that gives it substance. The identity is therefore more difficult to display and maintain, and visibility is more difficult to achieve.

In Amateurism and anarchism in the creation of autonomous queer spaces, Gavin Brown[192] says:

> "(...) in recent decades anarchist resistance has been generalised such that it no longer focuses predominantly on the state and capital, but attempts to expose and undermine all forms of domination operating in society (including racism, patriarchy and heteronormativity). The goal of anarchism has shifted from the abolition and replacement of existing political institutions towards the redefinition of every aspect of social relations. (...) In the process of building prefigurative experiments, the desires for personal liberation and social change motivate each other. This in turn promotes anarchism as a culture, a rhizomatic lived experience that pops up everywhere, adapting to specific situations and cultures."

As Brown indicates, when speaking of prefigurative experiments in some forms of anarchism, relationship anarchy also approximates the concept of "prefigurative lifestyle politics." This term was coined in 1977 by Carl Boggs in[193] reference to "the embodiment, within the ongoing political practice of a movement, of those forms of social relations, decision-making, culture, and human experience that are the ultimate goal" and which authors such as A.J. Elliot Ince and[194] Paul Raekstad[195] examine historically, assessing its relationship with proposals ranging from programmatic aspects of the First International, the first anarchist movements that applied it in isolated communities, to post-war approaches that proposed expanding the concept to broad social contexts, and finally, contemporary currents

---

192 J. Heckert and R. Cleminson, *Anarchism and Sexuality*, op. cit.
193 C. Boggs, "Marxism, Prefigurative Communism, and the Problem of Workers' Control," *Radical America*, 1977.
194 A. J. E. Ince, *Organising anarchy spatial strategy prefiguration and the politics of everyday life*, doctoral thesis, Queen Mary University of London, 2010.
195 P. Raekstad, "Revolutionary practice and prefigurative politics: A clarification and defense," *Constellations*, 2018.

such as Zapatismo, the movements taking place in public spaces, *Occupy*, etc., which are already widely recognized, though not necessarily taken on by significant majorities.

In the reference cited, Elliot Ince proposes that the daily policies practiced by radical prefigurative groups are oriented around autonomy in its anarchist sense, not isolationist forms of autonomy. That means that it advocates for the practice and promotion of collective self-organization with the intention of reaching all of society, not upholding one community as an example or experiment. Ince indicates that prefigurative politics are linked to the conception and configuration of everyday spaces. Coinciding with my approach in the book's introduction, he relates prefigurative trends to the decline of anti-capitalist, anti-globalization, and global justice movements. Ince suggests that its failure should be used as inspiration and a warning, as well as a source of creativity and flexibility, weighing in by saying:

> "(...) the spectacular politics of street parties, blockades, squat raves and summit demonstrations. (...) showed that politics could be fun and exciting in the apparently hopeless aftermath of the brutal neoliberalisation of the 1980s and 1990s. However, the failures of the movement are clear: ghettoisation, a distinct lack of power to affect material conditions, and the movement's eventual stagnation. Graffiti in Seattle during the 1999 WTO summit – "we are winning" – now seems embarrassingly optimistic a decade later to those involved in the upsurge who have witnessed its faltering. (...) [and] "what next?" How do you 'move on' after decline, and where to? Throughout, I have argued that a return to the transformative potential of everyday life is an important shift that has begun to take place, and that it is underpinned by an increasingly serious approach to radical political organising around concrete, material issues."

The battle is being lost against the immense deployments of security forces at international summits; against the restrictions and infringement on freedom of expression, which haven't stopped growing; and against the educational and ideological control of the oppressed majorities by the powerful religious, political, and economic elites that already control most of the private and chartered education and that, through some shameful pseudo-media and social networks, end up submerging true journalism in a tide of fake news and ultraconservative reactionary communication strategies. It isn't about abandoning any paths of peaceful struggle, advancement, and progress, but we must recognize that things aren't at all easy. On the other hand, there are also those who signal important points of reluctance regarding prefigurative approaches. One of the most influential works that has questioned this type of politics is by Murray Bookchin; it very critically analyzes some forms of environmentalism, biocentrism, and lifestyle anarchism.[196]

In any case, it must be considered that relationship anarchy is not exactly a type of prefigurative anarchism but more indirect in its political aspirations, more in the line of the phrase attributed to Emma Goldman (though it is actually paraphrased), "If I can't dance, it's not my revolution,"[197] or from Bob Pop's reply to the question, "What is subversive today?" "Being happy. We're supposed to be sad, distrustful, and hopeless. When that's what we're up against, rebellion is happiness and affection. A rabid happiness that's militant against inertia."[198]

6.1 What activism, and why?

In terms closer to the current reality of relationship anarchy – which works in environments of everyday practice – I can make out, as I said at the beginning, two different motivations: when there is nothing more than a desire to approach relationships in another way, or when, in addition to that desire, there is the added political concern

---

[196] M. Bookchin, *Social Anarchism or Lifestyle Anarchism: An Unbridgeable Chasm*, AK Press, Edinburgh.
[197] Alix Kates Shulman, "Dances with Feminists," *Women's Review of Books*, 1991.
[198] Luz Sánchez-Mellado's interview with Roberto Enríquez (Bob Pop), *El País* 26 Jan 2019.

to seek ways to improve our societies. Both have a reading based in identity. I have addressed the latter in the previous section; the first could correspond to the description provided by Michel Foucault in an interview conducted by B. Gallagher and A. Wilson in Toronto in June 1982:[199]

> "Well, if identity is only a game, if it is only a procedure to have relations, social and sexual-pleasure relationships that create new friendships, it is useful. But if identity becomes the problem of sexual existence, and if people think that they have to "uncover" their "own identity," and that their own identity has to become the law, the principle, the code of their existence; if the perennial question they ask is "Does this thing conform to my identity?" then, I think, they will turn back to a kind of ethics very close to the old heterosexual virility. If we are asked to relate to the question of identity, it must be an identity to our unique selves. But the relationships we have to have with ourselves are not ones of identity, rather, they must be relationships of differentiation, of creation, of innovation. To be the same is really boring. We must not exclude identity if people find their pleasure through this identity, but we must not think of this identity as an ethical universal rule."

Here, working from other starting points, Foucault identifies what I called "dangers of identarian sense" in the previous chapter, which I've proposed redirecting from identity to sensitivity. This should lead to the configuration of dynamics of interaction that are especially sensitive to any forms of authority, domination, and privilege, and to the construction of spaces or networks of collective self-management. I'll develop these ideas in the following sections.

---

[199] M. Foucault, "Sex, Power and the Politics of Identity," interview in *The Advocate*, 1984. The quote is Foucault's answer to the question, "Is it significant that there are, to a large degree, identities forming around new sexual practices, like S&M? These identities help in exploring such practices and defending the right to engage in them. But are they also limiting in regards to the possibilities of individuals?"

Identity or cuddles

Simply by building networks of mutual support, environments with fewer privileges and more laughter and kisses, a form of activism, a way of life, visibility, and normalization is already underway. But it's also true that, as I look around, I may sometimes meet people, groups, entire sectors that seem to need reference points that go farther. People who have felt like they're on the outside of a relationship system that didn't fit them, people who have searched and found articles, books, videos, podcasts; they have tried to assimilate them and make them their own... and end up finding themselves in the same place as always. As much as they perceive personal growth and a richer, more critical awareness, what they see around them is precisely unnecessary suffering, general resignation, and power relations.

This, among other reasons, is why there is organized, operational, and functional activism aimed at finding spaces and setting up meetings and events. Interaction, reflection, sharing experiences and emotional closeness are key elements to maintain and improve how I face a personal challenge with a collective calling. This challenge involves dismantling many behaviors and lessons assimilated from the first stages of life on, and which is therefore very intellectually and emotionally demanding. Only with a support network can I travel this path of deconstruction and renovation.

The question of whether we can call this work activism makes perfect sense. The contemporary interpretation[200] indicates that activism depends more on the meaning that groups assign to the exercise of organizing and coordinating actions and messages than on the actual result of those actions. Sharing approaches, thoughts,

---

200 Many of the current styles of activism represent a departure from previous forms of political action that were directed directly at the state. The current LGBTIQ+, anti-globalization, anti-capitalist, and anti-speciesist movements address and include personal aspects, and it is with these that they support their radical criticism of the system. For these communities, lifestyle activism is natural, the only path towards a cultural revolution leading to real, radical, inescapable change in hegemonic canons.

and objectives that aspire to social change from outside any corporate, institutional, or media space – even if it is exclusively oriented to support, aid, and promote connections in the community (though this not usually the case, the intention is broader) – it is an act that possesses the will to change things, to make visible, and to normalize ideas and practices. In fact, another objective of relationship activism movements is to create materials and be available to convey a vision to the media that is as far as possible from anything rough or shabby, a temptation that arises from sensationalism. According to Portwood-Stacer:[201]

> "(...) cultural work is necessary to produce political resistance and, second, that resistant practices perform cultural work as well. Shared norms and discourses of identity enable individuals to coordinate their behavior into collective practices that resist dominant ideologies and structures. At the same time, these collective practices of resistance performatively reproduce the same norms and identities that enabled them."

However, Foucault's reflection quoted at the beginning of this section points, as I noted, to something I've already dealt with in previous chapters: the danger of identarian sense. Group dynamics are quite complicated to manage – or rather, they aren't managed; they happen on their own without it being easy to moderate certain drifts that occur. There's another risk from the outside, as well. When it comes to groups that challenge the most central part of a society's belief system, the way that relationships are considered, and how their most intimate behaviors and coexistence mechanics are structured, the external perception is normally associated with a feeling of fear and rejection. Words like "sect," "brainwashing," and "perversion" have replaced the old concept of "sin." Though sin has become passé as a signifier, its meaning hasn't faded at all, as it responds to a form of defending the unshakeable nature of the hegemonic social model.

---

201 L. Portwood-Stacer, *Lifestyle Politics and Radical Activism,* op. cit.

Another common reaction that's closely related to the previous one is ridicule, contempt, caricature. These are responses that many identity-related, ideological, intellectual, scientific, commemorative, and radical manifestations have received and continue to receive when their target is revolutionary or simply untimely and socially unthinkable. In any case, it's possible that this attention, in the form of rejection or satire, responds to a susceptibility, to the fact that a sensitive nerve has been struck, that visibility is possible and we're on the right track. After all, the elites who create opinions and hold a good portion of control over the media consist of people who have the ability to reproduce cultural mandates and their results in the form of social practices in a clear, accessible way; they can therefore impart those mandates with consistency and credibility to facilitate their assimilation. The elite notably does not include those with a greater capacity to propose new ideas.

Hermeneutical dissent

I've already spoken of the concept of hermeneutical injustice introduced by Miranda Fricker[202]. This appears when a group cannot find access to common resources of social interpretation, which puts that community at a disadvantage with respect to society in general. Without tools for constructing meaning and communicating differentiating ideas and experiences that set the group's approach and objectives apart, there is an imbalance and a significant lack of options to build reality. An example that Esa Díaz León cites in a presentation entitled "Amatonormatividad e Injusticia Hermenéutica" ("Amatonormativity and Hermeneutic Injustice") [203] is that of sexual harassment at work. Before this concept was widespread, it was more difficult not only to relay these situations but even to conceptualize, understand, and express the seriousness of this sort of experience. Díaz León also cites concepts such as "homophobia" in

---

202 M. Fricker, *Epistemic Injustice: Power and the Ethics of Knowing*, Oxford University Press, Oxford, 2007.
203 Roundtable on November 15 at the 2018 edition of the Barcelona Pensa philosophy festival, held at the University of Barcelona.

the negative sense and "gay," "queer," and "trans" in the positive. These notions' diffusion into common language provides very powerful tools for empowerment and thinking about difference in terms of both resistance and affirmation.

Another element I've discussed is that of sexual consent, which is beginning to be recognized as part of the general wealth of socially known and understood concepts (at least to some degree). There is a huge difference between facing a situation of sexual violence of any level without knowing this signifier (especially its meaning and its recognized, shared value), and facing it with the support that comes from understanding it. This reinforcement may contribute to rebelling against true exercises of humiliation at specific times, reversing years of subjection and abuse, raising alarms about situations of violence that had been normalized... Other signifiers like "bullying," "xenophobia," "aporophobia,"[204] etc. may act or eventually end up acting in this way, as well. In the realm of relationships, many examples of common language can be cited that give meaning and support to the hegemonic model: "fidelity," "commitment," and "respect" in positive lights, or "adultery," "betrayal," and "deception" in negative ones. These concepts qualify specific behaviors to underpin the mandatory features of normative relationships. If we don't respect couple privilege, that pedestal where the person we socially identify as a spouse or the like is placed above any other, then "we're not faithful," "we're not keeping our commitment," or "we're not being respectful."

Obviously, fidelity is a generic concept that refers to not violating trust, not sexual exclusivity; commitments may be very varied and refer to duties and responsibilities that have nothing to do with the

---

204 Aporophobia, rejection of the poor, is a term proposed by Adela Cortina in response to the fact that it's not a problem when a foreigner or someone of another race comes to invest, participate in tourism, or contribute resources of any kind. It is a problem when the person is poor. The existence of this word is invaluable for society to be aware of that reality. A. Cortina, *Aporofobia, el rechazo al pobre: un desafío para la democracia*, Paidós, Barcelona, 2017.

normative couple; respect is directed to the individual, not to a culturally normative model of behavior. Negative terms, on the other hand, place blame and define what can and can't be done. For example, "betrayal" and "deception" – as synonyms for behaviors that aren't approved by the norm – cast any deviation from that norm as harmful. "Adultery" characterizes the sexual exclusivity that must accompany the institution of the traditional couple, and so on.

So, what can activism do in this regard? Trystan S. Goetze introduces the term "hermeneutical dissidence"[205] to refer to the production of a personal set of interpretive tools capable of attributing coherent meaning to the universe of a group's approaches and experiences, in this case, a non-normative group. The idea is to give life to new meanings that positively reflect sensitivity; the ethical, anti-authoritarian perspective; the levels of consideration, respect, commitment, and care that underlie approaches like relationship anarchy (and which other proposals share, with differences and nuances, such as ethical non-monogamies, the LGBTIQ+ struggle, and feminist, anti-speciesist, and antifascist movements). Philosopher Komarine Romdenh-Romluc[206] delves into the importance of how meanings, signifiers, origins of meaning, arguments, and experiences form a structure that can compete with the hegemonic order as a vision of the world, particularly in the areas where these visions create conflict and a disadvantage for the minority that she calls "the object of injustice." This process aspires to turn this structure into a source of cultural authority.

From activism's point of view, the problem arises when the oppressed group, which is the object of hermeneutical injustice, proposes questions that in turn may appear unjust or contradict our principles. The author gives the example of Western feminism and

---

[205] T. S. Goetze, "Hermeneutical Dissent and the Species of Hermeneutical Injustice," *Hypatia*, 2018.
[206] K. Romdenh-Romluc, "Hermeneutical Injustice and the Problem of Authority," *Feminist Philosophy Quarterly*, 2017.

the difficulties involved in criticizing some practices of other cultures that are oppressed in the West. At times, this criticism fully enters the realm of cultural colonialism. Similar instances arise from certain feminisms' attacks on trans people or the abolitionist invective about unions and organized collectives of sex workers. There have also been certain misgivings on the part of LGBTIQ+ organizations regarding sex-positive movements and non-monogamies. This includes, for instance, the inclusion of those movements at events like Pride; such a move has been seen as a potential threat that could partially return a group that has, for decades now, made great strides towards normalization back to marginalization.

6.2 Support networks and civil and economic rights

The social and legal norm establishes that relationships considered to be a "couple" — as they include an affective-sexual component in their original formulation, regardless of the actual behaviors that occur within them — amass all legal privileges, rights, and benefits of a social nature. This comes from a tradition where the meaning of marriage was exclusively reproductive; it is still the concept of family, expanded in some legal codes according to cultural advances, that remains protected. In contrast, relationship anarchy starts out from the claim that this privileged treatment should not be provided.

When there is a a specific border that defines the types of relationships and unduly hierarchizes bonds, from the moment that border's existence is challenged, the aspiration to change the legal treatment of relationships is clearly justified. In *Minimizing Marriage*[207], Elizabeth Brake proposes ending the current concept of marriage and replacing it with the legal recognition of caring relationships between adults, which she calls "minimal marriage." This

---

207   E. Brake, *Minimizing Marriage: Marriage, Morality, and the Law*, Oxford University Press, Oxford, 2012, and elizabethbrake.com/after-marriage/

legitimation would be articulated through a series of particular commitments in each case, and recognized benefits would be associated with those commitments. The benefits would also be specific to each relationship, meaning they are non-normative in the sense that I've been using that term. The only applicable restrictions would be basic criteria of justice and equity. Brake also recognizes that the automatic, generalized application of these types of formulas may negatively affect the groups that are most vulnerable, specifically women. Therefore, she proposes that they should be established with caution and at a pace that society can keep up with, considering the axes of oppression at play and their intensity. Overcoming amatonormativity cannot come at the cost of other oppressions becoming more intense or chronic.

Liberation from or deregulation of relationships?

Brake's approach is framed in a set of proposals of a liberal political nature (liberal in the sense of civil rights, not economic liberalism – what is called progressive politics in Europe) such as Tamara Metz's intimate care-giving unions,[208] Clare Chambers' marriage free state,[209] and the legal recognition of friendship as a care-giving union as posited by Laura A. Rosenbury.[210] A vision more rooted in social anarchism would be promoting the establishment and legal recognition of support networks between people. This would be closer to the ideas of many activist groups, especially in Europe. Without relationship anarchy being the only frame of reference in these groups, a recent work by Pablo Pérez Navarro[211] investigates this issue, quoting several testimonies. Among them is that of Miguel Vagalume:

---

208 T. Metz, *Untying the Knot. Marriage, the State, and the Case for Their Divorce*. Princeton University Press, Princeton, 2010.
209 C. Chambers, *Against Marriage: An Egalitarian Defence of the Marriage-Free State*, Oxford University Press, Oxford, 2017.
210 L. A. Rosenbury, "Friends with Benefits?" *Mich. L. Rev,* 2016.
211 P. Pérez Navarro, "Beyond Inclusion: Non-monogamies and the Borders of Citizenship," *Sexuality & Culture*, 2016.

"Though it is convenient in some cases to achieve certain legislative objectives (unions, affiliations, family health insurance...), at the present, the legal recognition of these types of relationship is not a priority in these communities. (...) You don't get out of one corset just to squeeze into another."

And Brigitte Vasallo's:

"[(...)] [The fight for legal recognition] is a job that must be done, but let's see how it is done. Let's see if the law becomes a means, not a pact with a "shitty reality." Let's see if we're going to demand marriage between more than two people as a tool for survival (to obtain the recognition of children being raised by more than two people so that they are allowed to visit their partners in the hospital, etc.), or if that is going to be an end in itself and we're going to settle for it."

The example of marriage equality is a clear one. In LGBTIQ+ communities, concepts like "chosen family," as opposed to "family of origin," and the first experiences of care in networks emerged beyond traditional forms of coexistence (among other things, due to rejection and distancing from families of origin). Given this fact, it is paradoxical that the aspiration to fit into a normativity from which they were ejected has resulted in an already-effective return to that same normativity, along with the acceptance and reproduction of all its prescriptive guidelines. In this sense, I consider it important to remember that people with more economic and social power, with more resources, already have alternatives for access to care, comfort, company, and attention without changing anything. They have the skills, contacts, and time to look for all that, or even just pay for it. The most vulnerable people are the ones who are at the other end of the axes of power and influence, the ones who would get the most benefits out of another way of socially organizing bonds through networks of affection and care.

6.3 Collectives, spaces of socialization, and actions for visibility

Not everyone has an interest in connecting with communities of people they don't know. There are those who prefer to maintain a network of bonds and follow the evolution of ideas and experiences from the outside through books, articles, blogs, and social media. But there are also many people who, to a greater or lesser extent, enjoy approaching like-minded people to have activities and projects in common. The level of formality or spontaneity of the meetings is also an issue that is subject to the preferences of each individual and allows for many interpretations and formats. Different actions of any type contribute to a sense of community and to certain long-term collective dynamics. Whether they are local or broad in geographic scope, sporadic or periodic, or even if they set up permanent premises with space for events, a bar, a library, etc., the idea is for there to be the possibility of meeting and sharing experiences, readings, and reflections.

Communities for non-normativity

Stable, active communities that focus exclusively on relationship anarchy don't exist yet, as far as I know. The vast majority are grouped into larger communities identified under the common umbrella of "non-monogamies," of "non-normative ethical relationships," or the concept of "polyamory." Of course, the differences between these proposals are important, and in some respects, they're so markedly distinct that they're at the opposite ends of an axis for characterization: they range from having not one but several relationships of an amatonormative and privileged nature to not allowing amatonormativity and couple privilege. However, the act of jointly challenging the compulsory, heteronormative, monogamous system unites many sensibilities in communities that are plural but share some common identarian feeling.

In many cities in Spain, regular formal meetings are held, but they're often associated with a festive component. They are called "Policañas" or "Polibirras" (Poly-beers). Both in Valencia and in Madrid there are legally formalized organizations (respectively, "Associació per a les Relacions Afectives Ètiques Non-normatives de València," which is quite active thanks above all to the drive of Berta Fabra, and "Poliamor Madrid" which is backed by a group that is also very dynamic); in Barcelona, the most powerful organization is "*Amors Plurals.*" In rural areas, the *Amors Rurals* collective in Catalonia that I've already mentioned is particularly notable. In other European countries, there are slight variations, such as in France, Belgium, and Switzerland. There, the regular meetings are usually called *Café Poly* and are held in major cities. In Austria and Germany, they're called *Polytreff*, poly-encounters, and they take place in large urban areas as well. Other similar formats are *Poly-Connect, PolyTisch, and PolyWhonzimmer,* each with their own peculiarities.

There are more intensive arrangements: conferences with one or two days of lectures, workshops, and round tables, like the pioneering Polydays, which has been held in the United Kingdom since 2004, almost always in London; Openday in Madrid, and *Les Jornades d'Amors Plurals* (The Plural Loves Conferences) in Barcelona. There are also academic panels like the Non-Monogamies and Contemporary Intimacies conferences held at universities in Lisbon in 2015, Vienna in 2017, and Barcelona in 2019. The next one is scheduled for 2022 in Chile.

OpenCons

The most anticipated events in these communities are undoubtedly those that include two or three full days of interaction, usually at hostels or country homes, with spaces for workshops and activities and the ability to accommodate attendees. At these places, there is a significant level of coexistence over a weekend. The first of this kind in Europe was the *International PolyWeekend Girona* in 2010 and the *OpenCon UK*, which ran from 2010 to 2014 in Dorset.

The first OpenCons set a trend that continues to this day, not only in terms of the general format but also in almost all the details. This is the description that Ludi, one of the organizers of these first events, gave on polytical.org in October 2011, and which we could say has already historical value:

> "OpenCon will be a weekend of workshops, discussions, socialising and community-building among non-monogamous people in the beautiful Dorset countryside. It'll run from the evening of Friday 14th October until the afternoon of Sunday 16th October, and it costs £90 for a bed, full board and unlimited cups of tea over the weekend.
>
> OpenCon is envisioned and organised using the unconference model: the idea is that attendees bring their ideas and run workshops themselves on topics they'd like to see discussed. Essentially, we're trying to provide a space in which conversations can happen – we as organisers don't necessarily know what poly people should be discussing, but you do, so we've put the programme into your hands.
>
> A few workshops have been arranged in advance to kick off the weekend, including discussions on being bi and poly, poly activism, and feminism. When attendees arrive, they'll see a big schedule with a small number of pre-arranged workshops, a large number of empty timeslots in our five workshop spaces, and a stack of post-its and pens for adding their own sessions to the mix. We haven't published the schedule in advance because we don't want the small number of pre-arranged workshops to be the focus!
>
> It's not just workshops, either – there's loads to do to help make OpenCon a success, including publicity, arranging rideshares, evening entertainment, meeting and greeting, being a friendly face on desk and keeping people in touch after the event. There's now this awesome google doc, where anyone can sign up for (or suggest) anything!

After discussion, we've actively chosen to not advertise OpenCon very much because this is intended as a community event for people already practising non-monogamy, rather than an outreach or an introductory event. We're happy to let news spread slowly via word of mouth, because this is more likely to lead to a group of really awesome people making the event happen!

Last year's event included pre-arranged workshops on poly activism (which created Polytical.org), relationship anarchy, and poly and spirituality, and we also saw people arrange workshops on queer poly, sexuality, sci-fi and many more. It was a brilliant weekend! This year, we've more workshop space, more people coming and a shiny new chillout and craft area, and I think it's going to be even better! "

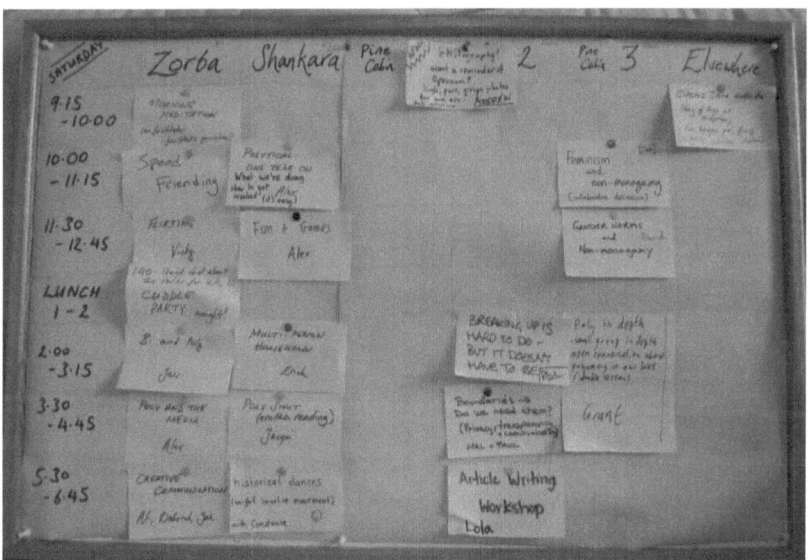

Contents of the first day of OpenCon 2011. Source: polytical.org (now in webarchive.org)

Since 2012, the *International OpenCon Catalonia* has been held in the region of l'Empordà in Girona, which had its eighth year in 2019. The format is quite similar to that of the original OpenCon; this in turn has been used in events of the same name held in Finland, Transylvania (Romania) in 2017 and 2018, and Perugia (Italy) from 2016 to now. In Spain, *OpenCon Madrid* has been held since 2015 in the province of Ávila, and since 2018, there has been *OpenCon València,* which most recently brought more than 100 people together for a weekend in the region of Foia de Bunyol. Another highly interesting event that presents the peculiarity of explicitly seeking an intersectional view that includes territory and language (Catalan, in this case), feminism, anti-capitalism, environmentalism, non-monogamies, diversity, and the LGBTIQ+ struggle is *Eixams*. It has been held since 2016 in the south of Catalonia, and the organizing team is associated with *Amors Plurals*.

Library of the second OpenCon València in June 2019. Source: Juan-Carlos Pérez-Cortés

The calling to include most of these questions, even if not explicitly stated, is present in all the meetings I've mentioned. There are always workshops on feminism, diversity, axes of oppression; there is a vegan option on the menu (or a vegan menu for everyone, except those with special needs), non-mixed workshops where people read as women can have activities without men present (and sometimes workshops for men to deal with topics on deconstructing hegemonic masculinity), and other similar topics.

In some groups, there are also periodic activities organized for women, such as polibirras and non-mixed encounters. In February 2020, Womanxé was held, the first weekend event, in an OpenCon, non-mixed style for cis and trans women and non-binary people. This trend reflects the necessary role that women and feminism play in the activist sphere, as an essential element for preventing affective diversity at the beginning of the 21st century from following the same path as the supposed previous revolutions, where men kept all their levels of power and leadership.

On other continents, especially North America, the style and dynamics of the events include highly varied encounters, some of them more magical, ritual, festive, spiritual, sexual, playful, BDSM-oriented, or esoteric in nature. There's such enormous diversity.

Alan MacDonald hosts a comprehensive list of upcoming events taking place worldwide[212]. These events range from intimate weekend retreats to multi-day camps, conferences, and even a special event at Burning Man.

In the United States, there is the Southwest Love Fest, a weekend event held in Arizona, and the Midwest Love Fest, a one-day conference on relationships, identity, community, and non-monogamy is held in Indianapolis, Indiana. Camp Menagerie (formerly PolyCamp Northeast) spans a full week in east-central New Hampshire. It offers a variety of self-organized talks and activities, including nonviolent communication techniques, general poly discussion, genderqueer topics, yoga, nightly campfire, board games, crafts, a kayak race, cuddle party, and talent show. The Rocky Mountain Polyamory Family Campout, held nearly every year for the past 20 years, takes place in the White River National Forest near Carbondale, Colorado, offering opportunities for hiking, exploring ghost

---

212   The most thorough lists at the moment are probably "Upcoming Events: next 12 months" on polyevents.blogspot.com, and "Polyamory Events" at findamunch.com.

towns, fishing, campfire cooking, conversations, and hanging out with other polyamorous families. Polytopia, a three-day weekend exploration of polyamory takes place in Portland, Oregon.

Black Poly Pride in Washington, DC aims to celebrate and empower the Black polyamorous community. Polyamory Unconference in Ohio allows participants to propose and run their own sessions, creating a dynamic and collaborative learning environment. Network for a New Culture camps in Virginia offer several-day retreats focused on building intimate and sustainable communities. Minnesota PolyCon provides a one-day event with sessions on various aspects of polyamory. Rocky Mountain Poly Living and Poly Weekend Retreats in Colorado offer relaxing getaways for polyamorous individuals to connect and enjoy the beauty of the Rocky Mountains. Rocky Mountain Polyamory Family Campout also in Colorado offers an informal gathering for polyamorous families to enjoy the outdoors.

Poly Big Fun in Texas and offer opportunities for connection and learning. Solo Polyamory unConference is a roving conference that caters to solo polyamorous individuals and those who support them. Loving More Oregon Retreat offers a weekend-long retreat for polyamorous individuals to connect and learn from each other. RelateFest in Miami, Florida is a wellness event focused on exploring relationships, learning new skills, and connecting with others.

Moving beyond the US, Polytreffen in Germany provides a platform for German-speaking polyfolks to network and share experiences. Love Is Love in Germany is a new conference that brings together polyamorous individuals and their allies. Polyday London in the UK provides a day for ethically non-monogamous individuals to connect, share knowledge, and build community.

In Canada, Polywood, a kid-friendly poly camping weekend, is held in Ottawa, Ontario, offers a chance to laugh, learn, and build community under the stars, according to their organizers.

Even at the iconic Burning Man festival, the Village of PolyParadise, a large theme-camp cluster running since 1999, typically hosts 250-300 campers, with about half being repeats from previous years. It offers a variety of workshops and events, including Poly High Tea, the Human Carcass Wash, Poly Friendly Social/Mixer, Ethical Slut Meet & Greet, Fire Flow Yoga, the Twisted Swan Celtic Pub, and the non-alcoholic Temple of Bacchus.

A meeting on relationship anarchy

The only monographic meeting specifically dedicated to Relationship Anarchy that I've heard of in Europe was held on July 16 and 17, 2016 (apart from workshops, lectures, talks, debates, etc.).

We called it the First Meeting on Relationship Anarchy, and it took place in a cozy dance school in Albacete in Castilla-La Mancha. With Roma and Lucas de las Heras initiative and organization, it was attended by activists from Albacete, València, Castelló, and Catalonia, and the work focused on identifying the structures, values, tools, violence, risks, axes, and relationship configurations that are at play in the field of relationship anarchy. With them, we made a conceptual map. As conclusions, it was suggested that work was needed that would allow us to delineate and differentiate Relationship Anarchy from other proposals, maintain ties with other communities, and continue scheduling specific meetings. It hasn't happened yet, but let's hope that the long-awaited second edition can be held soon.

In the USA, another monographic event, the Relationship Anarchy Discussions (RAD) Unconference[213] has taken place in Detroit in 2019 and online in 2021.

6.4 The future

We know the past. Until now, the world has experienced forms of organization, government systems, and power structures that have led to a reality of exploitation, inequality, war, crime, corruption...

---

213 http://radunconference.com.

Anarchist understanding has had no role in these forms of government and power, and yet "chaos and disorder" are still linked to anarchism and not the authoritarian models that have had a place in the administrations and powers that have steered history. Chaos is the staggering inequality, hunger; the lack of sanitation, essential services, clean water; people dying at sea; resources invested in weapons and armies. Disorder is the destruction of ecosystems, inhumane treatment of animals; discrimination against those who are different, who love differently, believe in different gods or none; disease and death from preventable causes that are rampant on the planet; the lack of opportunities, hope, and future that young people who don't have a rich, powerful family backing them find when they set out into real life, and the repression they are subjected to when they protest and demand equal opportunities, dignity, and rights. That is not anarchy. That is what anarchy was born to change.

Examples and reference points

But it is crazy to think that a handful of individuals who are dissatisfied with the way relationships are set up in our societies, who meet with smiles and spend hours talking to try to overcome their own contradictions, are going to change the world overnight. The only sensible ambition is to find ways to live differently, ways that are less focused on small bubbles of consumption, reproduction, repetition, and recreation... And make them visible.

In Carlos Iglesias's film *Un franco, 14 pesetas*, two Spanish emigrants in 1960s Switzerland take a train trip and, after finishing their sandwiches, throw the paper wrappers on the ground. An old woman sitting on the other side of the aisle notices and, without flinching, without any reproachful gestures or dirty looks, she walks over, picks up the papers from between the two stupefied men's legs, and throws them into the wastebasket that's right near their hands, easily within reach. They look at each other and can only mutter an inaudible, "What did she do?"[214] Our example, the way we act, support, and relate to each other is more valuable than any other political, repressive, or rhetorical tool. It is a slow yet pervasive form of revolution that soaks into the fabric of everyday life and makes it change color from within. To get to that point, we must live and visibilize, understand and recognize ourselves as a community, and then communicate that understanding. We must refine and sift through our own contradictions, but after having experienced them, not just through hearsay. At this time, not many of the people around us know that there are non-normative, ethical relationship models. And of those who do know of their existence, do they have an idea that is in the least correct, even if incomplete? Or is it completely distorted? And what do they think from a moral perspective? From a practical perspective? And from a political one?

The evolution of all these issues will determine the extent to which society is willing to accept a profound change in this area and in this direction and logic. It may not be the time or the way. Or perhaps there is a need, a capacity for cultural reconstruction, a social basis that's capable of making disruptive behaviors visible on a large scale, of overcoming the stigmas we will have to carry over to and use to create a new space, expanding the common sense of the time, and turning this proposal – now radical – into yet another option, perhaps a majority option at some point in future history.

Beyond bonds

And hopefully this new way of relating, with its solidarity, network, egalitarian and horizontal character free from authoritarianism, will influence the organization of societies, communities, and States, leading to a real change, an authentic revolution that starts with affection, with bonds. But it's also possible that something will befall even this hypothesis of an acceptance and normalization that may become significant, something that we've already seen so many

---

214 https://youtu.be/eVC8MyfIP10.

times... co-opting, assimilation by consumer societies, the conversion of a radical movement into a fashion, a trend, just another market asset. From committed activism to economic asset, careening downhill without brakes.

We've experienced this happening in the past, and it's happening now; we have the ability to fight it. We have the drive to live out our bonds in a different way and for that to serve as an example, without trying to convince those who don't see the need to change anything. Our reality has so many imperfections, so many problems, so much affliction, that it's quite difficult to be optimistic about the present. However, it's much easier to have that attitude about any future arising from a revolutionary change. At the beginning in the introduction, and throughout the book, I have repeated that I am convinced that revolutions are becoming increasingly difficult, at least in their classic format. So, the challenge is precisely to change challenges, styles, paths. More than 40 years ago, Michel Foucault said these words, and they still ring true. It is with these words and their realistic optimism that I'd like to end this last chapter.

"That revolutionary European thought (...) has lost its specific points of support. (...)

"So, if I understand correctly, you're quite pessimistic?"

"I would say that being aware of the difficulty of the conditions is not necessarily a sign of pessimism. I would say that if I see the difficulties, that is precisely the extent to which I am optimistic. Or, if you prefer, because I see the difficulties – and they are huge – it takes a lot of optimism to say, "Let's start again!" It has to be possible to start over. That is, to begin the analysis, the criticism again; not, of course, the mere analysis of the so-called "capitalist" society, but the analysis of the powerful state social system, which we find in socialist and capitalist countries. That is the criticism that must be done. It's a huge task, of course. We have to start now, and with a lot of optimism."[215]

---

[215] Knut Boesers's interview with Michel Foucault, 1977, in *El poder, una bestia magnífica: sobre el poder, la prisión y la vida*, Siglo XXI, Buenos Aires, 2012.

Epilogue

In *1984*, Orwell wrote that "The best books... are those that tell you what you know already." I would add that the best readings are those that reveal that what you already intuited... wasn't just in your mind. Those readings end up connecting you with more people and building something bigger, something more horizontal but with better outlooks. Something that doesn't just fit in one person's head and only makes sense and has room to grow when shared with many others. This book is a polyphonic composition of many of those readings. If I haven't managed to get these many in-tune voices to create a harmonious sound, it's entirely my fault.

I opened the preface with a quote from Toni Morrison, and I'd like to end the epilogue with words from this exceptional woman, who sadly happened to pass away during the writing of this work. From her autobiography, The Pieces I Am: "History has always proved that books are the first plain on which certain battles are fought."

That's where we're at.

Cheers, and relationship revolution!

Glossary

AFFECTIVE NETWORK: This is a set of affective nodes (see) linked by bonds of potentially very different degrees of intensity, yet they share characteristics of affectivity, consideration, and care.

AFFECTIVE NODE: In a model of relationships based in structural monogamy, the social fabric is a set of isolated bubbles that keep interests and caretaking separate and confined on each island. In a model like relationship anarchy, where all relationships are valuable (not equally important, but possessing value, without hierarchies), a network of bonds is established – a true fabric. In this network, each person is a node, and each relationship is different. However, no bond has the ability to override or eliminate others.

AFFECTIVE OR SEXUAL EXCLUSIVITY: One of the cultural mandates that most heavily influence the format of relationships in most contemporary societies is that of affective and sexual exclusivity. When a relationship considered to be intimate or a "couple" is established, the commitment of exclusivity or affective sexual fidelity is normatively imposed without the need for discussion. Neither person can maintain or establish other relationships of the same or similar type. In some formats that move away from normativity, sexual exclusivity is relaxed (open couples or swingers), and in others, affective sexual exclusivity is as well (non-monogamy, polyamory).

ALLOSEXISM: The normative prioritization of sexual relationships – that is, valuing relationships that include erotic attraction and sexual practices over other sorts of relationships. Like amatonormativity, allosexism assumes that important commitments and true depth of the bonds can only exist in these types of relationships. It is also associated with the conviction that everyone wants to experience erotic attraction and have sexual practices, and that those who don't respond to this "normality" have some sort of problem or illness.

ALLY: Someone who belongs to an oppressive group can take on a significant commitment in dismantling the oppressive structure. The process normally has to start with learning by listening to those who are oppressed. It then moves through introspection and confrontation of one's own prejudices, stereotypes, and automatisms; understanding and working on defense reactions and feelings of guilt and shame; developing the capacities needed to break with oppressive attitudes, expressions, behaviors, and assumptions; confronting the institutional structures and policies that uphold oppression; and finally, offering their modest collaboration (not their leadership) to those who belong to the oppressed group to fight by their side.

AMATONORMATIVITY: The normative prioritization of amorous relationships – that is, valuing relationships that include expressions of romantic love over other types of relationships. The important commitments and the true depth of the bonds are associated with this evaluation. Amatonormativity involves the conviction that these relationships are not only the "important ones" but that they're the "normal ones," and that everyone wants (or should want) to form romantic relationships that constitute the axis of their existence since, without them, life is nothing but loneliness and failure.

AROMANTICISM / ALLOROMANTICISM: Conditions that express the lack of or very low tendency to experience the feelings and conditioning that go along with romantic attraction (aromanticism) or the normal tendency, which is habitual in society, to experience them (alloromanticism). Heteroromanticism, homoromanticism, biromanticism, and panromanticism are also spoken of when referring to orientation (see "Pansexuality").

ASEXUALITY: The absence of sexual attraction or a strong decrease in it compared to what is considered "normal." This does not imply a lack of sexual desire or libido but a lack of attraction. It is different from abstinence as it isn't a decision or a repression, but a sexual orientation. In fact, it doesn't imply abstinence since asexual people can decide to have sex without an attraction, either to satisfy their sexual desire, someone else's sexual desire, or out of curiosity to experience the sensations of sexual activity (see also "Demisexuality").

AXIS, VECTOR, DIMENSION, OR GRADIENT OF OPPRESSION OR DOMINATION: Relationships between people always present power differences that affect different traits that are functional, emotional, symbolic, etc. When these differences are very marked, all operating in the same direction, and constant and unchanging – when they're chronic – we speak of submission, oppression, or domination. If this also occurs in the majority of society, repeatedly following the same model (for instance, always directed from men to women), we must talk about structural oppression (in the previous example, sexism).

There are different oppressions that work in parallel. For example, these may be directed from natural citizens to poor foreigners (xenophobia / aporophobia) or from heterosexual people to homosexual people (homophobia or homo-antagonism). We can represent these phenomena as gradients that are more oppressive with the more violence that occurs, or as vectors or axes in a multidimensional space if we want to understand their interactions. We can easily visualize up to three axes: horizontally, for instance, there's sexism, vertically xenophobia / aporophobia, and finally homophobia in the third dimension. My position in this three-dimensional space defines how much violence I have to bear: if I am a migrant lesbian woman, I will be located at a point of maximum oppression. If I'm a heterosexual man who's a natural citizen of my country, I will be situated at the point that has to bear the least structural abuse.

BINARISM: System of beliefs, attitudes, laws, etc., that entails a division of people, identities, traits, or other elements into two groups. This means that anyone who does not belong to one of the two designations is left out of that system. When used in relation to gender, it is specified in the male/female dichotomy. This forces any person (or behavioral trait) to adapt to one of the two labels, as being "in the middle" involves invisibility and marginalization. The answer is the defense of genderqueer, agender, or non-binary identities of resistance. In the context of this book, it also applies to relationships that are characterized as affective sexual or friendship, forcing any bond to adapt to one of the two options through the cultural mandate of amatonormativity (see).

CARETAKING: Caretaking is an essential concept in contemporary feminism. This represents an ethical, practical reference point that must be reclaimed because it has traditionally been taken on by women without any visibility or compensation. Co-responsibility in terms of caretaking, recognition, and redistribution is defended. In the field of relationships, caretaking is given an important place to face the possibility that designing or practicing new types of bonds would eliminate the need for this element, which is central and necessary at many times life, to be considered and valued. The emotional dimension of caretaking is also an important issue in this context.

CISGENDER/TRANSGENDER: Traditionally, the binary criterion is applied to babies in that they are assigned female at birth or assigned male at birth. Cisgender is used for someone who identifies with the same binary gender that was assigned to them at birth. Transgender applies to someone who does not identify with the binary gender they were assigned at birth. They may be a trans man *(afab)* or a trans woman *(amab)*. Some trans people decide to take hormones or resort to surgery to modify their body, and others don't need to. The alternative is to identify as non-binary or genderqueer.

CLOSETS: The expressions "being in the closet" or "coming out of the closet" refer to publicly communicating an aspect of life (often, one's sexual orientation) that is kept secret or relatively private for fear of social rejection or some sort of negative consequence. The aspect that is kept hidden or made public is, by definition, outside of hegemonic normativity.

CONSENT AND CULTURE OF CONSENT: Consent is the action of clearly and explicitly expressing acceptance of something, usually a more or less intimate act of an emotional, physical, or intellectual nature. The culture of consent is a movement originating from feminist activism that considers scrupulous respect for individual boundaries to be the most important aspect in the analysis and practice of relationships that have a sexual or emotional component. This culture rejects anyone seeing their boundaries overstepped or feeling forced to do anything, setting up alarms if this should occur. It absolutely emphasizes individual sovereignty and bodily and emotional autonomy, and it maintains that I am the only person who can judge and decide on my own wants and needs.

According to this culture, consent must be given in positive, active, and explicit terms. The expression of consent is specific – that is, it is only valid exclusively for one particular situation and moment, and it does not extend to other cases or moments. It is also procedural, meaning that it must be expressly maintained throughout the process for which it is expressed. And it is reversible, so it can be revoked at any time without explanation.

DECONSTRUCTION: The term deconstruction, in its philosophical and literary sense, is relatively obscure, technical, and academic. It is a form of semiotic analysis that's associated with poststructuralism and postmodern philosophy. One of the characteristics of this style of inquiry and criticism of the field of communication is the question of essentialism and reassessing the ambiguity of language and thought. Therefore, it is often used in simpler and more direct terms to refer to critical, conscious revision of the elements of our personality that we've considered essential and part of our identity up to now. Dismantling what we think we are is one way of ensuring that we aren't obeying cultural mandates. The goal is to get closer to what we want to be, beyond what we've been told we are.

DEMISEXUALITY: This is the sexual orientation of someone who does not often experience physical or sexual attraction, but does experience emotional attraction. It's common for a demisexual not to have sexual relations or only to have them with people they have an intense, established emotional connection with. Like asexuality, demisexuality implies a limited physical or sexual attraction (to bonds with the proper sentimental connection), but not necessarily less sexual desire. The rest of the considerations expressed in the definition of asexuality are also applicable.

DESCRIPTIVE / PRESCRIPTIVE: This refers above all to labels, the terms we use to refer to relationships, identities, roles, etc. A label is used descriptively when the intention is to portray, explain, or add detail to a reality. This use is neutral, purely expository. Often, though, labels, words go beyond describing to draw borders delineating what things are within the concept and what things are outside it. This delimitation produces a prescriptive effect, one of obligation, confinement, a cage that imprisons the possibilities of building and self-managing a relationship, an identity, or a behavior. What you say you are thus limits what you can be and what you can do.

FAKES (POLY-FAKES, ANARCHO-FAKES...): The communities where experiences with alternative relationship models are reflected on and shared also serve to facilitate meetings with people who are going through similar times, have similar concerns or questions, or can contribute with conclusions from experiences they've enjoyed and suffered through. At these meetings, emotion and feelings are highly present, and that circumstance makes the authenticity of the interactions very important. However, the idea of finding people, especially women, who have relationships without the normative armor, arouses the curiosity and interest in heterosexual cisgender men, above all, who are seeking gratuitous sexual relationships with no strings attached out of lack and pettiness. These characters, who are fortunately usually easy to spot, are called poly-fakes when they intervene in meetings under the label of "polyamory." In the case of relationship anarchy, they could be called anarcho-fakes, though this word is not currently in use.

FAMILY OF ORIGIN / CHOSEN FAMILY: The term "chosen family" originated in Kath Weston's research in the 1990s on the relational aspects and formats of assistance, protection, and caretaking in the LGBTIQ+ community. The contempt and rejection of homosexuals by their families of origin led to the need to form support networks outside the social umbrella of the biological family. A chosen family can function as a less normative version of the traditional family, replacing it, or it can constitute a complementary network.

FLAMING: Exhibiting characteristics, gestures, expressions, and styles of behavior that don't match one's assigned gender can be described as flaming. It is predominantly used to refer to the gay men, indicating effeminacy, but it is also applicable to the inverse phenomenon, when someone read as a woman has manners and an expressive pattern closer to the stereotype of the male gender. These sets of mannerisms are frequently the object of ridicule and attack, as one example of social violence that results from heterocentric normative hegemony to which any deviation poses a threat and a form of dissent.

GENDER: The set of expectations, norms, customs, and practices that apply to people based on differences in physical appearance that correspond to diverse biological traits. The factor most commonly used to divide people into two groups is the anatomical manifestation of the cellular presence of two X chromosomes or one X and one Y chromosome. Other known circumstances that cause anatomical variants and which are assigned to one of these two groups with varying degrees of difficulty are the mutation or differential expression of the genes SRY, DAX-1, SOX 9, SF-1 WT1, WnT4, or the presence or absence of the hormones and enzymes MAH, 5-alpha-reductase, and dihydrotestosterone at different stages in development. The combination of all these factors gives rise to multiple bodily configurations that make up a bimodal – but not binary – distribution. Generally, all these bodily configurations are compatible with a healthy and (what should be) socially normal life. In societies today, the assigned group (boy or girl, man or woman) will entail clear variations in the treatment, education, value, opportunities, and expectations in life that an individual will receive.

GENDERQUEER OR NON-BINARY: A gender identity that corresponds to those who are not represented by their assigned sex at birth nor by the opposite one. They thus reject the normative gender binary and locate themselves somewhere on the spectrum between the two conventional genders. Other identities that have been described and which share some nuances with it are "agender," "gender-fluid," "third gender," "bigender," "pangender," and "trigender."

GRAY-ROMANTICISM OR GRAY-AROMANTICISM: This orientation is halfway between romantic and aromatic orientations. People with this orientation may experience romantic attraction rarely, or they may feel romantic attraction but not want romantic relationships or want relationships that are not very romantic.

GRAY-SEXUALITY OR GRAY ASEXUALITY: This orientation falls between sexual and asexual orientations. People with this orientation may feel sexual attraction only on certain occasions or desire relationships that are less sexual than is normatively accepted.

HETERO-/HOMO-/BI-/PANSEXUAL: Sexual orientation describes a person based on what they find sexually attractive. Using many of the standard terms implies acceptance of the sexual binary. Someone who is only attracted to people of the opposite sex is heterosexual.

Those who are attracted to people of the same sex are homosexual. Someone who is attracted to both sexes in a binary manner (identifying those interests as men and women and perceiving their attraction as differentiated) is bisexual. If one's attraction to people doesn't explicitly identify and differentiate the sexes, they are pansexual or omnisexual. Someone who doesn't identify with a gender (genderqueer or non-binary) but does feel specific attraction to those they perceive as belonging to one of the binary genders is gynosexual, if attracted to women, or androsexual, if attracted to men.

There are other orientations that don't characterize the object of attraction based on the person's sex but on other traits, such as sapiosexual, when the basis of attraction is intelligence; androgynosexual, when based on androgynous appearance; demisexual, when based on emotional connection; and autosexual when oriented around oneself, meaning the preferred sexual activity is masturbation. This list is not exhaustive.

HIERARCHY: This is an organization in a structure applied to people, things, concepts, symbols, etc., on an ordered scale that establishes a criterion of subordination. In contexts of people and bonds, subordination is considered in terms of interrelation, meaning it implies that one of the elements of the hierarchy has the ability to influence what happens to another. Hierarchical structures must be distinguished from other concepts like preference, importance, affinity, complicity, dedication, time spent... A bond may exhibit a higher (or lower) degree of affinity, complicity, or any other of these qualities, than another bond and not be in a superior (or subordinate) hierarchical position, as long as there is no capacity for influence in terms of direct effective power.

INTERNALIZED OPPRESSION: This phenomenon affects oppressed groups, whose members come to believe that the stigmas, prejudices, and stereotypes attributed to them are true. According to this internalization, these people adjust their attitudes, practices, and language to reflect these stereotypes. Internalized oppression leads to loss of confidence in one's own possibilities, low self-esteem, insecurity, and even self-hatred and hatred of the group to which one belongs.

KINK: This refers to any unconventional sexual practices or fantasies. It encompasses practices like BDSM (Bondage, Discipline, Dominance and Submission, Sadomasochism), fetishisms, the leather subculture, etc. It is considered one of the manifestations of the queer phenomenon and would therefore be included in the last letter of the acronym LGBTIQ+. In the kink universe, conventional sexuality is called vanilla, implying normal, ordinary.

LABELS: In this book, these are the terms we use to refer to different elements of the world or of thought. See Descriptive / Prescriptive.

LIMERENCE: This is an involuntary emotional state that surfaces when desire and romantic attraction for someone develops. It is characterized by generating thoughts focused on the other person, obsessive fantasies, desires for the attraction to be reciprocal and to be near to and interact with them physically. This is related to variations in certain levels of hormones and neurotransmitters.

LIMINALITY: This is the sensation that occurs when crossing a significant threshold or going through an important change or rite of passage. During the liminal moment, the person is on the threshold between one state and the next, between one identity, perspective, reality... and the other that is expected subsequently. In this phase, certainties disappear or are temporarily blurred, and doubts and fears usually appear.

METAMOURS: In the lingo of consensual non-monogamies, metamour is used to refer to my intimate relationships' intimate relationships. In the context of relationship anarchy, given the desire to avoid hierarchizing relationships and binarizing them into two sets – intimate and non-intimate – the concept loses meaning, though it could be reclaimed to refer to the most intense bonds of those with whom I have a stronger bond, that is, the people closest to me in my network of affections who I don't relate to directly.

MONOGAMY (STRUCTURAL): Besides being a specific practice or relationship style, monogamy can be considered a cultural expectation that sets up a social structure linked to the concepts of a heterosexual reproductive couple, romantic love, or the nuclear family. This structure, sometimes called compulsory monogamy, marginalizes other forms of more or less intimate connection in terms of what is considered acceptable. Therefore, it is necessary to distinguish between monogamous relationships that are explicitly chosen and consensual by those who make up the bond, and monogamous relationships that are the product of cultural, social, and institutional coercion, and which give rise to monogamy as a hegemonic system or structure.

MONOSEXUALITY / PLURISEXUALITY: A classification of sexual orientation that is alternative to the classic categories of heterosexuality versus homosexuality. Monosexual describes someone who experiences attraction to only one gender or to people who are at one end of the sexual spectrum, compared to plurisexual people who are attracted to both genders or, in non-binary terms, individuals who fall anywhere on the spectrum of identities and expressions of gender. Homosexual and heterosexual people are monosexual; bisexual and pansexual people are plurisexual.

MUTUAL AID: A classic anarchist concept that refers to the practice of giving and receiving freely from each person according to their ability and to each person according to their need. Mutual aid is horizontal in nature, which means that it is established between equals, and does not mean barter (a "tit-for-tat" attitude) or imply obligation or reciprocity. In any event, it implies indirect reciprocity: when I offer help, I don't expect it to be "returned" to me by the same person, but rather it is the group, generally one or more different individuals, who will help me solve a problem in the future.

This way, the support is reciprocal, but not on a personal level; it is indirect, in relation to the group or support network.

NORMATIVITY AND HEGEMONY: We accept normativity when we uncritically and automatically adhere to the dominant vision regarding some topic of great relevance. It is similar to accepting a license or a standard contract without evaluating each aspect of it or reflecting on its consequences or whether it's possible to try to modify some clauses, even though it may not be easy. I've called the attitude of defining our own clauses, rather than accepting the standard form, self-management. The concept of cultural hegemony was developed by Antonio Gramsci, who argued that some elites have the oligopoly of influence over the rest of society, and through this influence, they maintain control based on beliefs about normality and common sense. That is to say, these elites shape the adhesion contract that configures normativity. The normativity and common sense of an era (which varies as the years go by) give rise to the ideological repertoire of legitimizing or hegemonic identities, which encompass the meaning, thoughts, and practices that are adopted automatically, invisibly, and unconsciously on a daily basis, without us realizing it.

NRE (New Relationship Energy): This term used in circles of consensual non-monogamy to refer to the altered emotional state that arises from falling in love or limerence (see) when a new intense relationship appears in someone's life. Along with jealousy, this is one of the most analyzed and debated problems in meetings, blogs, and articles in these environments. It's important not to use NRE as an excuse to stop caring for, attending to, and showing consideration for those I've had bonds with for a longer time, abusing the trust that a longer relationship provides.

OBJECTIFICATION: It is treating people as if they were things, objects... without considering their feelings, their desires, their decisions, or their boundaries. In a patriarchal system like in our societies, objectification is often a masculine trait that is aimed at women, turning them into sexual objects, though any other axis of privilege may support objectification. Sometimes, the phenomenon is limited to language or abstract consideration, which is serious insofar as it is a symbolic violence and a performative factor; other times, though, it reaches physical behaviors, being the basis of abuse and violence in its most literal expression. One cannot generally feel empathy for an object, so objectification is a dangerous, serious disturbance in thought, given that empathy is the main mechanism that makes coexistence, consideration, and respect possible.

ONE PENIS POLICY: The OPP is a terrible example of ideological co-optation of a relationship model by patriarchal masculinity. It is a relatively common form of non-monogamy, especially in some countries, where a couple usually consisting of a heterosexual man and a bisexual woman is opened only to other women. A network may form, but there can only be one man in it. The ethics of this approach reflect very little respect for any sense of justice; it reveals a rudimentary, insecure masculinity and, at the same time, a strong gradient of domination (and submission on the part of the women involved). This model is also frequently anchored in the tremendously sexist and homophobic idea that sex and love between women is not "real" and therefore isn't a threat to men.

OPEN COUPLE: This relationship style doesn't confront the ideology of the couple; it inherits all of its elements but tries to avoid the problem of sexual monotony by opening up the possibility of establishing secondary relationships, normally limited to bodily interaction, with the prohibition (a rather naive one) on affectivity developing in them. This restriction is the result of consensus between the members of the couple. Secondary relationships have no say in that agreement.

PATRIARCHY: A patriarchal society maintains a structure with multiple axes of power in most of which people read as men have privileges by virtue of being recognized as men. In Western societies, progress has been made in the fight for equal civil, legal, economic rights, etc., and that has led many to believe that the patriarchal structure has disappeared. However, the level of symbolic and physical violence, practices of submission and domination, power quotas, and rights that are not enforced equally is still towering. There continues to be a systematic, widespread bias in all measures and dimensions that works in favor of men. The concept of patriarchy must be distinguished from that of patrilineality, although both occur at varying degrees of intensity in today's societies. A society is patrilineal when surnames, titles, and economic and social capital are inherited primarily through lines recognized as masculine.

PERFORMATIVITY: A statement is said to be performative when it goes beyond representation or description, since the act of being expressed entails an action. Verbs like committing or prohibiting are clear examples. A commitment or prohibition arises from the speech act itself. The action is performed by stating it. It was the philosopher of language J.L. Austin who defined the term and ended up concluding that any expressive act is performative: speaking is always a way of acting. In the '90s, Judith Butler built a complete theory around Jacques Derrida's contributions and Austin's performativity regarding the deconstruction of gender, which she presents as a cultural construction and not as an essential part of a person. When a baby is assigned a certain gender, this is done through a speech act (one that's then repeated for years, throughout their life): we say "it's a boy" or "it's a girl." The child's chromosomal, hormonal, and anatomical profile is a complex reality, but we turn it into a marker, the gender, which will give rise to a set of behaviors that will continue throughout all the years of that individual's life. Judith Butler proposes reappropriating those labels by changing those behaviors according to our wishes. Turning this challenge of deconstruction into a collective strategy of corporal expression and behavior would act as a constant performative, communicative act that can transform society's power structures.

PERSONAL BOUNDARIES: Within the framework of the culture of consent (see), boundaries establish the explicit limits beyond which there is no acceptance. Personal or individual boundaries are defined in relation to one's own body, space, dignity, or personal well-being. When one's own well-being is dependent on what other people do, the distinction between a boundary and an imposition becomes blurred. For example, if I set my boundary by specifying that someone else can't come near me, this is a clear case of an individual boundary. But if I specify that they can't get close to a third party or drink alcohol or leave the city, arguing that this affects my well-being, I'm twisting the sense of personal boundaries and prescribing an imposition that goes beyond my body and my space, even if it does affect my well-being or my happiness. Keeping the margins of what we consider personal boundaries clearly differentiated isn't easy, but it is essential to fit autonomy and personal sovereignty within the framework of care, affection, coexistence, and the concept of mutual support.

PERSONAL SOVEREIGNTY: Personal or individual sovereignty is a core notion of anarchism, both historically and philosophically. It refers to the concept of possession of one's own person in terms of the moral or natural right to one's bodily integrity and to be the exclusive owner of one's own body and life. It connects with the concepts of voluntariness, self-agency, freedom, and responsibility.

PHOBIA / ANTAGONISM: The suffix "-phobia" originally referred to an irrational fear that may become pathological. In words like homophobia or transphobia, though, it represents a form of violence and oppression (sometimes fear and the feeling of threat are what trigger violence, but, while they are necessary ingredients, they alone are insufficient). In these cases, using "-phobia" may infringe on the respect and dignity of those who experience actual phobias and suffer their consequences without being able to do anything to prevent it, except undergoing medical and psychological treatments that don't always work. It can be a way of trivializing or blaming those realities. Thus, a recent proposal has been made to replace this suffix with "-antagonism" (homoantagonism, trans antagonism), though the original form is much more widespread. In this book, I've used both interchangeably.

POLYGAMY / POLYANDRY / POLYGYNY: Polygamy is the formation of non-dyadic affective sexual unions, meaning they take a form other than that of a relationship *(-gamy)* between two people. From the binary perspective, it can be categorized into polyandry, which is a union where there are several men and only one woman, and polygyny, where there are several women and only one man. Polygamy is often used to automatically refer to forms of social organization accepted in cultures like that of Christian Mormons or Muslims, where specifically polygyny is practiced. In the Western world, the term *polygamy* is often emphatically rejected as a label for consensual practices of non-monogamy, such as polyamory. This rejection is incomprehensible in a literal sense, and it is based on moral supremacism, racism, and xenophobia that creates a strong reaction of rejection and contempt, even genuine hostility, especially towards polygamy practiced in Muslim societies, or rather, directly towards that religion as a manifestation of Islamophobia. In all societies, especially in less secular and democratic ones, there are surely aspects that are ethically indefensible when seen from a perspective of reason, equality, and human rights. However, in this case as in so many others, we see the speck in our brother's eye and not the beam in our own (to paraphrase The Gospels, the books considered sacred by two of the biggest monotheistic religions: Christianity and Islam).

PRIVILEGE: Privilege is a phenomenon that involves people, relationships, cultures, and institutions and provides advantages and benefits to those in the dominant groups over those in the oppressed groups. Western societies assign privileges to white people who are read as being men, heterosexual, free from disease or functional diversity, natural-born citizens, and neither very young nor advanced in age; belonging to the Christian religion; and possessing economic means and the ability to express themselves in the majority language. Privilege is characterized by being invisible to those who enjoy it or by being considered deserved by them, earned on their own merits and accessible to anyone who tries hard enough. Oppression, on the other hand, is easily perceived, although sometimes there is a type of injustice called epistemic or hermeneutic injustice that makes oppressed people not understand exactly what that disadvantage, violence, or misery consists of and where it comes from, nor know how to convey their perception and evidence of what they suffer through. There is also a phenomenon of blaming oneself for oppression (see internalized oppression). One domination strategy that's been used with great success by elites, and which has turned into a hegemony of (common) sense in many places, pits whoever is next-to-last against the last. In other words, it makes those who are highly vulnerable (for example, workers at a low cultural level) believe that the cause of their ills stems from those who are still more vulnerable (such as immigrants arriving in search of work).

QUEERPLATONIC: The term queerplatonic describes a more intense intimate bond than what is usually considered friendship but which doesn't conform to the expectations, commitments, behaviors, practices, and limits of the traditional model of the romantic couple, such as obligatory sex, total and constant dedication, exclusivity, etc. Still, it is characterized by the inclusion of feelings of affection and emotional commitment. The prefix "queer-" doesn't indicate that the people involved identify as queer or non-normative; rather, it is the type of relationship that goes beyond normativity. Those who sustain this type of relationship may label each other as "my partner," though terms like "my zucchini" are also used to underscore the lack of a proper label or even the convenience of dispensing with specific labels. This is really the only type of relationship described and widely known that challenges amatonormativity as a cultural mandate.

RACIALIZATION: The concept of race or ethnicity is strongly contested from various points of view. In fact, the characterization of race as a biogenetic concept is highly problematic and only fits neatly into a reality of social and cultural interpretation. The concept of racialization refers to the processes and consequences of defining people by their race. This social mechanism attributes racial meaning to people's identity and their interaction with society, its structures, and its institutions. Racial assignments establish a hierarchy, which results in violence and structural inequalities that are sustained over time. These consequences are anchored in the belief, held at various levels of consciousness, that people's behavior is determined by their genetics or because it is more likely that a person with certain traits has been brought up a certain way.

The approximate characteristics (pigmentation, external facial and body features, etc.) of the individuals who hold economic, political, and social power correspond to non-racialized traits, meaning that the people with those traits aren't racialized, even if they don't have power.

RADICAL: The etymology of this term refers to change starting with the very root. A radical approach focuses on transforming social structures and value systems from the bottom up in a fundamental way. The opposite tendency is immobilism or reactionary thinking.

RESPONSIBLE / CONSCIOUS VOLUNTARY COMMITMENT: A voluntary commitment from the person who agrees to it is not the result of a negotiation or an exchange but of the deep conviction that they want to maintain a certain level of care, attention, affection, support, presence, dedication in terms of life, emotion, logistics, etc. This conviction has to go through a process of reflective analysis in order to be conscious. Commitments are responsible when they aren't arbitrary; they respond to specific reasons, and the consequences of agreeing to them and the harm that breaking them would entail have also been assessed (since they aren't associated with a normative sanctioning regime, as are contracts and agreements). This does not mean that they're forever, engraved in stone. Rather, they are reassessed in a conscious, responsible way with dialogue and reason.

ROMANTIC: Romantic relationships constitute the hegemonic model of a bond in its heteronormative, monogamous, and reproductive iteration. They are based on the sublimation of emotional feelings of love and attraction in a stereotyped courtship ritual that functions as a form of expression of those feelings and emotions. The aim is twofold: forming a unique, eternal (or at least lasting), idealized, intimate bond that almost always involves sexual relations; and forming a family unit that is relatively independent of the rest of society. The romantic relationship is put above all else: for richer, for poorer, in sickness and in health. This system of thought began to develop in Europe during the Middle Ages with stories of chivalry and courtly love. It reached its highest point of expression in the 18th and 19th centuries with the emergence of Romanticism as an artistic movement, as the name suggests.

SELF-MANAGEMENT: Self-management or work collectivism is a term traditionally used by anarchism that challenges the organization that arises from the power of the State and Capital. In the context of this book, it refers to the organization of relationships and networks of bonds in non-normative terms – that is, according to guidelines established by the members of those relationships or networks in a voluntary, conscious, and responsible manner. It's about not adhering to the standard contract offered by social normativity as a pre-printed agreement and labeled with titles like "couple," "friendship," "family," etc. Instead, voluntary commitments and individual limits are defined to configure a model of behavior where there is no authority beyond that implied by fulfilling commitments. There is no hierarchy or authority of some over others, nor are social norms accepted as rules by default. If any questions or conflict arise that aren't included in the commitments and limits explicitly established, they are discussed, and new commitments are established to address the problem.

SEXUAL / GENDER IDENTITY, ORIENTATION, AND EXPRESSION: Gender identity is an individual perception that gives rise to the awareness of belonging to a gender, either in binary terms (male or female) or non-binary terms, such as a point on the spectrum between conventional femininity and masculinity. In many cases, this perception coincides or fits with the sex assignment given at birth (cisgender), but for others it does not (transgender, non-binary, etc.). People who have genitalia or chromosomal or hormonal profiles that do not fit the supposedly pure male or female forms are called intersex (see "Gender"). They are assigned one of the two binary sexes at birth (as has historically been the case), sometimes resorting to surgery to bring their anatomy closer to this assignment. Gender expression is the externalization of gender identity, including behavior and appearance: gestures, voice, body language, style of dress, hairstyle, use of makeup, name, preferred pronouns, etc. Sometimes, gender expression is experienced in a fluid way, changing circumstantially for recreational, social, political, or other purposes. Sexual orientation refers to sexual attraction (see "Hetero-/homo-/bi-/pansexual"). Romantic or emotional orientation may be different from sexual orientation (see "Aromanticism / Alloromanticism").

SWINGERS: Swinging, also called partner swapping, is a type of relationship that includes sexual activity between one or, more commonly, both members of a couple and other people or couples, together or separately, as a recreational or social activity. Like an open couple, it is a model based in monogamy where the restriction of sexual exclusivity is relaxed in response to the problem of monotony and routine in intimate relationships. However, the mandate of affective exclusivity is upheld, and great importance is placed on respecting couples' integrity. It is, therefore, an amatonormative lifestyle.

UNICORN: In the field of non-monogamy, this refers to a bisexual woman who is willing to have an intimate relationship with an established couple without any demands to participate in that couple's agreements and with the commitment not to do anything that may cause trouble or any upsets. The term refers to the rarity of finding such a person (the unicorn being a mythological being), and it is used pejoratively towards those who seek this arrangement since it clearly implies objectifying, sexist thought.

UTOPIA: This is what writer Thomas More dubbed an island in his work now commonly known by the same name; its original title was *A truly golden little book, no less beneficial than entertaining, of a republic's best state and of the new island Utopia*. For More, Utopia was a rationally structured society where everything would be owned collectively rather than individually, and where people would spend their days reading and practicing the arts. A society of peace, happiness, justice, and complete harmony of interests. The author himself created the title by juxtaposing two Greek particles that together mean "a place that does not exist" or "nowhere." It is such an optimistic story that the word now means something impossible yet attractive, with a strong idealistic component. Eduardo Galeano recounted that he was once at a conference in Cartagena with Argentine filmmaker Fernando Birri, a good friend of his, and a student asked what utopia was good for. After a few seconds of silence, Birri replied, "What's utopia good for? That's a question I ask myself every day. I ask myself what utopia is good for, too. And I tend to think that utopia is on the horizon. So, if I go ten steps, utopia moves ten steps away, and if I go twenty steps, utopia is twenty steps farther away. As much as I walk, I'll never, ever reach it. So, what is utopia good for? For just that, walking."

About the author

Juan-Carlos Pérez-Cortés, Ph.D. Researcher in Artificial Intelligence with extensive scientific production in this field. He is a full professor at the Universitat Politècnica de València, Spain, founder and director of the Perception, Recognition, Learning, and Artificial Intelligence research group. He has served as scientific director of the University Research Institute on Computer Science, where his group has been based since 2004.

Outside his academic field, he has participated in events and spaces related to non-normative relationships since 2010; he was the author of one of the first translations into Spanish of the Relationship Anarchy Manifesto and actively contributes to its dissemination in different spaces of debate. He is co-founder of the Association for Affective, Ethical, Non-normative Relationships of València (ARAEN Valencia), which organizes, among other activities, one of the most attended relational activism meetings in Europe, the OpenCon Valencia, which in 2023 will reach its third edition (after the 2020, 21 and 22 editions were cancelled due to the pandemic). It has participated in the first Meeting on Relationship Anarchy in Spain, other national and international meetings, and workshops and conferences on relationships and normativity.

www.ingramcontent.com/pod-product-compliance
Lightning Source LLC
LaVergne TN
LVHW091617070526
838199LV00044B/834